JOHNNIE JOHNSON'S GREAT ADVENTURE

For Johnnie

JOHNNIE JOHNSON'S GREAT ADVENTURE

The Spitfire Ace of Ace's Last Look Back

by

Air Vice-Marshal James Edgar
'Johnnie' Johnson CB CBE DSO** DFC*
&
Dilip Sarkar MBE FRHistS

AIR WORLD

AIR WORLD

JOHNNIE JOHNSON'S GREAT ADVENTURE
The Spitfire Ace of Ace's Last Look Back

First published in Great Britain in 2020 by
Air World
An imprint of
Pen & Sword Books Ltd
Yorkshire – Philadelphia

ISBN 978 1 52679 174 0

A CIP catalogue record for this book is available from the British Library.

Typeset by SJmagic DESIGN SERVICES, India.

Printed and bound in the UK by TJ Books Limited.

Pen & Sword Books Limited incorporates the imprints of Atlas, Archaeology, Aviation, Discovery, Family History, Fiction, History, Maritime, Military, Military Classics, Politics, Select, Transport, True Crime, Air World, Frontline Publishing, Leo Cooper, Remember When, Seaforth Publishing, The Praetorian Press, Wharncliffe Local History, Wharncliffe Transport, Wharncliffe True Crime and White Owl.

For a complete list of Pen & Sword titles please contact

PEN & SWORD BOOKS LIMITED
47 Church Street, Barnsley, South Yorkshire, S70 2AS, England
E-mail: enquiries@pen-and-sword.co.uk
Website: www.pen-and-sword.co.uk

Or
PEN AND SWORD BOOKS
1950 Lawrence Rd, Havertown, PA 19083, USA
E-mail: Uspen-and-sword@casematepublishers.com
Website: www.penandswordbooks.com

FSC www.fsc.org MIX Paper from responsible sources FSC® C013056

Contents

Introduction

As I wrote in the introduction to *Johnnie Johnson's 1942 Diary: The Wartime Diary of the Spitfire Ace of Aces*, Air Vice-Marshal James Edgar Johnson, the RAF's officially top-scoring fighter pilot of the Second World War, was the ultimate character from the *Boys' Own Paper*. Fearless and forthright, a gifted Spitfire pilot and born leader, 'Johnnie', as he was universally known, was also much more. He was highly intelligent and a thinker, and immensely knowledgeable and well-read regarding the subjects that interested him. He was also a talented writer, as confirmed by this passage from his 1956 autobiography, *Wing Leader*, regarding a ground-attack sortie on 21 April 1944:

> Two days later we tried the same tactics but nearly came to grief. The tactical bombers were operating in the Paris area and I led a section of Spitfires back down to the deck to sweep the numerous airfields scattered around the French capital. After twenty minutes at low level I was lost, although I knew we were a few miles south of Paris. I put away the map and concentrated on flying the various courses I had worked out before leaving base.
>
> About another five minutes of this leg and then a turn to the west to avoid getting too close to Paris. Our horizon was limited to about three miles over level country but was considerably reduced when we dipped into a valley. We crossed a complicated mass of railway lines which indicated that we were close to Paris. We sped across a wide river and ahead of us was a heavily wooded slope, perhaps rising 200 feet from the river. We raced up this slope, only a few feet above the topmost branches, and found ourselves looking straight across a large grass airfield with several large hangars on the far side.

> The German gunners were ready and waiting. Shot and shell came from all angles, for some of the gun positions were on the hangar roofs and they fired *down* at us! I had never before seen the like of this barrage! It would have been folly to have turned back and make for the shelter of the wooded slope, for the turn would have exposed the vulnerable bellies of our Spitfires. Enemy aircraft were parked here and there, but our only thought was to get clear of this inferno. There was no time for radio orders. It was every man for himself, and each pilot knew that he would only get clear by staying at the very lowest height.
>
> It seemed that our exits were sealed with a concentrated criss-cross pattern of fire from a hundred guns. My only hope of a getaway lay in the small gap between two hangars. I pointed the Spitfire at this gap, hurtled through it and caught a glimpse of the multiple barrels of a light flak gun swinging onto me from one of the parapets.
>
> Beyond lay a long, straight road with tall poplars on either side, and I belted the Spitfire down the road with the trees forming some sort of screen. Tracer was still bursting over the cockpit, but with luck I should soon be out of range and I held down the Spitfire so that she was only a few feet above the cobbled roadway. Half a dozen cyclists were making their way up the road towards the airfield.
>
> They flung themselves from their bicycles in all directions. If you're Frenchmen, I thought, I'm sorry, but I've had a bigger fright than you! I pulled up above the light flak and called the other pilots. Miraculously, they had all come through the barrage, and when the last one answered I pulled the Spitfire into a climbing roll with the sheer joy of being alive.

Johnnie's breathtaking account provides a vivid glimpse of war through the armoured windscreen of a Spitfire. In his log book, Johnnie wrote 'Spitfire below poplar trees! Very accurate flak from Brétigncy!!!'

In the winter of his life, Johnnie, who was very much a 'people person', and I became good friends, despite our difference in age. Johnnie enthusiastically supported my writing and research, enormously enjoying our various symposiums and book-signings throughout the 1990s. Often we watched the sun go down in the conservatory of his Buxton home, talking of 'The Great Adventure', of battles and pilots. In truth, as the child who had so many models of Johnnie's Spitfire suspended from my ceiling, it was not uncommon for me to have to pinch myself! It really was true: here, in front of me, with his flying log book, photographs and papers was no less than 'Greycap Leader' himself, the RAF's wing leader *par excellence* of the Second World War and my boyhood hero of heroes – now a good friend to me, a nobody in the bigger scheme of things, considering the circles in which Johnnie moved. But that, of course, was the measure of the man. Johnnie cared not for what a man *had*, what mattered to him was whether he was *reliable*. Thankfully Johnnie must have found me to be so, otherwise I would not be writing this now, having been entrusted with the great man's memory by Johnnie's youngest son, Chris. A great privilege.

The Great Adventure was a book Johnnie and I originally planned together, at his suggestion. 'OK, Greycap,' said I, 'If you write your memories bit, I will add the historical detail.' 'Deal,' said Johnnie, ever with a sharp eye for business, generously adding '50/50 on Royalties?'

'Roger that, Greycap.' Sadly the project was unfulfilled. Johnnie became ill, largely withdrew from public life, and died on 30 January 2001, aged 85. There the matter lay – until now. In the interim I produced the biography *Spitfire Ace of Aces*, but often wondered how far Johnnie had got with his 'bit'. The answer lay with Chris Johnson, in whose possession rested *The Great Adventure*.

So, here we have it, at long last. Some of it Johnnie has taken from his original *Wing Leader*, but what makes *The Great Adventure* unique is Johnnie's various observations, opinions and stories of certain personalities. Of special interest to me, for example, was the first-hand material from Johnnie's old AOC, 'Broady' – something rarely seen. Johnnie's 'Last Look Back' provides unique comment, but a nagging doubt remains. Did 'Greycap' intend to finish the book where the last full stop is, or did he mean to share more, fascinating reflections.

The answer to that question we will never know, which makes *The Great Adventure* all the more intriguing.

Dilip Sarkar MBE FRHistS

Prologue

In my previous book on the great Johnnie Johnson, *Johnnie Johnson's 1942 Diary: The Wartime Diary of the Spitfire Ace of Aces*, it was necessary to provide a prologue describing Johnnie's background and experience up to 31 December 1941. This was largely extracted from my biography of Johnnie, *Spitfire Ace of Aces: The Wartime Story of Johnnie Johnson*. Because the diary finished, naturally, at the end of 1942, it is now necessary to provide context to Johnnie's account *The Great Adventure*, which starts after his posting away from the Kenley Canadian Wing in 1943. Again, this is extracted from *Spitfire Ace of Aces*, which remains the only biography of this great British fighter ace.

Johnnie, the policeman's son from Melton Mowbray, was a surveyor who, having been rejected by the socially elite Auxiliary Air Force, learned to fly with the RAF Volunteer Reserve. Mobilised on the outbreak of the Second World War, Johnnie successfully completed service flying training, was commissioned, and converted to Spitfires. Posted to 19 Squadron at Fowlmere during the Battle of Britain, because the squadron was engaged on active operations against the enemy, Pilot Officer Johnson and other replacement pilots were sent away to 616 Squadron, which was refitting and rebuilding to strength at Kirton, and therefore better placed to provide further operational training. So began a long association with 616 Squadron, with which, the following year, Johnnie would join the Tangmere Wing, flying in Wing Commander Douglas Bader's leading 'Dogsbody Section'. At Tangmere that 'season' Johnnie scored his first victories and learned air fighting from the 'great man'. Later made a flight commander, Johnnie was promoted to command 610 Squadron in July 1942, with which he fought over Dieppe that August. So, we now join Johnnie and 610 Squadron at Castletown in January 1943…

Chapter 1

Greycap Leader

On 13 January 1943, Johnnie flew to Chedworth and attended No 1 Fighter Leader Course. After a local flight over the River Severn on 16 January, and aerobatics the next morning, on 18 January, he was recalled to Castletown: the Commander-in-Chief had not forgotten his promise to Johnnie that early in 1943 his squadron would get a place back in the frontline. On 20 January, 610 Squadron relieved 131 Squadron at Westhampnett. Johnnie was home again, back at Tangmere: 'While at Castletown we had received a number of replacement pilots, so these chaps were keen to see action, to prove themselves. It was an exciting time for the Squadron, a challenge which 610 was ready for.'

On 26 January 1943, Johnnie flew with 485 Squadron on a Wing patrol of Hardelot, covering the withdrawal of bombers. North of Le Touquet, due to, according to Johnnie, 'Excellent controlling by Appledore', the Tangmere Wing intercepted 2/JG2. In the short sharp fight that followed, Wing Commander Brothers and a 165 Squadron pilot both destroyed Fw190s. On 3 February, Johnnie led 610 Squadron on a sweep with 485 Squadron between Berck and Le Touquet. The trip was uneventful, although the Northolt and North Weald Wings were heavily engaged. Three days later, 610 suffered its first loss since returning to 11 Group: Sgt H.R. Parker, a New Zealander, was missing from a Rhubarb, the pilot last heard of about twenty miles north of Cherbourg. The fourth Westhampnett pilot to be lost in just three days on Rhubarbs, Sergeant Parker's body was never found, despite an extensive ASR search led by Johnnie. The 10th of February, however, was, according to the unit's ORB, 'A black day. On bomber escort to Caen, Squadron was jumped by Fw190s. Squadron Leader AE Robinson (supernumerary), Flying Officer LA Smith DFC and Sergeant HR Harris (NZ) all reported missing, while Pilot Officer KS Wright managed to stagger home with an aircraft badly shot up about the tail.' Johnnie recorded in his log that the 'Bombers flew at cloud base and this made it impossible for 610 to give them cover support. Bounced by 190s on the turn.' To lose three pilots on one sortie was a bitter blow indeed. All were married men.

Johnnie:

'Yes, that was a particularly bad trip. The problem was that, so as to provide as small a target as possible to the flak gunners, the Ventura leader flew just below cloud, meaning that we had no room to position ourselves above his formation. I therefore placed 610 Squadron at the bombers' rear, as other escorting Spitfires were on each flank. My intention was to sweep the target after the Venturas had bombed, but the 190s carved us up during the turn. About thirty fell on us through a gap in the cloud, so they had the advantage of height, surprise and speed.' In the ensuing combat, the tail was shot off Flying Officer Smith's tail, the pilot being seen to bale out over the sea, about three miles from the French coast. The Polish Sergeant Lisowski's Spitfire was also hit, and was smoking badly, but he ignored Squadron Leader Johnson's order to turn around and crash-land in France, instead staggering back to England and safety. Pilot Officer Wright's Spitfire was hit by a cannon shell and flung upside down, but by some miracle his controls responded sufficiently for him to drop to sea-level and head for home, alone. So ferocious was the attack by I/JG2 that diving for the deck was the only option for Johnnie and his remaining pilots. The CO of 610 Squadron knew that in the past the Germans had shown a marked reluctance to engage at sea level, so it was just above the waves that the Spitfires levelled out. If necessary they would turn tightly, just above the wave tops, enticing the Germans to follow; only the most skilful pilot would survive. As the Spitfires streaked across the waves towards England, Johnnie was too late in shouting a warning to two Spitfires flying ahead. A pair of 190s hit them hard, both Spitfires going down. That flown by Squadron Leader Anthony Robinson, serving as supernumerary with 610, suddenly became enveloped in flame. As the horrified pilots watched helplessly, the pilot screamed all the way down over the R/T. Seconds after impact, the sea had closed completely over the aircraft, of which there was no trace. Johnnie: 'That incident was awful, and will always remain pretty much etched into my memory. It was shocking, we had never experienced anything like it before. None of us spoke for the rest of the way home. It seemed at the time that there was no solution to the 190 menace. As we have previously said our radius of operations was reduced to the enemy coastline for some time, and all of this because of one fucking aircraft type! We were losing a lot of chaps, far too many. It got to the stage that we had to avoid combat unless the Controller gave us the perfect bounce. We needed the Spitfire Mk IX – badly. Although some squadrons were flying them, it was frustrating for the rest of us.'

On 13 February Johnnie probably destroyed an Fw190 over Boulogne: '610 Squadron, led by myself, was flying as top cover to 485 Squadron and formation was under Appledore Control. Wing started to climb off Shoreham and crossed French coast just South of Boulogne at 1310 hours with 610 at 21,000 feet and 485 at 17,000 feet. After several vectors during ten to fifteen minutes, about fifteen Fw190s were seen flying West in the Montreuil – Stella Plage area at approximately 10,000 feet. Squadron Leader Grant, leading 485 Squadron, called up saying he was going to attack, and I led the Squadron down, still maintaining height above 485. Before 485 could engage the E/A they ran into approximately twenty more 190s, which were at 13,000 feet south west of Boulogne, and immediately turned head-on to engage them. 485 Squadron was considerably outnumbered and as Squadron Leader Grant called for assistance I led 610 Squadron into the general melee which was developing. After some time at 12,000 feet, I singled out a 190 which was climbing to the South, above the main engagement, but was out of range and so I did not open fire. The 190 then made a 180° left-hand turn and dived down, and I got into position by executing a steep turn, and opened fire from port quarter from above with cannon and machine-gun from 350 – 400 yards. As I closed gradually, giving several short bursts, I saw a large piece of the E/A fall away. The 190 then dived vertically, streaming black smoke. As I broke away and turned, I saw a crashed aircraft burning to the South of Montreuil woods, just before the Squadron left the French coast. Combat was broken off at 9,000 feet. Several pilots saw this E/A diving down but none can confirm that it was this 190 that crashed, but Sergeant Lisowski, flying at 2,000 feet, saw a 190 pass him at fifty yards in a vertical dive, just before the former crossed the coast on the way back. Cine-gun was exposed and I claim this Fw190 as probably destroyed.'

The Tangmere Spitfires had been led into a trap by Hauptmann 'Wutz' Galland, Kommandeur of II/JG26 and brother of the legendary Adolf, whose *Gruppe* was operating with 7/JG2. Galland and two of his pilots destroyed three 485 Squadron Spitfires, while Pilot Officer Skibinski, of Johnnie's 610 Squadron, was picked off by a 7/JG2 pilot. 485 Squadron claimed two 190s destroyed in response, in addition to Johnnie's probable, but in reality the enemy withdrew unscathed.

Early in March, Wing Commander Brothers was posted away. Before another wing leader was appointed, on 8 March, the Tangmere Wing was led by Wing Commander Duncan Smith DSO DFC, who was actually Wing Commander (Flying) at North Weald. On this sortie 610 and 485 Squadron provided withdrawal cover to Fortresses which had bombed Rennes. There were no combats. On 10 March, Johnnie led the Wing on Rodeo 180. Again the trip passed without incident. Changes, however, were afoot. Johnnie: 'I had been getting an increasing number of calls from a staff officer, asking me how many operational hours I had, how many sweeps had I done, so I told him, and he asked "When did you last have a rest?" I said "Well, I've just had one, we've been up to Castletown, no operational flying up there whatsoever, shot lots of grouse and downed a fair bit of malt!"

He said, "Oh, so you count that as a rest, do you?"

I said "Yes I do, and the salmon fishing was pretty good too!" Well, it was better than going to be an instructor at some bloody OTU, wasn't it, teaching a lot of ham-fisted buggers how to fly! He said, "Oh, I'll call you back". I was concerned that this interest was because they intended to rest me from operations, which was the last thing I wanted. The staff officer called me back and said "The Commander-in-Chief (who by that time was Air Marshal Sir Trafford Leigh-Mallory) sends his congratulations; you are to put up your Wing Commander's stripe immediately and take over the Canadian Spitfire Wing at Kenley".'

On 19 March 1943, Wing Commander J.E. 'Johnnie' Johnson DFC & Bar left 610 Squadron, which he had successfully commanded for eight months. With his faithful black Labrador, Sally, for company, he set off in his old Morris for Kenley and the Canadians. A whole new era was about to begin.

By the time of Johnnie's promotion and appointment as Wing Commander (Flying), his personal score of enemy aircraft destroyed was just into double figures. Being a Wing Leader, however, was not about a personal score, but that of the team. Now was the chance for Wing Commander Johnson to demonstrate the depth of his leadership qualities. Johnnie: 'It was a quantum leap from being a squadron leader to becoming a wing commander. The dream of every fighter pilot at that time must surely to have been getting a wing in 11 Group, which I had now achieved. To say that I welcomed and looked forward to this new challenge was an understatement! The RAF, in my day, taking my career from sergeant-pilot in the VR to Wing Commander (Flying) in three-and-a half years would have been impossible in the army. No-one in the Life Guards, for example, could have gone from trooper to lieutenant-colonel in three years. Never. Rank and privilege, and class and breeding was very much to the fore in the army in those days, and in the RN to some extent, but it wasn't by now in the RAF. In the RAF, if a man could do his job and hold his own in the squadron and that sort of thing, then that is all we required of him. He had equal opportunities for promotion whether he had been to the local grammar school or Eton or Harrow. That was the great thing about our service, equal opportunities.'

Kenley was a long established fighter station in Surrey. The personnel of the Spitfire Wing now based there were Canadian, as Johnnie remembered: 'The Canadians? They had a reputation for lacking discipline, bloody-mindedness and so on and so forth. Stan Turner, for example, a very prickly pear. Bader could handle him, Bader knew that Stan Turner, when the chips were down, would be there when lesser men had fled because he was such a fucking obstinate bastard, wouldn't give in, but he was ill-dressed and wouldn't shave occasionally, and when he was pissed he always had a six-shooter somewhere on him. When he was pissed he used to let this fucking gun off in the Mess or wherever he was! Of course on the old Bader Wing, 145 was taken out of the line and Stan was very pissed off about this, so he went up to Catterick and they'd got an old man commanding Catterick called Beisegal, who was very dyed in the wool, pre-war regular, and old Stan got his six shooter out and started loosing off, shooting pictures off the wall, and there was talk of a court martial, and Leigh-Mallory himself had to get on the blower and put the thing right! Funny thing was about Turner, later on in life he went out to the Mediterranean where he was still scruffy, ill dressed, but he finished up in 1944, beginning of 1945 as our Group Captain! He took over 127 Wing and he comes up from the desert in all his khaki, he's still got the fucking gun, and then he became the toughest disciplinarian that you ever met: "Must Court Martial the bugger, can't have that, put him under close arrest, he's not properly dressed", and *this* from bloody Turner! Talk about the change over from poacher to gamekeeper! What I am trying to get at is that the Canadians had a reputation, through people like Turner, of being tough and obstinate and difficult to handle. When I got the Canadian Wing, the Group Captain down at Tangmere said "Oh Christ, they'll all have six-shooters and they'll be shooting stuff off the wall, they'll never take any notice of you!" But in fact they were the finest bunch of people you ever did meet. They flew well, beautiful discipline in the air, they'd all done a lot of flying hours in Canada, many as instructors, and they could *really* fly.'

As Johnson motored to Kenley, many thoughts occupied his mind, but uppermost was that the Kenley Wing was equipped with the new Spitfire Mk IX – the answer to the Fw190 threat: 'Really, when I had commanded

610 Squadron, flying the Spitfire Mk V, we were cut to pieces by the 190s. So having the Spitfire IX, which was a different aeroplane altogether, you've got a chance of getting stuck into these bastards. The IX was far more powerful, the Merlin Sixty-One engine matched the airframe (there was no undue torque or bad flying characteristics like there was later with the Griffon marques). The IX was a very good combination of airframe and engine. The IX was the best Spitfire. When we got the IX, we had the upper hand then, which did for the 190s! We could turn inside him and hack him down, which we did. Those cannon shells were about as thick as your wrist, and when you sent them crashing through his armour, he didn't fucking like it one bit! There were two Spit IX squadrons at Kenley in March 1943, 403 and 416, and two of Spit Vs, 411 and 421, at Redhill. I was supposed to look after the flying of the Redhill squadrons too. Kenley's squadrons were both Spitfire IXs, the Redhill squadrons still being on Spitfire Vs. This did not become a "Big Wing" affair, however, because, due to the difference in performance, you could not operate Vs and IXs together, and also Kenley could not take any more than two Spitfire squadrons anyway.'

Group Captain H.A. 'Jimmy' Fenton, who had commanded 238 Squadron during the Battle of Britain, was the Station Commander: 'Kenley seemed to have everything: comfortable quarters, entertainment including a camp cinema, and an abundant source of girlfriends for the boys!' Hugh Constant Godefroy was then a pilot officer serving with 403 'Wolf' Squadron and remembers Johnnie's arrival: 'Charlie Magwood was made CO of 403 Squadron, and we were told that we were getting an RAF Wing Leader, Wing Commander JE Johnson DFC & bar. Group Captain Fenton brought him in at lunchtime, and with Squadron Leader Bud Malloy's help introduced him around. He made a positive first impression. When he spoke, it was firm and decisive. He was a wiry sort of fellow who walked with almost a cocky swagger. There was none of that fishy eye aloofness about him. He looked at the person talking to him as though he was paying attention. His face broke into a smile, which emphasised the chip out of a top tooth. He called the Wing into the Briefing Room for an introductory orientation. Using short crisp sentences and slow, almost Churchillian emphasis, he stated that he expected implicit obedience to his flying orders. Flying discipline was the only discipline he was interested in; he didn't give a tinkers damn what we did on the ground. He favoured the "fluid four" formation to provide better cross cover. He stated that he expected it would take a little time for us to get used to each other, but that he looked forward to leading a Canadian Wing.

"Any questions?"

There was dead silence.

"OK, chaps", he said with a broad grin, his eyes twinkling, "Give me a chance for a quick squirt, and I'll see you in the bar."

There was a roar of laughter, and as the gathering broke up, it was evident that he had won the pilots' respect immediately.'

On 22 March 1943, Johnnie flew Spitfire Mk IX, EN398 for the first time, a sortie of fifty minutes of 'Local flying'. He also made four landings and immediate take-offs, just to get used to the Mk IX. EN398 became the Wing Leader's regular mount, a Canadian maple leaf painted below the cockpit and the initials 'JE-J' painted on the fuselage. For ease of identification in the air, it had become customary for Wing Leaders to have their initials so painted, although the practice not always found favour with intelligence officers, as Johnnie recalled: 'To see your initials painted on a Spitfire was really something, you really knew then that you had made it, as it were. The "Spy" suggested, however, that I should not conform for fear of the enemy identifying and singling me out in the air. I told him… well… you can imagine what I told him, and "JE-J" was duly applied!' Johnnie also had to select a radio call sign and chose 'Greycap'. The scene was now set for excellence.

The weather was slowly improving, and with better flying conditions the daylight fighter war was due to increase in both tempo and ferocity. To his dismay however, Wing Commander Johnson had found that his new wing still flew the antiquated line astern formation; he remembered: 'Yes, that it is true. We had a long talk about it early on and naturally I intended that we should fly in line abreast. Syd Ford of 403 favoured the line astern, and Foss Boulton of 416 couldn't make up his mind. We agreed that for the first few shows I would lead the Wing with 416, which would fly in finger-fours. 403 was to fly top cover, some 3,000 feet above us, in whatever formation Syd chose. I agreed to review the position after a few sorties so that a decision could be made for the whole Wing. Of course I could have insisted that we flew finger-fours from the outset, but that was not really my way. I wanted to win them round by showing them the benefits of the finger-four in action. It was more democratic that way and more likely, I thought, to motivate and encourage. In respect of one matter, however, I did follow Syd Ford. His guns were harmonised on the "spot" principle, rather than the more usual shotgun type spread pattern. Syd's combat films showed the devastating effect of his particular choice of harmonisation, so I made it mine too.'

Until this point, the winter weather had been unfavourable to offensive fighter operations, but was now starting to turn. Action was not far ahead, and the afternoon of 25 March showed promise when Rodeo 194 was ordered. At 1650 hours, the Wing, led by Greycap, took off from Kenley but headed independently through cloud to RV over Dungeness. The Wing swept the area of Boulogne, St Omer, Sangatte, between 25,000 and 28,000 feet. As Johnnie led his Canadians over the French coast at Boulogne, they passed the Northolt Wing's Spitfires heading back to England. Visibility was poor though, and no reaction was forthcoming from the enemy. By 1830 hours the Kenley Wing was landing back at base. When dawn broke on 28 March the weather was bright and sunny, with only scattered cloud, the wind blowing gustily from the west. Soon the teleprinter clattered away and the Form 'D' came through: the Kenley Wing would fly on Ramrod 48 and provide high cover to American bombers attacking the railway marshalling yards at Rouen. As we have seen, the American bombers' first missions were tentative probes to targets close to the French coast, mainly those connected with the Directive's primary target: the U-boat. The Biscay-based submarines, however, were protected in massive concrete bunkers, built by the Germans using slave labour. Anti-aircraft units also heavily defended them, St Nazaire soon becoming 'Flak City' to the Americans. Railway marshalling yards were also important targets because through them passed supplies to the U-boat bases. Having already struck at an important marshalling yard in Germany itself, in March 1943, the 'Mighty Eighth' began attacks on such targets in France. The attack against Rouen on 28 March, in which the Kenley Wing was involved, was one of those raids. On that day, Wing Commander Johnson led the Kenley Wing off at 1230 hours and headed for Beachy Head at 26,000 feet. There the Spitfires met the bombers, eighty B-17s and twenty B-24s, orbited right and set course for Hastings. Johnnie later wrote in his log book: 'American bombers straggled badly and the 100 covered about twenty miles.' When twenty miles off Dieppe, the bombers were instructed to 'pancake', so Johnnie hauled the Kenley Wing round and swept the Channel behind the bombers. The operation was not, therefore, a success.

The following day was another sunny one, with only scattered cloud and variable wind. Wing Commander Johnson led the Kenley Wing off at 1245 hours on Circus 277, an attack on the marshalling yards at Abbeville. High over Beachy Head the Spitfires met twelve Ventura bombers that immediately began climbing, contrary to plan. For some unrecorded reason, five minutes later six of the bombers turned back with the Spitfire Mk V Wing. The remaining box continued on course, bombing the target from 10,000 feet. Abbeville aerodrome was a famous Luftwaffe fighter base, from which four FW190s were seen to scramble, but no engagements took place. The German flak gunners hammered away all the while however, although there were no hits due to shells exploding at the wrong height. On the way out, Squadron Leader Ford reported the position of a six-inch coastal gun, and six E-boats were noted in the Somme Estuary as the Beehive passed out over Cayeux. By 1405 hours the Spitfires were back at Kenley, their guns again unfired.

On 31 March the morning weather was fair but cold, with a gusting westerly wind, the Kenley Wing was detailed to fly Ramrod 47. This time the B-17s were bound for Rotterdam, and the Kenley Spitfires rendezvoused with seventy bombers over Harwich at 1105 hours. Ten minutes later the wing crossed the French coast at 26,000 feet and swept the area Dunkirk–Le Touquet–St Omer. At 31,000 feet over St Omer, twenty Fw190s were sighted. Later Johnnie wrote in his log book, 'Could not engage as Huns going NE and we were short of gravy.' Despite the improvements that the Spitfire Mk IX enjoyed, limited range remained a problem. The Wing returned over Dunkirk and Hawkinge, landing at 1220 hours. Flight Lieutenant Charlie Magwood wrote with frustration in his log that the Germans 'wouldn't stay and play'. Johnnie himself recognised that his Canadians needed action, and soon. He wrote, 'We wanted a full-blooded scrap with the Abbeville boys to weld the Wing together.' The unsettled spring weather, however, continued to make this difficult. On 3 April, 'Ops' were on with Ramrod Forty-nine. The plan was for the Hawker Typhoon fighter-bombers of Squadron Leader Denis Crowley-Milling's 181 Squadron to make a low-level attack on the enemy airfield at Abbeville-Drucat. As the 'Bombphoons' turned for home, the Kenley Wing was to sweep the area between Le Touquet and St Omer, engaging any scrambled German fighters. Such a Ramrod was bound to provoke a lively reaction, and anticipation was high. Kenley was the only fighter wing involved and would be controlled by Squadron Leader Hunter, the Senior Controller of the new radar station at Appledore in Kent (codename 'Grass-seed'). Appledore's radar was of a higher resolution than existing appliances, which were designed for home defence, and could therefore detect bandits over France and beyond. For the first time, wing leaders would have the great advantage of advance information in the air regarding the presence, size and direction of enemy aircraft.

At 1445 hours the Kenley Wing crossed the French coast at Le Touquet, the eight Typhoons being well below and racing home having given the hornets' nest a violent stir. As the Spitfires swept over St Omer between 24,000 and 26,000 feet, Grass-seed vectored Greycap on to fifteen to twenty Fw190s of II/JG26. The bandits, having taken off from Vitry, were still climbing and flying west, towards the coast in finger-fours and at staggered heights. In a demonstration of excellent controlling and teamwork between Squadron Leader Hunter and Wing Commander Johnson, the Kenley Wing was soon positioned over Montreuil, 3,000 feet above and up sun of the enemy, in perfect position for a bounce. The only problem was that Grass-seed also reported more bandits behind the Spitfires. Although reportedly some miles away, no one knew how accurate this information was given that the radar was operating at its maximum range. What was Johnnie to do? On seeing the 190s below, his mind was made up: it was too good an opportunity to miss. First, remembering the fate of Wing Commander Bader, Johnnie satisfied himself that the 190s concerned were not merely bait, then led 416 down to attack on the port side while 403 dived on the starboard. Johnnie's combat report subsequently related that he 'attacked an Fw190 from astern using cannon and machine-gun. Opened range at 400 yards and closed to 200. I saw cannon strikes on the wing roots and fuselage of the enemy aircraft that flicked over and went down smoking and burning.' Unteroffizier Hans Hiess (6/JG26) baled out but his parachute failed to open. A veritable mêlée ensued as the Canadians fell on the unsuspecting Germans. Flying Officer Fowlow and Flying Officer Cameron, both of 403, saw a 190 go down, having been attacked by Squadron Leader Ford, pouring black smoke and flames from the cockpit, later enveloping the entire machine like a 'ball of fire' (ORB). Flight Lieutenant Charlie Magwood blasted a 190 from fifty yards. There was a succession of long flashes and flames from cannon strikes all round the centre section of the fuselage and wings, chunks flew off just before the aircraft disintegrated – completely. Just a black cloud hung in the air. Flying Officer H.D. MacDonald fired at another 190 from 100 yards, which soon streamed white smoke, dropped an undercarriage leg and was abandoned by the pilot.

416 Squadron fared not quite so well. Squadron Leader Boulton claimed a 190 destroyed, Flight Lieutenant R.A. Buckham and Flying Officer N.A. Keene sharing a probable, and Flying Officer J.A. Rae one damaged. Oberfeldwebel 'Adi' Glunz of 6/JG26, however, shot down Flying Officer A.M. Watson over Le Touquet, this being the Germans' only victory in this engagement. The pilots of the two 190s hit by the COs of 403 and 416 Squadron, Unteroffiziers Heinrich Damm and Albert Mayer, were both killed, but the other three 190s claimed destroyed by the Wing all managed

to struggle back to land safely at Vitry and Merville. Now in a very hostile sky with more 190s hurrying to the scene, Grass-seed advised Greycap to withdraw. Johnnie: 'We didn't need telling twice! We got out as quick as we could and raced across the Channel. After the combat the Wing had naturally become fragmented, so we came home in pairs and fours. News of our success had spread rapidly and naturally the pilots were jubilant – this was what we had all been waiting for. It was a great shame that we lost Watson, however, but nevertheless we had gone over there and given the 190s a clobbering. We were all delighted and I telephoned Appledore and thanked Hunter for his excellent controlling.' Both the new British 'Wingco' and the Canadians had shown each other their mettle. Richard Booth was a pilot in 416 Squadron: 'Upon conclusion of a Wing operation we would have a re-hash of the day's activities with "JEJ". At the end of one of these early sessions he invited suggestions. We complained that we had difficulty understanding him on the R/T, at which point Johnnie volunteered to try and talk more like a Canadian over the ether! At the next de-brief he inquired as to whether he was clearer over the air, but to a man we advised him to go back to normal!' Eileen Steel was a young WAAF working Kenley's Pass Office, situated immediately above the Station's main entrance. From that vantage point, Eileen and her colleagues, all 'starry eyed youngsters, often watched Wing Commander Johnnie Johnson coming and going. We hero-worshipped him even then.'

The 4th of April was another fine and sunny day, perfect for Ramrod 51. The Kenley Wing was ordered to provide First Withdrawal cover to the leading box (of seventy) B-17s returning from a raid on the Renault factory at Billancourt, Paris. Greycap led the Wing out over Beachy Head at 24,000 feet, crossing the French coast at 1432 hours over Quiberville. When Johnnie reached the RV, near Rouen, 'Fw190s were attacking bombers heavily when we sighted them.' Major Oesau, Kommodore of JG2, had intercepted the bombers with his I Gruppe and the operational squadron of a training unit, JG105, after they had successfully hit their target. Before the Spitfires arrived, II and III/JG26 also joined in, charging the B-17s head-on. The 'Forts' were tightly grouped in two large boxes, providing mutual fire support, but one Fortress was seen spiralling downwards; only one parachute emerged. The backdrop was provided by way of a huge pall of smoke rising some 7,000 feet high over Paris, and flak bursts here and there. Greycap despatched Squadron Leader Ford and 403 Squadron, who were ten miles away, to attack the 190s and 'sort them out'. From 200 yards, Squadron Leader Ford delivered a long burst at a 190, causing a large explosion and fragments to fly off. The undercarriage soon dangled limply and the front of the aircraft became engulfed in 'solid yellow flame' (ORB). The port wing broke upward and the 190 dropped towards the ground over 20,000 feet below. Flight Lieutenant Magwood thumbed the trigger at a 190 that had hurtled vertically through the bombers, while Pilot Officer EL Gimbel DFC, an American, and Flying Officer WJ Cameron saw a B-17 destroy a 190 before diving themselves onto a 190 a couple of thousand feet below. Gimbel fired and Cameron watched pieces fall off the 190, which rolled and went straight down. As the two Spitfire pilots broke away they were attacked by three 190s, flying in close line astern, from 200 yards astern. Cameron shouted 'Watch out, Ed!' (ORB) and broke sharply right and upwards. Gimbel did not reply but Cameron saw a Spitfire going down 'in a gentle dive streaming black smoke' (ORB).

At 1435 hours, Flight Lieutenant Magwood fired at a 190, which dived away and crashed on the edge of a big wood near Bellencombre. Together with his Blue 2, Sergeant LJ Deschamps, Magwood climbed to 23,000 feet and got in a short burst at another 190 from 200 yards astern but without result. Deschamps gave chase and hit the 190 around the cockpit area that immediately became enveloped in flame, the stricken enemy fighter plummeting earthwards. A few minutes later Deschamps was bounced by two 190s from out of the sun. Magwood watched helplessly as Blue 2 'skidded off to starboard, streaming glycol' (ORB). Magwood himself then started a running engagement until crossing the coast about St Valery where he dived beneath a 190 that he attacked from astern. Delivering a short burst, Magwood saw 'flashes of flame from cannon strikes all around the cockpit and along the starboard wing, chunks flew back, the cockpit was enveloped in flames and he fell off, diving vertically followed by two splashes' (ORB). As the 190s pursued the B-17s across the Channel, Flying Officer MacDonald followed twenty of them, singling one out which he attacked. The 190's starboard wingtip fell off and 'bright scarlet flames' (ORB) were seen in the cockpit. This enemy fighter also crashed into the sea, witnessed by Flying Officer Aitkin who also saw both splashes.

Although Squadron Leader Boulton exchanged blows with a 190 that attacked him head-on, 416 Squadron, with which Greycap was flying, made no claims. The wing crossed the English coast 8,000 feet above Shoreham, landing at 1525 hours. Two Spitfires were missing. Ed Gimble had collided with a 190, baled out and successfully evaded; he was safely back in England by August. Although it was hoped that Leo Deschamps would make a safe forced landing, he was in fact killed. Four B-17s were lost, all before the Spitfires' arrival. Again, this emphasises the extra danger faced by the Americans when they ventured beyond the range of their fighter escort. The need for a long-range escort fighter was becoming ever more pressing.

403 Squadron claimed five Fw190s destroyed and one damaged. From available German records we know that JG26 lost Karl Fackler to either Magwood or MacDonald (and two other pilots to the B-17s). Obergefreiter Jürgen Birn of 4/JG54 was also killed in this battle, but by whom is not known. Five 190s, two each of II & III/JG26 and one of 4/JG54, returned to base with combat damage. All of the claims for 190s destroyed by 403 Squadron appear accurate however, so it is possible that they belonged to I/JG2 or JG105. In return, the pilots of JG26 claimed eight Spitfires destroyed (six of which being confirmed), and I/JG2 two. Fighter Command actually lost eight Spitfires in total that day, two of 403 and six of the Northolt (Polish) Wing. It is worth reflecting on the sad fact that during the raid on the Renault factory, in support of which the Kenley Wing was flying, 200 Parisian civilians were killed. The death toll of civilians caused by Allied bombing in the occupied lands was high. A heavy price was therefore paid for their freedom. Quite rightly, however, Johnnie and his pilots felt flushed with success. That morning, Squadron Leader Syd Ford had presented the 'Wingco' with Canadian shoulder flashes to be sewn on his battledress. This was a clear indication that Johnnie had won the Canadians over.

On 5 April, another fine day, the Americans sallied forth to attack the ERLA aircraft factory at Antwerp. Ramrod Fifty-two saw the Kenley Wing flying first fighter cover to the first box of a force comprising 104 B-17s and B-24s. In an effort to extend range, Johnnie had first led his wing down to Manston, near the Kent coast, and refuelled; those few extra miles might mean life or death to a bomber crew. Just west of Ostend and ten minutes early, due to a strong tail wind, the wing rendezvoused with the bombers, which were outward bound, at 25,000 feet, formating down-sun and above the leading box. The Americans had firstly feinted towards Abbeville before turning towards Antwerp, thus forcing the shadowing FW 90 pilots to waste fuel. Nevertheless Major 'Pips' Priller led 8/JG26 and III/JG26 straight to Antwerp and formed up for head-on attacks, the Germans' favoured method against the heavily armed American bombers. Priller charged almost immediately after Greycap and his Spitfires arrived on the scene. The 'Wingco' and 416 Squadron challenged the 190s and became engaged in a running battle on the bombers' starboard side. Johnnie subsequently claimed three 190s damaged, Squadron Leader Boulton and

Flying Officer Rae one each. The 190s did not attack the port side, where 403 Squadron was positioned. Later, 403's pilots were agreed that the 190s' attacks 'were determined and persistent and were mostly from ahead, above and below in singles, fours and sixes'. Priller, of course, was an *experte* and clearly knew what he was about.

Just north of Ghent, the Spitfires were ordered to return, with fuel states very much in mind, and had to abandon the bombers to their fate. An increasing number of enemy fighter units were scrambled to attack the American 306th Bomb Group, which lost five B-17s. The 306th, based at Thurleigh, claimed the destruction of five enemy fighters, although JG26 only actually lost one Fw190: Hauptmann Fritz Geisshardt, Kommandeur of III/JG26. This was an important loss as Geisshardt was an experienced *experte* with 102 victories (75 of which in Russia). Nevertheless, the day was the most successful so far for the *Jagdwaffe*, especially considering that, for the first time, German fighter controllers had managed to coordinate the combined forces of three different commands (JG1, JG2 & JG26) throughout the interception.

At midday on 7 April the wing was released and most of the pilots went up to London. Hugh Godefroy describes one such 'sortie' with the ever-popular 'Wingco':

'In the air, Johnnie Johnson was "Greycap Leader", cool, commanding, and as aggressive as a bull terrier. But when the sun went down, he didn't mind being called "Johnnie". He was one of us. His responses seemed Canadian, pure and simple." What we need is a pissup! I've had my fill of liver and onions. Monty!"

"Sir!"

"Call the Red Lion at Redhill and tell them to kill the bloody fatted calf. We're on our way. Come on lads, fill up the vans and follow me. Hughie, you'd better come in mine. I may need a second pair of eyes on the way home!"

'Chuckling with anticipation, everybody grabbed their caps and piled into the vans. As expected, it was a hair-raising ride. What with the masked headlights and my poor night vision, I didn't see obstructions until we were almost upon them.

"Get out of the bloody way, you stupid bastard!", Johnnie would shout, as he suddenly overtook a vehicle.

"Clear the road, the Kenleys are coming!"

"That's original, Hughie, I rather like that."

"Look out Johnnie, there's a man in the middle of the road!"

"Bloody Canadian, you obviously haven't learned to drive in England yet!"

I was greatly relieved when we pulled in the parking lot of the Red Lion.

"There we are – my kingdom for a pint of Guinness!"

'To the amusement of most of the regulars we took over. There was plenty of beer, games of darts and skittles. Johnnie, with the help of Walter Conrad, led a singsong around the piano with old favourites like 'Roll out the Barrel', 'Waltzing Matilda' and the South African Zulu war dance, 'Hey zinga, zumba. Zumba, zumba'. There was food for those who wanted it: smoked salmon and excellent steak-and-kidney pie.

'When the proprietor shouted:

"Time gentlemen, please!" there was a chorus of:

"A-w-w-w-w-w-!"

"Time gentlemen, for one more for the road!"

"Right you are", said Johnnie. "OK lads, you've 'ad it. Bottoms up! There's work to do in the morning".

'I offered to drive.

"What?" said Johnnie. "You drive in your present state of public drunkenness? Not bloody likely! What we need is a sober man at the wheel. Look, some stupid clot has boxed me in. I'll show the bastard!"

'With a crunch, Johnnie backed the van into the car behind, shunting it a good six feet to the rear.

"That's better. All aboard, chaps!"

'When the van was full, we were off in a cloud of dust. But now, with a few pints of ale and a steak-and-kidney pie under my belt, somehow it didn't seem to matter. After a while, in the dim light of our shielded headlights, I saw half-a-dozen women walking on the right side of the road. With a squeal of tyres, Johnnie slammed on the brakes.

"There they are chaps, same level, 12 o'clock, get into them and don't let any of them get away!"

'Tittering with laughter, Johnnie led us in pursuit of the women who had now broken into a trot. Johnnie caught the hand of a young lady straggler and as he spun her round she butted her cigarette in his left ear.

"O-w-w-w", he said, "You nasty little bitch!"

'The ladies in front stopped, and from their midst we hear a querulous voice say "Nobody calls my daughter a nasty little bitch. I say, what's all this in aid of?"

"They've got us outnumbered, return to base!"

'To the sound of Johnnie's giggling laughter, we all piled back in the truck again and took off. It was a happy light-hearted evening, full of harmless fun, and in the Johnson tradition punctuated with the unexpected. There wasn't a man who didn't waken refreshed and ready to follow him in the morning.'

Johnnie:

'Personalities at Kenley? Ford I was very impressed with. He got a DFC & Bar, he had flown a lot up at Digby. We had some good flight commanders, but the rank and file had not a lot of experience. When I got there they had not done a lot of flying over France, of course you can't in the winter months because of the weather. Buck McNair had a bit of the Stan Turner in him, I remember going into the Mess one night, we hadn't done much flying then, he was promoted about May time and he had a few beers. I went into the bar after dinner and he shouts out "Hey Wingco, when are we going to do some flying? The fucking guns are rusting up!" So all eyes switched to the "Wingco" wondering "How's he going to handle this one?" So I said "Get me a pint, Buck, and we'll talk about it." It was the only way to deal with it, he was a bit aggressive was Buck. Fortunately, I got there at the right time: we had the Spitfire IX, the weather was getting better all the time and these guys could fly very well, they knew how to handle their Spitfires and don't forget that Kenley was in a built up area, very difficult to find in murky weather. "Batchy" Atcherley, who had been the Station Commander sometime before, had erected a series of tents around the circuit and painted them white. If you saw the tents you just kept turning inwards and the runway appeared! It was one of the first landing aids that I ever came across. The impressions were that the Canadians were actually a very well disciplined outfit, both in the air and on the ground, except, of course, when they got pissed. Then some pissed pilot officer would come and clobber a squadron leader or something and it all went pear shaped! Fortunately they mostly got pissed in the Mess, so it was all kept in house, and the following morning there would be an apology or whatever. There was still a leavening of peacetime guys, who had been through Kingston, the Canadian equivalent of Cranwell, "Iron Bill" MacBrian, for example, who took over as Station Commander from Jimmy Fenton, he had been to Kingston, and he was a very nice chap.'

Johnnie was making progress with fighter formations: 'By now I had the Wing flying finger-fours. To me, the two squadron wing was ideal, being far more manoeuvrable than a wing of three or more squadrons. In the air, there would be fifty yards, say, between my number two and me, 100 yards then the other pair, then about a quarter-of-a-mile the other four and so on. Then stepped up, down sun so that they could see, two or three thousand feet higher, would be the other squadron. We covered a lot of sky, a mile or so.' There was still no standard formation operating procedure within Fighter Command however. The Kenley Wing became noticeable in the air, and Johnnie's formation became known as the 'Wolfpack'. Johnnie: 'The climb out of Kenley would depend on what the job was. If it was a fighter sweep then we would keep low level until we could see the Dutch or French coast, then climb as hard as we could to cross it at a reasonable height to get above the flak, say 12-14,000 feet, or 24-25,000 feet, which was our best height. If we were escorting Fortresses then we would climb high from base, because the higher you were the greater the range. The fighting height was 24-26,000 feet. The Germans always seemed to have a little bit of height on us due to the fuel injection.'

More clear and bright weather on 15 April saw Greycap leading the Kenley Wing on Rodeo 204. The wing crossed the French coast at 25,000 feet over Berck-sur-Mer and swept to port. Vectored by Appledore to St Omer, the wing manoeuvred to attack various forces of enemy aircraft but without sighting any of them. As Johnnie wrote in his log book, 'They were under 9/10ths cloud at 20,000 feet and we were over.'

By now, American fighters were entering the arena. By the first week in April, three P-47 Republic Thunderbolt Fighter Groups, 4, 56 & 78, were ready for operations. The P-47 was a huge, radial-engined beast of an aircraft. At 15,000 lbs gross, it was twice the weight of a Spitfire and soon nicknamed the 'Juggernaut', or more commonly the 'Jug'. In comparison trials against the RAF's captured Fw190, the P-47 appeared capable at 20,000 feet and above, but was found wanting below. To its advantage, the P-47 was armed with eight .50 calibre machine-guns, the standard American aircraft weapon of the war. This packed a heavier punch than the RAF's .303 'pea-shooters' and would serve the Americans well. The P-47s made their first, uneventful, sweep, from Debden in Essex on 10 March 1943. Technical problems delayed the next incursion until 8 April, when the 'Jugs' sallied forth over the Pas-de-Calais. During these early trips the P-47s were escorted by Spitfires, as was the case on 15 April when all three P-47 groups swept Ostend and clashed with II/JG1. The soon-to-be 'ace' Don Blakeslee shot down a 190, and two other 190s were also claimed destroyed by the P-47 pilots. One 'Jug' was shot down however, and two more failed to return due to engine failures. Later the 'Jug' would earn an enviable reputation as both a long-range bomber-escort fighter, as was intended, and a low-level ground-attack fighter-bomber in support of the Allied armies. To start with, however, the P-47's range was similar to that of the Spitfire, some 170 miles, so the immediate difficulty of finding a long-range offensive escort fighter remained unresolved.

The entry of another new American fighter, the P-38 Lockheed Lightning, was delayed firstly due to it being difficult and slow to build. The Lightning, featuring an unorthodox design, was, however, brilliant in concept and promising in performance. When the P-38 equipped 78th Fighter Group arrived in England during 1942, and took over Goxhill, the situation in North Africa dictated them being redirected to that theatre. Further supplies of P-38s were sent not to England but to North Africa and the south west Pacific. It would not be until the autumn of 1943 that the Eighth Air Force would receive the Lightning for operations in the European Theatre. As things turned out, the twin-engined P-38, like the Me110, proved no match for single-engine fighters. American bomber losses, however, indicated that if they were to continue their task then increased protection from the German fighters was *essential*. The Luftwaffe had 800 fighters in the West, and the energetic *General der Jagdflieger*, Adolf Galland, was doing his level best to increase that figure. As things stood, the Germans were still able to carefully coordinate and time their interceptions to coincide with that point in time when the bombers' 'Little Friends' had to turn back due to the constraints of fuel.

On the morning of 17 April, Wing Commander Johnson flew over to West Malling to examine two Fw190s that had landed there by mistake during the early hours. By 1417 hours, Greycap was back at Kenley and taking the Wing up on Circus 285, providing escort to twelve Venturas attacking the marshalling yards at Abbeville. The RV was at zero feet over Beachy Head, the bombers being four minutes late. While the Beehive proceeded to the French coast, a Defiant and a Mosquito were observed shadowing the raiders. Wing Commander Johnson broke radio silence and sent a section to investigate what turned out to be 'friendlies'. At 1453 hours the formation crossed the French coast at Cayeux with the Spitfire Mk Vs of 411 Squadron flying as close escort to the Venturas at 13,000 feet. The target was duly 'pranged', and Greycap wrote in his log 'Excellent bombing'. He had positioned his fighters to the east of the bombers, providing such an effective screen that *Hauptmann* Wutz Galland was heard by the British Y-Service ordering his 190s to remain in formation as there were 'too many Spitfires'. While 411 Squadron and the bombers re-crossed the French coast, homeward bound, between Le Tréport and Cayeux, Johnnie led his Mk IX squadrons back around at 24,000 feet towards Abbeville – spoiling for a fight. As the Kenley Spitfires continued to climb inland, Greycap was informed by Appledore that the Hornchurch Wing was engaged. When the Kenley Wing was up sun and at 33,000 feet, Flight Lieutenant Godefroy, Yellow Leader, asked Greycap's permission to take his section down to attack three 190s that he could see climbing out to sea some 10,000 feet below. The Wingco agreed, and Godefroy's finger-four peeled off to attack. Yellow Leader fired at the right-hand 190, with cannons and machine guns, causing the port cannon magazine to explode and flashes of flame along the fuselage in front of the pilot. The 190 pilot was unable to recover his aircraft from a spin and baled out; both pilot and aircraft ended up in the Channel. Meanwhile, Yellow Two, Pilot Officer P.K. Gray, opened fire from 200 yards astern on the port 190. The German pilot half-rolled, was hit by Gray again, and entered a spiral dive pouring white smoke. This pilot also baled out, his 190 likewise crashing into the sea. The rest of the wing made no claims, but Johnnie recorded in his log book that the 'Wing was involved in a general dogfight over the French coast'.

Having landed back at Kenley by 1552 hours, there was more action ahead for the 'Kenleys'. At 1745 hours, Greycap and his Spitfires were off on Circus 286. The Spitfire pilots' task was firstly to provide target support for twelve Venturas bombing the marshalling yards at Caen, and then sweep the general area. The Beehive crossed out at less than 500 feet above Brighton, climbing to 21,000 feet, crossing the French coast at Dives and turning south for Caen. The bombing was accurate once more but the flak was equally on target and intense over the target. The Spitfires then flew at 22-25,000 feet to twenty-five miles north-west of Fécamp. Appledore then informed Greycap of a gaggle of bandits apparently engaged on an ASR operation near Dieppe, so Johnnie led the wing down to 2,000 feet. Coming along the coast were four Fw190s and four Me109s, which were attacked by the whole wing!

Flight Lieutenant Magwood had just given lead of 403 Squadron to Flight Lieutenant Godefroy on account of his R/T suddenly becoming unserviceable. Godefroy, having 'Tally Ho'd', led the charge of Yellow and Red Sections, being followed by Magwood with Blue Section which engaged a single 109 from another enemy formation before also attacking the 190s. One of the 'Butcher Birds' actually pulled up vertically and went through the surprised Spitfires, breaking sharply right and racing towards France.

Magwood reacted swiftly and half-rolled onto the 190 which did likewise but, being too low, crashed into the sea while 'trying to aileron out of it' (ORB); Magwood had not fired a shot! As Godefroy was about to fire at a 190 he suddenly had to break to avoid colliding with several Spitfires that cut across in front of him. Having recovered, he noticed two splashes in the sea, one of which was Magwood's 190, the other, smaller, probably being a pilot. Flying Officer Fowlow then fired at a 109 that pulled up in front of him, but it then dived away with no results being observed. Pilot Officer Dean Dover saw a 109 climbing into the sun and fired at it, but likewise would make no claim. As the Canadian turned away from France he suddenly found himself head-to-head with a 190. Dover immediately thumbed the trigger and Sergeant Brown, flying behind, saw the 190 dive into the sea. According to the squadron ORB, 'On the evidence available it appeared that various sections of the Squadron were all involved with the same Fw190, with no one pilot appearing to have accounted for it in clear-cut or definite style. For that reason the whole squadron shared the credit for destroying one Fw190.' Squadron Leader Foss Boulton, leading 416 Squadron, had fired a long burst of cannon at an Me109F which was confirmed as destroyed following an analysis of his combat film. All of the 'Kenleys' returned safely to base and were all down by 1930. By the close of play on what was a busy day, the Germans had lost a total of eight Fw190s, offset against just three Spitfires. To the great credit of their escorts, remarkably not one Ventura was lost.

On 20 April a complete change in the weather brought clear, still and sunny skies. The day's first operation was Rodeo 209. The wing swept the Le Touquet and Abbeville area, coming out at Dieppe. Appledore recalled the wing, however, when 'Seventy-five plus E/A were reported in the vicinity of our Wing all alone' (ORB, 403 Squadron). Johnnie, as we have heard, insisted on iron discipline in the air, for obvious reasons, and this included the matter of radio silence. In his log book he wrote, 'Rodeo 209 with the Polish Wing jabbering Russian over the R/T!' Next came Ramrod Sixty-seven, target support to eight Typhoons bombing Tricqueville aerodrome, which was successfully attacked. Afterwards the Spitfires were taken over by Appledore Control and vectored to a formation of twenty-one plus bandits at 29,000 feet over Dieppe. Six 190s subsequently made a head-on attack against 416 Squadron, but Boulton and his men reacted swiftly, the CO himself destroying one, Pilot Officer R.D. Phillip damaging another, all for no loss. Appledore then informed Greycap that fifteen Fw190s were closing from behind to attack. Low on fuel, Johnnie ordered the wing out, this command being 'smartly obeyed' (ORB, 403 Squadron).

On 1 May, a cloudy May Day which threatened rain, Wing Commander Johnson led the Kenley Wing down to Portreath in 10 Group, from which airfield the Spitfires were to provide top fighter cover for Circus Twenty-eight. Again, the movement to operate from a forward airfield was to extend the Spitfires' range. The B-17s of the 306th Bomb Group were to bomb the U-boat installations at Lorient, an important target given that the commander-in-chief of the *U-bootwaffe*, Admiral Dönitz, had his headquarters nearby at Kernaval. The Lorient boats were amongst the most successful operating from the Biscay coast, and therefore anything to impede or prevent their operations was helpful. Greycap's Spitfires rendezvoused with the Portreath and Exeter Spitfire Wings on time before flying first to Ushant, thence to the north of Brest at 26,000 feet. The German-occupied French port put up a protective screen of intense light flak as the Spitfires passed overhead and swept the area inland. Just before the Spits recrossed the coast on the way home, five Fw190s were seen above and about two miles behind. The Kenley Wing turned about to engage but the 190s' leader sensibly chose to make off to fight another day. The Germans half-rolled and dived away. Although this was the only incident of note so far as the Kenley Wing was concerned, it was a different story for the American bomber crews. As always, Jagdfliegerführer (Jafu) Brittany waited until the Spitfires had turned back before unleashing his fighters which rapidly fell on the B-17s. Of the seventy-five participating in this attack, seven were destroyed and two more were damaged.

On 4 May, Flying Officer J. Danforth 'Danny' Browne joined 403 Squadron. Although serving in a Canadian fighter squadron, Dan was in fact an American: 'I signed up in the RCAF in 1940, I was called up to the Commonwealth Air Training Plan in the February of 1941, and then I got my 'wings' in late August of 1941, and went home on a month's leave in New Jersey, said "goodbye" to my mother. We were in Halifax at the time of Pearl Harbor, and sailed a few days later. I was on a ship called the *Letitia*. I think that Atlantic crossing was some of the most terrifying experiences of my life! We ran into 108 knot winds off Iceland, my God those waves were huge and so they decided to really hunker everything down. We had the *Normandie* lose all its lifeboats during the storm, and several destroyers literally went straight through those huge waves, which was amazing. It was very frightening, especially when I climbed up the mast to watch proceedings. I would look down and see the green Atlantic, look the other way and just see froth! Eventually we got to Bournemouth, from where I thought that we would go to Singapore, which is why I thought we were on the High Seas. As we left Gibraltar we were attacked by FW Condors. We were picked up by the Condors two days out, and attacked by submarines on the third. We lost a couple of ships out of the convoy, although my ship, the old P&O liner *The Viceroy of India*, was safe. We went into Cape Town, picked up the Vichy French in Madagascar. Then we heard that Singapore had fallen to the Japanese, which was frustrating as I wanted to get into combat, which is why I, an American, had volunteered before my own country came into the war. It was an exasperating time, as they then posted me to fly Gloster Gladiators in Iran, in defence of certain oil refineries. We were then shipped back, going all the way round Africa without anything exciting taking place. Back in the UK, I was then posted to the OTU at Rednal in Shropshire, near Wales. Got through the course and then had good fortune to be posted to the Canadian Spitfire Wing at Kenley in 11 Group. This was better than Gladiators, to say the least! So, with no operational combat experience I joined the Kenley Wing, which turned out to be one of the happiest events of my life. I later had the opportunity to transfer from Kenley to the American air force, but I stayed where I was. My mother was Canadian and I enjoyed their company. One thing, we had some fine Canadians at Kenley. Some had been miners and lumberjacks, just roughnecks all their lives, so it was a weird combination. It was perhaps a stroke of genius to put Johnnie in command, although he was an Englishman. I was delighted to find Spit IXs at Kenley, which had a two-stage, two-speed engine. When you got up to about 19,000 feet, that second stage kicked in, at which point it was *your* air and no longer the Germans' air. Also, being "green", it was an incredible experience to go on your first operational sortie with Wing Commander Johnnie Johnson, who was definitely headed for great things.'

The 7th of May dawned fine and no time was lost in the planning of operations. In the morning, 416 Squadron carried out various local flights, searchlight cooperation exercises, and convoy patrols. Johnnie flew his usual Spitfire, EN398, on a test flight to jettison an auxiliary fuel tank. This was probably a flush-fitting 'slipper' tank, fitted beneath the cockpit section and containing either forty-five or ninety gallons of extra fuel, which designers had found to be the best option. The idea was that, with the ninety gallon tank, the pilot would take off and for the first hour and twenty minutes draw fuel from the auxiliary tank. When the enemy was sighted, the 'slipper' was jettisoned, normal flying characteristics thus resuming. Using the forty-five gallon tank, the Spitfire Mk IX's radius of action was 240 miles, 270 miles with the ninety gallon example. Johnnie: 'Owing to the lack of foresight by the fucking Chief of the Air Staff, Portal, the Spitfire could have had the same range as the Mustang, but he told Churchill that it would impede its performance as a defensive fighter, which of course is quite wrong. So the Spitfire never really had the range, and we should have done, simple as that. What pissed us all off so much is that we still had the same range in a Spitfire as we had in 1940, although Churchill himself is on the record writing a minute to Portal saying "Cannot the range of the Spitfire be improved?", and Portal writes back saying, "Not without detriment to its performance as an interceptor", which was absolute rubbish. That really needs highlighting. We did have auxiliary tanks, the largest being of ninety gallons, but that meant that there was more fuel outside the aircraft than in given that the Spitfire normally carried eighty-five gallons. Sometimes the bloody tank wouldn't come off, so they devised a little plunger in the cockpit which, if the tank got stuck, you kicked down. The Americans also fitted tanks to their Thunderbolts and Lightnings, but although it sounds fine in theory, doubling the range and so on, in practice it was not the answer. Dolfo Galland could attack our fighters as they were on the way in, making the pilots jettison their tanks, in which fuel was still plentiful, thus defeating the whole object of the exercise. No, it wasn't the answer, but the lack of range comes back to the English way of thinking, which is all about defence. Our lack of range was a big concern, and as the summer of 1943 progressed, so too did our frustration.'

On 9 May, Flying Officer Bob Middlemiss joined 403 Squadron on what was his second tour of operations: 'From soon after my arrival, whenever Johnnie Johnson led the Kenley Wing it was often with me flying as his Number Two. He was a great leader and had the knack of knowing where the Huns were, and was always there, personally, leading the squadron in for kills. Flying with him was great and of course as Number Two your job was to ensure that the Wing Leader was not attacked by the "dreaded Hun".'

The 11th of May was sunny and warm with a light southerly wind. First thing, Wing Commander Johnson flew another tank-jettisoning test, a sortie of forty minutes in his usual Spitfire, EN398, and 416 Squadron practised deck landings at Dunsfold. Then came the briefing for the day's operation: Circus 295, in which the Kenley Wing would provide 'second fighter echelon' (ORB, 403 Squadron) to a formation of B-25 Mitchells bombing the port of Boulogne. At 1210 hours, Greycap led the wing to North Foreland at 500 feet before making a wide orbit off Dunkirk at 14-16,000 feet. The Spitfires, however, were recalled by 'Wytex' (Codename for Kenley, ORB, 416 Squadron) and then vectored under Appledore to cross the enemy-occupied coast at Mardyck, there being, as Johnnie recorded in his log, 'Huns about' inland. Having orbited St Omer, by which time the other aircraft involved in the Circus had withdrawn, as Greycap prepared to leave France via Gravelines a gaggle of bandits was 'Tally Ho'd', as Johnnie's combat report relates: 'Fw190s were sighted above when the Wing was over Gravelines, so we turned to engage in order to avoid an enemy bounce. Eight 190s flying in fours line abreast passed under my section, followed by a further three 190s in line astern. I turned after these three E/A and attacked number three from 10° starboard astern, with cannon and machine-gun – range 300 yards. I saw a piece of E/A fall off near the perspex hood, and E/A climbed steeply for 200-300 feet and then fell over and dived vertically. I broke away and immediately afterwards searched below in order to locate this aircraft. I saw an aircraft go into the sea about two miles off Gravelines.' Greycap's wingman, Flying Officer R. Wozniak, confirmed the victory, adding, 'I saw a splash in the sea in the area of Wing Commander Johnson's combat immediately after he had fired.'

Red Section of 403 Squadron was also engaged, attacking eleven 190s which were sighted beneath the Canadian Spitfires. As a high-speed running fight developed, Squadron Leader 'Foss' Boulton of 416 Squadron managed a long burst at a 190, but made no subsequent claim. As quickly as it had begun the engagement was over, and the wing returned safely to Kenley at 1335 hours. For Johnnie, the day's flying was not over. In his log he recorded a local familiarisation flight of twenty minutes in a Spitfire Mk XII (serial number not given). This is interesting given that this flight was his first in a Griffon-powered Spitfire. Although the Rolls-Royce Merlin was extremely successful, having proved capable of development, there were nevertheless limits to the power that could be obtained from a twenty-seven litre engine. This had been recognised very early on in the Spitfire's development programme and work had begun on a new engine shortly after the outbreak of war. The new engine was another of twelve cylinders, called the Griffon, but the capacity was more: 36.7 litres. The resulting output was a potent 1,700 horsepower. Pilots would find the main handling difference from the Merlin being that the Griffon rotated in the opposite direction, so instead of swinging to the left on take-off, the Griffon variants swung to the right.

After more poor weather, on 13 May it was sunny and warm with a light southerly wind. The Kenley Wing's first task of the day was to provide 'second fighter echelon' (ORB, 403 Squadron) on Circus 296. Greycap led the Spitfires out over North Foreland at 5,000 feet, crossing the French coastline over Dunkirk at 22,000 feet. Heading east towards Cassel, control passed to

Appledore and the Spitfires climbed towards St Omer, which was reached at 27,000 feet. Given that in total fifteen Spitfire squadrons were active over France, escorting just six B-25s to Boulogne, the Germans wisely refused to engage *en masse*. Nevertheless, the Kenley Wing was attacked by some twenty Fw190s from both above and below. Another running battle ensued. 403 Squadron's CO, Squadron Leader Charlie Magwood DFC, leading Yellow Section, was attacked by a *schwarm* of 190s from 4,000 feet below. The Canadian half-rolled out of the sun, forcing all but one of the one-time 'Butcher Birds' to take evasive action. With Magwood 350 yards astern and closing, that 190 broke to port, but it was too late: Yellow One opened fire with cannon and machine guns. The 190's hood and bits of wing flew off as the missiles found their mark; it then rolled over and spun down with 'smoke and flames billowing from the cockpit' (ORB, 403 Squadron). The outcome was in no doubt, and Magwood later claimed this 190 as destroyed. On the way out, he engaged and hit another Fw190, which was claimed as damaged. 416 Squadron also enjoyed success, 190s being claimed destroyed by Squadron Leader Boulton, Flying Officer R.H. Walker and Flying Officer J.A. Rae; Boulton also claimed another as damaged. There were no personnel casualties, but three 416 Squadron Spitfires landed back at Kenley having sustained varying degrees of damage.

The next offensive sortie for the Kenley Spitfires was Ramrod Seventy-one, the AOC-in-C Fighter Command, Air Marshal Sir Trafford Leigh-Mallory, sitting in on the pilots' briefing. He gave a short address, complimenting the Canadians on their good morning's work and explained a little of the current strategy of aerial warfare as it affected all fronts. In this afternoon sortie, Johnnie's Kenley Spitfires were to meet B-17s of the Eighth Air Force's 1st Bomb Wing attacking the Potez repair facility at Méaulte. Covered by three P-47 Fighter Groups, the B-17s of the 4th Bomb Wing made a diversionary attack on the already pockmarked airfield at St Omer. The Luftwaffe did not react however, watching closely the progress of the larger 1st Bomb Wing force which, after zig-zagging northwards up the English Channel, finally turned for France. Over Berck, the Kenley Wing joined the last boxes of Fortresses, watching 'nibbling' (ORB, 403 Squadron) attacks by enemy fighters on the lead bombers before the force reached Amiens. On the way in, one B-17 was seen to go down fifteen miles inland of Berck. Between the target and the approaching Fortresses was now a strong force of JG26 190s led by Major 'Pips' Priller. The 91st Bomb Group soon lost two Flying Fortresses to Major Priller and Leutnant Hoppe, while another went to flak. Amongst eleven B-17s damaged during these attacks, one was hit by a bomb dropped by a 190, so determined were the Germans to defeat the Americans by whatever means available. Nonetheless, the B-17s' target was soon wreathed in brown smoke and completely hidden to the aircrew fighting for their lives high above. For one American crew, violent death came suddenly when their B-17 exploded and disintegrated over Méaulte.

By now the Kenley Wing was heavily engaged, fighting off attacks as best the Spitfire pilots were able between burning Méaulte and the Channel at Le Touquet. Red Section of 403 Squadron was bounced by a *schwarm* of 190s; one of the assailants attempted a head-on attack against Red Two, Flying Officer R.D. 'Trapper' Bowen, but Red Four, Pilot Officer H.J. Dowding, responded in like fashion, opening fire at 200 yards and closing *rapidly*. Hits were seen around the 190's cockpit and it was soon going down. As Fortresses approached the French coast on their homeward journey, Greycap saw a *schwarm* of 190s approaching, clearly bent on attacking the bombers from the starboard side: 'I closed in on the leader and gave him several short bursts from the starboard beam, closing to starboard quarter, strikes being seen near his wing root. The enemy aircraft turned left and flicked right over. He dived and I followed for three or four thousand feet. E/A flicked over twice more and I gave him a short burst although at this stage I was almost out of range. I then broke away and rejoined the bombers but my Number Three (F/O Foster of 416) followed the aircraft down and saw the pilot bale out.'

After their respective combats, Flying Officer Bowen and Pilot Officer Dowding, of 403 Squadron, then formed up with Greycap and Flying Officer Foster who were heading home. Minutes later the four Spitfires were attacked by two 190s when half way back across the Channel. One of these the three Spitfires isolated and 'chased into the sea' (ORB, 403 Squadron). Red Three, Pilot Officer W.T. Lane, dived on two other 190s, giving several bursts of cannons and machine guns, strikes being witnessed by Greycap. Flight Lieutenant H.D. MacDonald, Blue Three, attacked the last of two Me109s at 23,000 feet, striking the target with his second burst of cannon and machine-gun fire. A lone Me109 flew below Yellow Section, positioning himself down sun, attacking above and to port. Flight Lieutenant H.C. Godefroy, Yellow One, fired at the 109 and saw hits on the tail and rear fuselage. Back at Kenley, the pilots of 403 Squadron excitedly made out their combat reports, but three Spitfires were missing: Sergeant W.G. Uttley of 403, who had last been seen over Doullens (and was possibly the Spitfire reportedly seen going down over that location (ORB, 403)), and both Squadron Leader Foss Boulton and Sergeant C.W. McKim of 416.

The latter had been heard to shout over the R/T that he had been badly hit and was seen to ditch his Spitfire in the Channel twenty miles west of Le Touquet, but of Boulton nothing had been heard or seen. Immediately their Spitfires could be turned around, Greycap led a number of his pilots to sweep back over the Channel, searching for their missing comrades. An 'oil patch, pieces of aircraft wreckage and a barrel or unexploded torpedo with red and white circle at one end' were seen, but no trace of the three missing Kenley pilots. Uttley and McKim, both 21, were both dead. The 416 Squadron CO, however, was more fortunate: having baled out at 26,000 feet in spite of head, back and arm wounds, Squadron Leader Boulton was captured. The likelihood is that all these three Kenley Spitfire pilots were those victories claimed by Major Priller, Hauptmann Naumann, the Staffelkapitän of 6/JG26, and Leutnant Leuschal, Staffelkapitän of 10/JG26.

On 14 May, the Kenley Wing was not to be amongst those able to afford the luxury of enjoying this 'hot and very lovely day' (ORB, 403 Squadron), the morning's Form 'D' having provided all necessary details for Ramrod Seventy-three. The Canadian Spitfires were to escort forty B-17s of the 4th Bomb Wing attacking the base of III/JG26, the airfield at Wevelgem, just across the French border into Belgium, near Courtrai. Greycap's Spitfires rendezvoused with the bombers at 8,000 feet over South Foreland, and set course for France. Another beehive could be seen, this being the 1st Bomb Wing and a B-24 group bound for the shipyards at Kiel. Some enemy aircraft were sighted shortly after the Courtrai force crossed the French coast over Dunkirk, and when fifteen miles inland a B-17 turned back, although not due to enemy action. As the bombers approached the target, Me109s and Fw190s began harassing the formation but, in the main, were driven off by the Spitfires. Flight Lieutenant Buckham of 416 Squadron shot down a 190 which became a fireball, and Greycap nailed another. Some ten miles west of Courtrai on the homeward run, Flight Lieutenant Godefroy of 403 Squadron pressed home an attack on a 190 and watched with satisfaction 'the cannon mounting and perspex hood come off and then a big ball of black smoke enveloped the E/A, as though it were disintegrating' (ORB, 403 Squadron). Flight Lieutenant MacDonald, also of 403, dived onto an Me109 that was flying with two Fw190s, fired and noted strikes on the cockpit and wing roots as chunks of debris span into the air. Flying Officer Bowen saw this 190 spin into the sea.

In spite of the Spitfire pilots' best efforts, two Fortresses were shot down. Hauptmann Hans Naumann, Staffelkapitän of 6/JG26 claimed one of these, having fired at a 351st Bomb Group B-17 near Wevelgem with his last twenty rounds. The crew baled out however, and these may have been the American parachutes later reported by 403 Squadron. Wevelgem had nonetheless been hit hard. Enemy aircraft had been destroyed and damaged, and a number of personnel, including both pilots and ground staff, were killed or wounded. The airfield was also badly cratered. A newcomer to the western front, Oberleutnant Erwin Leykauf, Staffelkapitän of 12/JG54, actually tried to get up in his 109 during the attack, but the aircraft's undercarriage legs were sheared off by a bomb crater. So badly damaged was Wevelgem in fact that III/JG26 was forced to move temporarily to the smaller field at Lille-Nord. It was the first, but not the last, time that a JG26 airfield was rendered unserviceable by Allied bombing. The Americans had made another first this day by putting 200 bombers in the air. After their earlier losses, an ever-increasing quantity of replacement aircrew and aircraft, including fighters and both heavy and medium-bombers, had been arriving in England from America, despite the U-boats' best efforts. The process was even afoot to convert certain B-17s and B-24s into heavily armoured and armed 'destroyer escorts'. At the time, given the limited range of the single-engined fighters available and considering that auxiliary fuel tank tests had yet to be finalised, this was the only realistic short-term option to afford the bombers greater protection all the way to the target and back. All of this indicates the resolve of the Eighth Air Force to succeed and see the job through. As Johnnie said, 'You couldn't help but admire them, could you?'

On the morning of 15 May, Greycap flew a Spitfire V, 'DN-O', across to Horsham St Faiths where he liaised with the P-47 Thunderbolt-equipped 56th Fighter Group. At this stage of the game it was vital for the Americans to listen to the experiences of RAF pilots like Wing Commander Johnson who had been 'at it' for a long time before Pearl Harbor. These liaisons were also important for morale and developing a spirit of mutual cooperation. Johnnie remained with the 56th Fighter Group for two days, leaving on the morning of 17 May for Bassingbourne, where he lectured fighter tactics to the 91st Bomb Group, a B-17 unit.

In his log book on 23 May, Johnnie wrote simply 'Awarded DSO'. The citation for this was more descriptive, and read, in part: 'Acting Wing Commander Johnson has led a Wing on a large number of occasions and has displayed outstanding skill and gallantry. During an operation one morning in May 1943, his formation was heavily engaged by a large force of enemy fighters. In the ensuing combats four enemy aircraft were destroyed without loss. The same afternoon he took part in a similar sortie and three enemy fighters were destroyed, one of them by Wing Commander Johnson. The next day, this officer took part in another successful sortie. By his skilful and courageous leadership, Wing Commander Johnson contributed materially to the success achieved. He has personally destroyed at least thirteen enemy aircraft.'

In addition to his flying prowess having been recognised by the award of a double DFC, Johnnie's contribution as a leader had also now been rewarded. Dan Browne added his view regarding the successful combination of Johnnie and the Canadians: 'We had some fine Canadians at Kenley. Some had been miners and lumberjacks, just roughnecks all their lives, so it was a weird combination. It was a stroke of genius in itself to put Johnnie in command, although he was an Englishman, and they gave us these Spit IXBs, and I suspect that there was some politics behind that to keep us colonials quiet. Johnnie got along with them beautifully, he'd go out and shoot crap with them. Johnnie has the most extraordinary vocabulary of evil songs, drinking all night long you know, we'd draw off that oxygen bottle in the morning, it just revived you! Johnnie's leadership was not about iron discipline, it was just that everybody wanted to do things the way that he wanted them done, because they were so proud of being in that Wing. All Johnnie had to do was ring London and say "I want this pilot off my Wing". No questions would be asked and when the guy landed he would just be ordered to report to some obscure duty in the middle of nowhere! Johnnie would shoot crap with us on the ground, and everybody would call him "Wingco".' Hugh Godefroy: 'As a leader, Johnnie Johnson was like the Pied Piper. We found ourselves bounding out of bed repeating his catchy phrases like "OK chaps, get into 'em!"'

Johnnie: 'Yes, it was quite something to get the DSO, especially on the same day as a chap like Al Deere, who I admired and respected enormously because he had been at it for such a very long time.' Air Marshal Leigh-Mallory wrote a letter of congratulation to Johnnie saying that he 'was very much impressed by what I saw of your work during my short visit to Kenley the other day, and I am satisfied that the high standard of the Kenley Wing is very largely due to your high qualities of leadership.' Another letter arrived from Air Vice-Marshal 'Dingbat' Saunders, the AOC 11 Group: 'My heartiest congratulations on your well-earned DSO. The Kenley Wing has done marvellous work recently under your leadership, and I am quite sure will continue its good work. Good luck and good hunting!'

On the night of 23 May the 'Kenleys' headed for London to celebrate their wing leader's DSO. The Biggin Hill Wing Commander (Flying), the New Zealander Al Deere, had also been awarded the DSO and arrangements were made for a joint celebration at the Kimmul Club in Burleigh Street. A popular venue with aircrews, the club was run by a former RFC Captain, Bobbie Page, and the DSO party was soon in full swing. Also present that night, with a crowd of 'Bomber Boys', was Wing Commander Guy Gibson DSO & Bar, DFC & Bar, who had led the highly publicised 'Dambusters' raid only the previous week. Five days after that night in the Kimmul Club, when he bought Johnnie a pint on account of his DSO, Guy Gibson's Victoria Cross was gazetted.

The daily grind of bomber escort sorties continued without respite. On the afternoon of 31 May, for example, Johnnie led the wing on Circus 309, at 1655 hours. The Kenley Wing was to mount the second wave of a fighter sweep while twelve Venturas bombed Zeebrugge from 12,000 feet. The Spitfires crossed out over Deal at 100 feet, climbing to 18,000 feet and crossing the French coast at Nieuport. Sweeping towards Bruges and Ostend at 21,000 feet, twenty-five Fw190s of II/JG26 were seen by Greycap some 500 feet below and diving on the port side. Followed by two 403 Squadron Spitfires, Johnnie headed for the 190s. 421 Squadron came down to cover 403 but also became engaged. Five of the squadron's pilots fired their guns, damaging two 190s. One minute after the combat began, Greycap saw a 190 dive vertically past him, its pilot apparently trapped in the cockpit, and watched it crash into the sea. Flying Officer N.R. Fowlow then shouted at Sergeant G.R. Brown of 403 Squadron to 'break hard port' on account of their section being attacked by two 190s. The first overshot, but the second, Oberleutnant Sternberg, Staffelkapitän of 5/JG26, hit Brown who skidded to port, his Spitfire pouring black smoke. With relief, Fowlow saw a white parachute blossom at 8,000 feet, off Nieuport. According to the 403 Squadron report, 'Three other pilots of the Squadron heard someone say "Goodbye" in a debonair manner', which was presumed to be Sergeant Brown. Three splashes were seen in the sea, all so large that crashing aircraft could be the only possible cause. One was Brown's Spitfire, the other two 190s, one of which had been seen by Greycap. The latter was later credited to Flying Officer Fowlow, who had seen a 190 'go straight down' after he had hit it from 200 yards. The second 190 was associated with a brown parachute seen later in the combat and was shared by Pilot Officers Isbister and Horten of 421 and Sergeant Small of 403. These claims were perfectly accurate given that II/JG26 lost two 190s, both of which went into the sea, their pilots being killed (Leutnant Georg Mondry, 5 Staffel, and Feldwebel Hans Danneburg, 4 Staffel).

Squadron Leader Hall and Flight Lieutenant Quint, both of 421, also claimed one damaged 190 each. The Spitfire pilots experienced heavy flak over Ostend, with moderate heavy flak at Bruges and Nieuport. This was 'exceptionally accurate', and one shell exploded between Johnnie and his No 2, Flying Officer R.D. Bowen. Hugh Godefroy remembers: 'A shell went off behind and to port of Greycap, blowing him almost over on his back. There was a pregnant silence as we all watched him come back straight and level. For a second his aircraft dodged around a little bit like a bird that had experienced a near miss. Finally he came on the R/T: "Makes you bloody think, dunnit?"'

On 1 June the weather was 7/10ths cloud, perfect for the search and destroy mission, Rodeo 225, that the Kenley Wing found itself flying at 1130 hours. The wing was the second wave of a fighter sweep of Hardelot–Doullens–St Pol controlled by Appledore. *Jafü* 2 scrambled I/JG27 from Poix, and all available JG26 fighters, to intercept, attempting to sandwich the Spitfires between the two German formations. Greycap's pilots, however, saw some thirty plus bandits climbing from the direction of Albert, so 421 Squadron provided cover while 403 went down to attack. The enemy broke right, and a huge dogfight began involving some eighty aircraft. Warrant Officer A.V. Hargreaves, of 403, damaged one of a pair of 190s flying in close line astern at 10,000 feet. Flight Lieutenant Harry MacDonald saw 'an FW firing at an Me109 from close range astern. This was seen by Blue One to go into a moderate steep dive and explode between St Pol and Hesdin. It was claimed as destroyed by the Squadron because the Squadron's attack led to the FW mistaking the 109 for a Spitfire and attacking it' (ORB, 403 Squadron). On the way back, Greycap personally scored again: 'After engaging thirty plus enemy aircraft in the Doullens–St Pol area, the Wing reformed and we headed towards the French coast on the outward journey flying at 23,000 feet. When four to five miles inland of Berck-sur-Mer I saw about eight Me109s behind 403 Squadron. We turned to engage and all enemy aircraft dived away except two 109s which went into a shallow dive towards Le Crotoy. Enemy aircraft were flying line abreast and I opened fire with cannon and machine-gun on the starboard aircraft from 500 closing to 300 yards. I saw several cannon strikes on the rear portion of the fuselage and on the tail plane. At 9,000 feet I broke off the attack as E/A was now diving vertically; he did not recover and I saw him crash onto the north bank of the Somme. My Number Two, Flying Officer Bowen DFC, also fired at this enemy aircraft and I claim it as destroyed, shared with him.' In total,

I/JG27 lost three Me109s, including the Kommandeur, Hauptmann Erich Hohagen, who baled out wounded, but it is impossible to ascertain who shot down who.

On 11 June an early ground haze cleared and the sun came out. At 1605 hours Wing Commander Johnson led the wing on Rodeo 229 at the head of 421 Squadron. In this operation the Kenley Wing was to be the second wave of a fighter sweep between Abbeville and Poix. At 25,000 feet over the latter, fifteen plus bandits, mainly Me109s, were seen flying from the direction of Abbeville and 1,000 feet below. Greycap turned his Spitfires to starboard and engaged with 421 Squadron, the fighters whirling around between 26,000 down to 7,000 feet. Squadron Leader Hall shot the tail unit completely off a 109 and damaged another, but although other pilots of 421 Squadron fired their guns there were no other claims. As the squadron's ORB states, it was a 'good show'.

On 13 June, the Kenley Wing's pilots were given a talk about the new 'Tactical Air Force in Great Britain' by an army officer. The pilots concluded that this was 'very interesting' (ORB, 421 Squadron). Fighter Command had originally been created as a defensive force, but when the long awaited invasion of enemy-occupied France eventually came, there would clearly be a change of role. Then RAF fighter pilots would not be defending their homeland, as in 1940, but on the contrary providing tactical support to the advancing British and Canadian armies (the American Ninth Air Force would similarly support American troops). The Allied fighters would also have to ensure aerial supremacy over the battlefield, and become mobile units able to keep up with the advancing armies. The idea was, therefore, to create a composite, tactical, force of fighters, bombers, fighter-bombers and army cooperation aircraft, independent of existing Commands. This tactical air force would exist exclusively for deployment in support of the Allied Expeditionary Force, which was being formed to undertake the proposed invasion. On 1 June 1943 this new aerial entity officially became the 2nd Tactical Air Force (TAF), comprising largely units formerly of No 2 Group Bomber Command (the RAF's light bomber force) and various squadrons from Fighter Command. Soon Fighter Command itself would cease to exist altogether, the responsibility for home defence becoming that of 'Air Defence Great Britain'.

On 14 June, Wing Commander Johnson analysed his operational flying on this tour, which had started on 13 July 1942, and wrote the result in his log book:

Operational Flying Times this Tour	120.30
Circuses	37
Ramrods	16
Rodeos	20
Roadsteads	NIL
Rhubarbs	2

At the other end of the spectrum at this time was Flying Officer Danny Brown, who had only recently started flying on operations with 403 Squadron. Of that early period he remembered: 'Getting into the combat experience, you were first treated like a mother treats a chick, get your feet under you and then start to think up there in the air. I remember telling Johnnie, the first time that I flew in combat, which was with him, that if someone had asked me what my name was I was not sure that I could have remembered it! He bounced a 109, and my job was to stay with him and cover him. I saw this plane right in front of us, right close, and all of a sudden I saw little tiny puffs of something, all the while thinking in nano-seconds, all the while thinking "Well, I wonder what in the world that is?", when I realised, idiot, that he was shooting a plane down! We watched it take on fire and smoke and watched it crash into the Somme delta. With that, you steadily gained more experience, but when you first start, you just don't get the opportunities. Remember that the German Air Force was not to be sneezed at. One of the great things about war is that you have to learn to get along with and be trusted by your fellow pilots. If you're not accepted then you might as well go home.'

Although a showery day with a good deal of low cloud, on 15 June the Kenley Wing flew Ramrod Ninety-five. The Canadians provided the second wave of high cover to a force of forty B-17s bombing Bernay aerodrome. Due to adverse weather however, the bombers aborted before reaching the RV over Fécamp, so Greycap was given permission to proceed inland at his own discretion. Climbing towards Rouen, Appledore informed Johnnie of bandits nearby. Going down to 24,000 feet, the Spitfire pilots saw fifteen Fw190s of I/JG2 flying in line abreast. Johnnie: 'I flew at 24,000 feet in order to avoid making smoke trails… I ordered 421 to remain top guard and led 403 to attack. I myself attacked the starboard 190 with cannon and machine-gun, closing to 200 yards. I registered several cannon strikes on this E/A, which pulled violently upwards, almost to a stall. The hood was jettisoned and I saw the pilot drop out but did not see his parachute open. This E/A is claimed as destroyed. I then saw a further fifteen Fw190s on my port side and they had gone into line astern – all turning port very slowly and covering about two miles. I closed in on the last E/A and attacked him with cannon and machine-guns from five to ten degrees port astern, closing to good range. I registered several cannon strikes and pieces flew off this E/A. As he went into a slow spin the magazine in his starboard wing exploded, blowing off huge pieces of the wing and fuselage. He was soon completely enveloped in black smoke and this E/A is also claimed as destroyed.' This was remarkable shooting. Unsurprisingly the propaganda process later made much of the fact that Wing Commander Johnnie Johnson, the fighter ace from Melton Mowbray, had got 'two Huns before breakfast', his Wing described as 'one of the busiest in Fighter Command'.

The next noteworthy operation took place on 17 June. From dawn until 0830 hours, 421 Squadron was at readiness, but there was no scramble. The squadron's CO, Squadron Leader Hall, was posted on rest to 58 OTU, the ORB recording: 'All sorry to lose our chief who was a good fellow and well liked by all personnel.' His place was taken by Squadron Leader Philip Leslie Irving Archer DFC, who had reported to 421 Squadron as a supernumerary squadron leader just two days before. Archer had flown with the highly successful 92 Squadron from Biggin Hill during 1941, thence 416 Squadron the following year. He had now returned to operations after a rest with five enemy aircraft destroyed and one damaged to his credit. His last claim was a Do217 on 18 July 1942, and all his previous victories were Me109s; he had not yet scored against the Fw190s.

The weather was reportedly 5/10ths cloud and very windy, but nevertheless the Kenley Wing received orders to fly Rodeo 231. In this operation the wing was to provide the third wave of a fighter sweep of the Pas-de-Calais. Greycap led the Spitfires out over Dover at 15,000 feet, crossing into France at 24,000 feet over Gravelines. Operations informed Greycap of the presence of some thirty plus 190s climbing from Ypres towards Dunkirk. Earlier in the day a dozen Bostons had attacked Vlissingen, and elements of JG26 had engaged the Spitfires providing rear cover off Zeebrugge. When the first wave of the afternoon Rodeo swept in, *Jafü* 2 expected bombers to follow, but when this did not happen two *Gruppen* of JG26 were vectored towards the last wave of Spitfires – the Kenley Wing. The Spitfires slowly orbited until the bandits were sighted climbing towards the French coast, strung out in line abreast, and some 10,000 feet below. This was the *Geschwadergruppe*, acting as bait, while Hauptmann Wutz Galland, Kommandeur of II/JG26, climbed his 190s with the intention of bouncing the Spitfires as the latter took the bait.

As predicted, the Spitfires pounced. Wing Commander Johnson led 421 Squadron down and attacked the last *schwarm* of 190s: 'I attacked number two on the starboard side, and as I commenced fire with cannon and machine-guns he turned slowly to starboard. I closed in to 150 yards range and saw cannon strikes on the cockpit and wing roots. As I was overshooting, I gave him a final burst and pulled steeply upwards, the enemy aircraft caught fire and started to burn, spiralling slowly down.' Johnnie had hit Unteroffizier Günther Freitag of 8/JG26, who crashed and was killed at Steenvorde in Flanders. A confused fight followed, involving 80 to 100 Fw190s and some 24 Spitfires.

By this time, Galland was diving into the Spitfires' rear, so the two Kenley squadrons turned to face the attack. Flying Officer K.P. Marshall, Yellow Three of 403 Squadron, saw Squadron Leader Archer of 421 Squadron flying alongside him at about 21,000 feet. Marshall saw two 190s closing in on Archer, and was about to yell 'Break!' when his own aircraft was hit. He broke upwards and to port but did not see 421 Squadron's new CO again. Flight Sergeant G.M. Shouldice, Yellow Four, fired a long burst of cannon and machine gun at Yellow Three's assailant, but had to break due to being attacked himself. Shouldice's kill was confirmed by Pilot Officer Bullick of 421 who saw a '190 with bits flying off and streaming black smoke, going straight down' (ORB, 403 Squadron). Having disengaged, Blue Section of 403 Squadron came out over France at 16,000 feet, while Red and Yellow Sections turned back inland over France to allow Marshall and Shouldice time to catch up. The former's aircraft was damaged, but the young Canadian managed to land safely at Redhill. Squadron Leader Archer of 421 was credited with having destroyed a 190, but sadly the new CO failed to return. Flying Officer McNamara of the same squadron was awarded a 190 'damaged', but he too was missing. The 27-year-old Squadron Leader Archer was buried at Longuenesse Souvenir Cemetery, St Omer, but Flying Officer James Emmett McNamara was never found.

Oberleutnant Horst Sternberg, Staffelkapitän of 5/JG26, was awarded a Spitfire destroyed, five kilometres south-west of Hazebrouck, and Unteroffizier Paul Schwarz, of 6/JG26, made his first 'kill' ten kilometres south-west of St Omer. Both German kills were made in roughly the same area therefore, which makes sense given that both of the Kenley Wing's casualties were from the same squadron. It is impossible to say which German shot down which Spitfire pilot. Sternberg's kill was timed at 1545; he later reported having collided with a Spitfire, forcing him to bale out, wounded. As none of the Kenley pilots reported having witnessed such a collision, the probability is that Sternberg collided with the crashing Spitfire of either Archer or McNamara. Back at Kenley, the wing claimed three Fw190s destroyed and one damaged. The Germans had lost two: Freitag to Johnnie and Sternberg to an alleged collision. The following day the British press reported: 'A Canadian Spitfire Wing added three more Fw190s to its score during a sweep over Belgium yesterday afternoon, bringing the day's score of our fighters up to a total of nine enemy aircraft destroyed. The Canadians' three victims were destroyed in a series of combats between Ypres and the coast at heights varying from 22,000 feet to 26,000 feet. The Wing was led by Wing Commander JE Johnson DSO DFC & bar, who himself shot down an Fw190, bringing his score to seventeen. The Spitfires first encountered a formation of about 30 enemy aircraft. Shortly after a dogfight with them about twenty more enemy fighters were seen. The Spitfires immediately dived in amongst the Fw190s and scattered the formation. Two of our Spitfires are missing.'

The following day, Kenley's popular station commander, Group Captain Jimmy Fenton, left for pastures new. He considered that: 'As Wing Leader, Johnnie Johnson was undoubtedly type-cast for the role, being outstandingly successful both as a fighter pilot and leader. As we were the most successful Sector in the Group, some reflected glory came my way, of which I was always happy to be the recipient! We were in a well organized and well-led Group with Air Vice-Marshal "Dingbat" Saunders as AOC. Morale was at its highest. It was the lead up to the invasion, still a year ahead, and the phase was vitally important in providing the disciplined and experienced fighter force that we were, in the event, lucky to have.'

At 0500 hours on 22 June, the 'Wingco' briefed his pilots on Ramrod Ninety-nine, in which the Kenley Spitfires were to meet and escort a formation of B-17s returning from attacking industrial targets in Germany's Ruhr Valley. By now the Americans had accepted that if the daylight offensive was to continue, especially in the absence of a long-range offensive escort fighter, priority must be given to targets connected with the Luftwaffe. These included not only enemy airfields but also targets connected with the German aviation industry, such as aircraft factories and other associated depots. The target today, for 235 Flying Fortresses of the 381st and 384th Bomb Groups, was the synthetic rubber plant at Hüls. As Germany was cut off from supplies of natural rubber, this *Chemische Werke* was of vital importance to the aircraft manufacturing industry given that it produced thirty per cent of the nation's output of synthetic rubber. This trip to the Ruhr was the deepest penetration so far attempted by the Americans. The Ruhr flak belt, as RAF Bomber Command knew only too well, was lethal, and this time the bombers also had to run the gauntlet of *Jafü* Holland-Ruhr.

At 0540 hours, the Kenley Wing took off, 'pancaking' at Manston at 0615. At 0930 the Spitfires were up again, bound for the Dutch coast. Greycap set course for Schouwen Island, which was reached at 20,000 feet, and from there inland to Sleidrecht, over which the Spitfires arrived at 24,000 feet. Six boxes of B-17s were seen coming out over the Dutch coast, escorted by 'Little Friends', crossing out over Schouwen between 24 and 27,000 feet. The Kenley Wing remained over the exit point until the last box of bombers had left. Although some twenty Me109s and Fw190s were seen, no substantial attacks were made and the Canadian Spitfires were not engaged. The bombers had hit the target accurately. Just under a quarter of the total tonnage of bombs dropped had fallen within the factory itself, the damage arising rendering the factory completely useless for a month, and normal production was not resumed for a further six. Sixteen bombers were lost and 170 more B-17s were damaged. Over the North Sea, about forty miles west of Schouwen, the Kenley pilots saw a Fortress at 5,000 feet, covered by eight Spitfires. Later a large flash was seen mid-Channel, and when the Spitfires arrived over the area shortly afterwards, large patches of oil marked the last resting place of more brave American airmen.

Another show was planned for the afternoon, the wing being led off by Greycap at 1554 hours on Circus 341. Together with the Hornchurch Wing, the Canadians were to support twelve Venturas withdrawing after bombing Abbeville aerodrome. While the Spitfires were in the Abbeville area, an aircraft was seen going down in flames, and a large fire was seen near Dieppe. Seven enemy aircraft were seen, but these were too far east and could not be engaged. The sortie was otherwise without incident and Johnnie's Spitfires were back at Kenley by 1728. As the 421 Squadron ORB commented, it had been a 'long day'. Of interest is that the Kenley Wing operated in conjunction with the Hornchurch Spitfires, led by the New Zealand ace Wing Commander W.V. Crawford-Compton DFC & Bar. The Spitfires often seemed outnumbered over France, so Johnnie thought it worth increasing numbers. Air Vice-Marshal Saunders agreed to an experiment and arranged that the Kenley and Hornchurch Wings would operate together. This represented a four-squadron force of Spitfire Mk IXs, some forty-eight aircraft in total. Johnnie: 'It was just that the Huns always had greater numbers, which didn't seem to cause them problems from a defensive viewpoint, which is perhaps worth studying, so we just thought that it was worth a go.' First thing in the morning of 22 June, Johnnie flew up to Hornchurch and worked out the finer points with Wing Commander Crawford-Compton, then returned to Kenley, all ready for Ramrod 100. Over Beachy Head, the Kenley and Hornchurch Wings met and rendezvoused with seventeen Flying Fortresses bound for Bernay aerodrome. After a penetration of ten miles into hostile airspace however, the bombers turned back due to unfavourable weather conditions. The entire Allied force returned without incident via St Valery.

The 24th of June was a clear, warm and still day. This would be the Kenley Wing's busiest day so far this year. After an early briefing, Greycap led his Spitfires up from Kenley at 0705 hours on Ramrod 102, a sortie not including the Hornchurch Wing. The Spitfires roared over Deal at zero feet, climbing to 18,000 feet en route to Flushing docks, which was being bombed by twelve 2 Group Bostons. The Spitfires swept over the target, which was smoking, at 25,000 feet, and experienced some accurate and heavy flak. After sweeping Nieuport and Ostend, the Kenley Wing returned via Deal, having seen not one enemy aircraft. The next sortie was Ramrod 103, in which the Kenley Wing was to fly the second wave of a fighter sweep over the Le Touquet, Fruges and St Omer areas, in support of more Bostons attacking railway facilities at St Omer. Greycap climbed the Spitfires hard immediately after take-off, at 1125 hours, crossing out over Rye. When ten miles off Hardelot, Appledore informed Johnnie that there were bandits off Cap-Gris-Nez at 25,000 feet. After several orbits, during which the Spitfires clawed for more height, the French coast was crossed at 24,000 feet over Le Touquet. Appledore then vectored Greycap north-east of Hazebrouck, where Flight Lieutenant H.D. MacDonald, Red Three of 403 Squadron, sighted what appeared to be three Me109s below at 14,000 feet. Together with Red Four, Sergeant D. Small, Red Three was despatched to engage the enemy, but the Germans dived away and escaped. Red Three and Four then re-joined Red Section, Red One being Greycap, and Red Two Flying Officer N.J. Ogilvie. The wing then proceeded to St Omer.

While the Spitfires cruised at 25,000 feet, fifteen Fw190s in several small formations were reported at 18,000 feet, so Greycap, leaving 421 Squadron as top cover, ordered Yellow Section of 403 Squadron down to engage while he led Red Section towards some other bandits. Again the Germans half-rolled away and refused to engage. While Red Three followed Red One and Two down however, a Spitfire suddenly cut between him and the leading pair. To avoid a collision, MacDonald immediately broke to starboard, and upon straightening out at 20,000 feet saw two formations of enemy aircraft being chased by Spitfires. A third gaggle of bandits broke starboard and went into a defensive circle. These six Fw190s soon straightened out, in pairs. Red Three dived out of a steep turn onto the port aircraft of the last pair and delivered a short burst of cannon and machine-gun fire from 150 yards. The Canadian noted strikes on his target's port wing, then, upon breaking away, saw the 190 doing a series of lazy downward rolls. At 6,000 feet a parachute opened adjacent to this 190, making MacDonald believe that he had destroyed it. What had in fact happened however, was that Red Four, Sergeant Small, had been attacked and shot down by Unteroffizier Gomann of 5/JG26, and it was he who MacDonald had seen bale out. The latter had hit and wounded Oberfeldwebel Alfred Günther, also of 5th Staffel, but the German managed to land his damaged 190 safely at Vitry. After Yellow Section's unsuccessful attack, the Spitfires were shadowed to the coast by some ten Fw190s, but no interception took place. Having left France over Cap-Gris-Nez at 27,000 feet, heavy flak had tracked the wing from St Omer to the coast. Throughout the entire proceedings, 421 Squadron had maintained top cover, but four pilots came home very short of fuel: Pilot Officer Linton force-landed at Dungeness, and three others landed at Redhill. By 1315 hours, the wing was all accounted for, excepting Sergeant Small who had been captured by the enemy.

Ramrod 106 was the next show that day, Greycap leading the wing off from Kenley at 1645 hours. The Spitfires were Forward Target Support Wing, sweeping the Rouen area, while twelve Venturas bombed Yainville power station. The English coast was crossed at zero feet over Newhaven, the wing then climbing until offshore at St Valery-en-Caux, where an orbit was made. Heading inland at 14,000 feet, Greycap received reports of forty enemy aircraft climbing up from Rouen towards Le Havre. Although the Germans had the tactical advantage, the Kenley Wing engaged to prevent them molesting the bombers. The brief clash was inconclusive, so the Spitfires re-formed and attempted to engage three Fw190s, flying from Rouen towards Fécamp, but again unsuccessfully. Two more 190s were then sighted shadowing the wing, apparently intending to catch the odd straggler. Johnnie: 'They were about two miles behind the Wing and I climbed both squadrons steeply into sun and carried out one orbit to port. The Fw190s, which were then down sun of us, appeared to lose sight of the Wing and flew beneath us, representing an excellent target. They were seen 1,000 feet below my Section and a mile ahead. I ordered my Number Two, Squadron Leader McNair, to engage these aircraft with me. The remainder of the Squadron (421) were told to keep high in order not to scare the Huns. I closed in on number two E/A from line astern and opened fire from 300, closing to 150 yards. Cannon strikes were seen on the fuselage and tail plane of this E/A and a large piece fell away from the starboard half of his tail unit. The E/A spun down and was seen to crash at Valmont.' Squadron Leader McNair destroyed the leading 190, these two enemy fighters probably being from *Jafü* 3's I/JG2. The two successful Spitfire pilots then re-joined the wing, returning home via Életot and Beachy Head. Two pilots of 421 Squadron had to put down at the coastal airfield of Friston, out of fuel. At close of play it had been another long, hot, day.

On 27 June cloud was 7/10ths but the day was otherwise bright. At 1015 hours Greycap led the wing on Rodeo 235, a free-lance sweep of the St Omer area in conjunction with the Hornchurch Wing and controlled by Appledore. The Hornchurch Spitfires were positioned to the port-side of the Canadians. Johnnie: 'After making rendezvous at Dungeness, I set course for Berck. When half way across the Channel, Appledore gave me a vector of 90° but I had to swing to starboard to avoid Boulogne. Appledore then warned me of bandits approaching and instructed me to steer 70°. Shortly afterwards in the St Omer area I saw approximately thirty Fw190s approaching from the port bow at 25,000 feet with a high cover of twenty Me109s to port and above them. Kenley bottom Squadron was then at 23,000 feet. I asked Hornchurch to engage and 403 also turned into the high cover. I climbed 421 steeply under the 190s, which split up and carried out a moderate turn to port. Six 190s, however, straightened out and flew in line abreast heading in the Nieuport/Ostend direction. I instructed my Section to engage these six enemy aircraft but just as I was within range they all dived steeply. I followed my aircraft and opened fire from 250 yards with cannon and machine-guns. Several strikes were seen on his fuselage, wing roots and tail unit and he commenced to emit thick black smoke. As I broke away I saw at least one half of a wing break off.' After the brief combat, the Spitfires re-formed over Gravelines before going home independently. When mid-Channel, the Kenley Wing was informed of bandits in the Dover area, so Greycap took the Spitfires down to sea level, sweeping towards Boulogne, but no enemy aircraft were seen. By 1140 hours the Spitfires were safely back at base

In his log book, Johnnie recorded that his total number of enemy aircraft destroyed to date was eighteen and two-thirds. It was an impressive score. Johnnie: 'My life as a Wing Leader was fantastic. It just revolved around fighter pilots, Spitfires, flying and fighting. The Wing Commander Flying appointment was excellent, not least because previously the senior squadron commander would lead, but then there was always argy-bargy about who was the senior! Being a Wing Leader was the best job in Fighter Command. You had no administrative duties whatsoever, apart to recommend chaps for a gong. I don't think I put pen to paper at Kenley for any other reason. All you had to do was look after your pilots and aeroplanes with a very simple chain of command. It was a marvellous job. The Station Commander was usually a Group Captain, who had to do the food and the clothing, the general well-being of the Station with perhaps 2,000 personnel. Occasionally, like Jimmy Fenton, he would fly with us, just to keep his hand in, but he had to fly a desk most of the time! So the whole command structure was simply Fighter Command C-in-C, the Group AOC, the Station Commander, then the Wing Commander Flying. A very short, sharp, chain of command. A very good one too, and a very good relationship between the guys at the top. I remember on one occasion we had come back from escorting some Fortresses and we had got into some rather stiff fighting, although we had done well, and I got back in my office about five o'clock in the evening and some staff officer from Fighter Command HQ rang up and said "Hello, is that Wing Commander Johnson?"

I said "It is."

He said "Well just a moment, the Commander-in-Chief would like a word."

All the Boss said was "I thought that I would call you up Johnnie and say how very well you have done today, thank you very much, goodnight."

'Marvellous, wasn't it? Leadership, *real* leadership. We held conferences at Uxbridge with the AOC 11 Group, Air Vice-Marshal "Dingbat" Saunders, or we'd go up to Bentley Priory when Leigh-Mallory called one. Mind you, these chaps, Leigh-Mallory and so on, were all the while coming down to see us. LM was very good at keeping a good liaison, he didn't fly much himself but he'd get flown down in some old Proctor or something about once a month. He'd always come down if you got a gong, he was very much a father figure who wanted to help all the time. What did used to happen was that if there was a good show, the chaps at Fighter Command would produce a document containing extracts of the relevant reports and circulate this amongst the Wings. They were very good at disseminating information this way and had really got it together by 1943. By mid-1943, Al Deere and I were the "Old Boys", so they had to listen to what we had to say. Old LM would say "So tell me, Johnnie, what did you do then", and so on, "Can we improve that, is there anything I can do? Do you want another squadron, perhaps? Do you want to lead more squadrons?" So we always had this backing. I held Leigh-Mallory in high regard. He could be a little bit pompous but he had a heart of gold, super chap, and we were all very sad when he was later killed.'

Due to his increasing number of aerial victories, Johnnie was starting to attract significant publicity: 'It wasn't until early May time, when we started to escort the Fortresses and hack a few Huns down, that I got a bit of publicity. They used to produce a Fighter Command score sheet, of which Sailor Malan was at the top, and it also showed you who was deceased! The public relations chaps used to push the score sheet out to the newspapers. Of course there wasn't much good news at the time, lots of disasters in the Middle and Far East, so the air fighters became a bit of news, "glamour boys"!'

Clearly it was a time for heroes, and Johnnie was now amongst the foremost 'knights of the air'. Dan Browne: 'We did these missions called the "Milk Run" and the "Mail Run", one of which was to Abbeville. We'd all cross over on the deck, with propellers no higher than an office desk above the water, to avoid radar detection. Of course, there was rigid radio silence. The bombers would then climb up, and we'd climb up and get above them. As you know, Abbeville was a very active fighter field so pretty soon the bombers would drop their bombs, the target being just eighteen miles from the coast. The bombers would then turn, dive back out and go home. We would be still climbing up, going inland towards Germany, and soon start getting reports: "There are 200 plus coming up over Cambrai", "There's 200 plus coming up over Lille" and so on. There were only twenty-four of us! We would keep climbing until we got to a safe altitude, then we'd turn around and head back. Of course we had superior altitude in the Spit IX, so as the 190s couldn't reach us they'd pull up vertical and fire at us from some way below. The trick was to stall and spin out.'

After Ramrod 117 on 1 July, Wing Commander Johnson was sent off on a fortnight's well-earned leave. Upon conclusion, Johnnie flew from Rearsby (in Leicestershire) to Kenley in an Auster, his co-pilot being a Squadron Leader Edwards. Bob Middlemiss, of 403 Squadron, had also spent some of that leave with Johnnie in Melton Mowbray: 'Johnnie organized a trip in the latest Auster IV at Rearsby, with the Chief Test Pilot, a Mr Waite. The latter was taking up a new Auster, MT454, and went along on the test flight. He taxied out to the runway in use and said that he would demonstrate a short field take-off. He applied the brakes, opened full throttle, got tail up into flying position, then let go of the brakes and after a very short run indeed we were up and flying. On completion of the air test he said "I will now demonstrate the very short field landing capabilities of this aircraft."

After touchdown he applied full brakes – needless to say we stopped after a very short run, and no doubt was left in my mind of the aircraft's short take-off and landing capabilities!'

Back at Kenley on 15 July, Johnnie re-familiarised himself with Spitfire JE-J, EN398, in which he undertook an hour of local flying. Greycap's first flight was a cannon test of fifteen minutes. On this day of scattered cloud and good visibility, the Kenley Wing was not up on operations until 1613 hours. The sortie was Rodeo 245, a sweep of Hardelot, Abbeville and Poix, controlled by Appledore. The wing began climbing soon after take-off, crossing out over Rye at 5,000 feet before making landfall over Hardelot at 20,000. From Boulogne, accurate and intense flak was sent up, after which Greycap was vectored to the Poix area, just south of Abbeville. Bostons of 2 Group's 107 Squadron had just bombed Poix airfield, escorted by Typhoons and Spitfires. Combat had been joined with losses resulting for both sides, the fight having just finished when the Canadians arrived on the scene. Appledore warned Greycap of bandits ahead however, and he immediately saw two *schwarms* of Me109s directly ahead and at the same height. Johnnie's combat report described what happened next: 'I turned slightly starboard to get advantage of the Hun but all E/A except two Me109s climbed and were not seen again. These two Me109s flew head-on towards the Wing and when not more than 1,000 yards away turned to port and away from the Wing. I led my Section to attack and when almost within range E/A started to climb steeply. We had the advantage of speed, after one dive, and so experienced no difficulty in overtaking the E/A. I instructed my Number Two to take the highest Me109, and I opened fire on the lowest with cannon and machine-guns from dead astern, range 300 yards. I gave him a four second-burst, strikes being seen on the port wing root, engine cowling and fuselage. E/A at once started to pour thick glycol vapour and went down in a wide spiral. His course was easy to follow as he left a strong trail of white glycol in the air. He was seen to crash in the Bangy-Senarpont area and continued to burn and smoke for some minutes. This E/A is claimed as destroyed.' As usual there was no doubt regarding the accuracy of Johnnie's claim. The other Me109 was attacked three times by Flight Lieutenant MacDonald, Red Three of 403 Squadron, with which section Greycap was leading the wing. On Red Three's second pass, the 109 half-rolled to port and dived, and on the third attack strikes were seen on its port wingtip, fuselage and cockpit. From 12,000 feet the 109 dived straight in. Three Fw190s were then sighted near Le Tréport, but these quickly dived away and escaped when a section of 403 Squadron Spitfires gave chase. The wing then re-formed and left France via Berck, crossing back in at 5,000 feet over Dungeness. By 1750 the wing was safely down with two more confirmed victories to add to a growing tally.

At 1945 hours the Kenley Wing was up again, on Rodeo 246, sweeping Hardelot and Poix, again under Appledore. When offshore at Hardelot, Greycap was vectored south and found six Fw190s flying south at 12,000 feet over Le Touquet. 421 Squadron dived after them but were unable to close the gap, the 190s having half-rolled and dived inland. After the unsuccessful chase, Greycap re-formed his Spitfires and headed home, landing at 2015. He wrote in his log book: 'Six Fw190s intercepted but E/A ducked as we were just opening fire!'

A dull and wet morning cleared by noon on 16 July, the weather improving steadily throughout the afternoon. The wing was up at 1915 hours, Greycap leading on Ramrod 144, a sweep with Hornchurch of Dieppe, Grandvilliers, Abbeville and the Somme Estuary, in support of Marauders bombing Abbeville marshalling yards. The Spitfires crossed out over Beachy Head, then climbed steadily, making landfall just west of Dieppe at 22,000 feet. The wings then flew to Grandvilliers and were given a vector: bandits below at Angels Twelve. The Spitfire Mk IXs dived and intercepted the 'enemy', which proved to be the Tangmere Wing's Spitfire Mk XIIs! The IXs then re-formed and climbed to 23,000 feet, the Hornchurch Wing slightly above and up sun of Abbeville. At this point, twenty Fw190s were seen coming head on, so Greycap manoeuvred to give Hornchurch the advantage. Although the Germans were bounced by Wing Commander Crawford-Compton and his men, no claims were subsequently made. The Kenley Spitfires then left France over the Somme Estuary at 20,000 feet, flying north to Berck before setting course for Rye. By 2050 hours the wing was safely down. In his personal log, Johnnie wrote: 'Hornchurch rather missed a good opportunity.'

Times were changing. On 20 July the 421 Squadron ORB recorded: 'Everybody preparing for move to 127 Airfield in 83 Group. Practically all Squadron personnel, except pilots, are already posted to 127 Airfield, which is forming here at Kenley.' This was all preparation, of course, for the proposed Allied liberation of enemy occupied Europe. It was clear that air power would play a decisive role on the battlefield, fighter-bombers and medium bombers flying in support of ground forces. To achieve that end the fighter-bomber units would lead a nomadic existence, able to operate from temporary airfields and move at short notice. The whole process was now being geared up to achieving that aim.

On 25 July, according to the 421 Squadron ORB, there was a 'big improvement in the weather', which perfectly suited the Allied air forces' purposes. In the morning, 100 B-17s bombed Hamburg, following up the RAF's nocturnal raid. To prevent the enemy fighters of *Jafü* Holland-Ruhr engaging the Americans, the RAF's No 2 Group despatched a dozen B-25 Mitchells to bomb the Fokker aircraft factory at Amsterdam, and Eighth Air Force B-26 Marauders bombed the coke ovens at Ghent. First off, the Kenley Wing flew across to Coltishall to operate from there on another escort sortie, Ramrod 158, this time providing target support to the Bostons attacking Amsterdam. At the Norfolk aerodrome, the pilots were briefed while their Spitfires were refuelled before take-off at 1415. The Spitfires crossed the Dutch coast at 24,000 feet over the target area and sighted the bombers. The wing skirted north of Amsterdam and followed the Bostons out over the Dutch coast. Greycap then led his pilots on a sweep along the Dutch coast to Noordwijk, but no enemy aircraft were encountered. By 1555 the Spitfires were back at Coltishall being 'turned around'.

At 1915 hours the Kenley Wing was up again, this time on Ramrod 158, providing forward target support to twelve Bostons bombing Schipol aerodrome. Crossing the Dutch coast at 22,000 feet between Noordwijk and Zandveert, the Spitfires then flew to Schipol, which was reached on time. Johnnie: 'At 1957 hours I was flying on the East side of Schipol at 22,000 feet, when I saw an Me109G, with under-slung guns in wings, flying in the same direction about three miles ahead of the Wing. Enemy aircraft turned to port and was obviously positioning himself to attack the beehive, which was then crossing the coast. I instructed the Wing to remain at their height and took my Section down to attack this E/A. I closed in on E/A, then at 12,000 feet, and opened fire with cannon and machine-guns closing to 170 yards. The 109 was flying directly into the sun and owing to this fact I could not see the result of my fire, but as I broke away he turned to port with glycol streaming from his starboard radiator. I saw him go down to about 6,000 feet and my Number Two saw him after this, diving vertically towards the ground. As I climbed away I saw an aircraft burning on the ground to the west of Schipol. As there were no Wing losses in the combat area I claim this Me109 as destroyed on this evidence.' The Wing Leader was supported by Pilot Officer Isbister, flying Black Two: 'Wing Leader opened fire, firing several bursts closing to point blank range. The enemy aircraft was pouring white smoke and taking no evasive action except medium turns. He then broke up and the last I saw of the E/A it was diving towards the ground at a very steep angle at 6,000 – 8,000 feet, pouring white smoke.'

Flying Officer L. Foster added: 'After the Wing Leader broke off his attack, I attempted to watch the E/A crash. I was able to see it still diving at about 3,000 feet but lost sight of it due to the thick ground haze. Shortly after, I saw what could have been the E/A burning in the area I last saw said E/A diving.' The Me109 concerned was probably from III/JG54, based at Schipol, the pilot of which was killed.

After this combat, the Spitfires re-formed and headed for the Dutch coast. When south of Ijmuiden, at 15-16,000 feet, eight P-47 Thunderbolts were seen above and behind the wing, flying the same course. The Americans misidentified the Spitfires and consequently one P-47 dived at Flying Officer Zary, White Four of 421 Squadron. At 200 yards the American pilot opened fire, but fortunately for Zary his marksmanship was poor and White Four was unscathed. The Thunderbolts were last seen heading towards Horsham. As the Kenley Wing Form 'F' later reported, 'Had this Section not been bounced by the Thunderbolts, they would probably have been able to engage two Fw190s which were seen below and to port.' Without further incident, the Kenley Wing landed back at Coltishall at 2055, returning to Kenley after the Spitfires had been refuelled. Four aircraft of 421 Squadron had been forced to return early from this sortie, having been unable to jettison their auxiliary fuel tanks. Red One of 403 Squadron, Squadron Leader Godefroy, had also returned early with a technical problem. By 2220 hours the wing was safely back at Kenley, and as the 421 Squadron ORB reported, 'It was a long day'.

Although the weather remained slightly uncertain, 28 July would see the Americans mount their heaviest attack yet against the German aircraft industry. The 1st Bomber Wing's 182 B-17s crossed the North Sea and bombed the Fieseler works at Kassell-Bettenhausen, while the 4th Wing's 120 were to make the deepest penetration into Germany so far: the AGO fighter assembly plant at Aschersleben, near Magdeburg. Both works produced the Fw190 and were therefore top priority aircraft industry targets. The lead force of the latter wing was the 94th Group based at Bury St Edmunds, led personally in the air by the Commanding Officer, Colonel Fred Castle who anticipated it being a 'hot' one. First the B-17s feinted towards Hamburg before turning south-east towards Aschersleben. Over the Continent, however, bad weather again caused problems, dispersing the Fortresses. Over the Dutch coast, JG1's Fw190s engaged the bombers, some of them using, for the first time, aerial rockets. These were actually 21 cm mortars adapted to be under-slung on both wings. Also, Me109s of the Jever based II/JG11, dropped 500-lb bombs onto the Fortress formations!

This was a new concept, only practical against tight formations, but devastating when successful. These new and perhaps somewhat desperate measures indicate the resolve with which the Germans defied the Allied CBO. It also emphasises how increasingly vulnerable the bombers were becoming without complete fighter support. As the Americans battled onwards and further into Germany, through a gap in the cloud Castle's bombardier in *Sour Puss* recognised a landmark from which he was able to accurately calculate time from target. Most of the other B-17s in this formation followed suit. When reconnaissance photographs were later taken, a large concentration of bombs was found to have been dropped within the target area, this causing sufficient damage to write off a whole month's production: fifty Fw190s.

To extend range, the Kenley Wing operated from Manston on Ramrod 165. Greycap's brief had been to meet the homeward bound B-17s three miles north of The Hague, but the rendezvous was changed, in the air, to eight miles south of Rotterdam. By then the B-17s were protected by a gaggle of Allied fighters, so the Kenley Wing did a couple of orbits before sweeping south-west along the Dutch and Belgian coast at 20,000 feet. A lone Fortress was seen coming out between Dunkirk and Nieuport, its crew no doubt being grateful for the escort provided by a couple of dozen Canadian Spitfires! For Squadron Leader Buck McNair of 421 Squadron it was to be a trip of high drama. At 1226 hours, over the inhospitable North Sea just off Knocke, McNair's Spitfire developed engine trouble. Unable to keep up, he dropped behind the wing, covered by Pilot Officer Parks. Slowly losing height from 20,000 to 10,000 feet, when twelve miles off Dunkirk and over the Channel, McNair's engine caught fire. Traumatically, the pilot lost control of his aircraft, which plunged seawards. At 5,000 feet, McNair managed to break free of his doomed Spitfire. At 2,000 feet Pilot Officer Parks saw with relief his chief's parachute open. McNair splashed into the Channel, Parks immediately taking a fix and transmitting a mayday signal. The young pilot then orbited McNair's position for an hour and a half until relieved by 411 Squadron. As the 421 Squadron ORB says of Parks' effort, it was a 'good show'. Immediately 421 Squadron landed at Manston and heard of their CO's predicament, the Spitfires were refuelled, the pilots taking off to participate in the ASR operation to rescue Squadron Leader McNair. A little while later, 421 Squadron watched a Walrus pick up McNair, the Spitfires then providing escort back to Hawkinge for the curious looking but life-saving seaplane flown by Squadron Leader Grove. As Greycap's log relates, the ASR sortie had lasted an hour and ten minutes, and McNair's ordeal in the water had lasted two hours. He was one of the lucky ones, as the 421 ORB reports: 'The Chief was burned about the face and had a real close call, but is now resting satisfactorily in hospital and should be back in a few days.' During this mission, the Eighth Air Force lost twenty-two B-17s (and some 198 men, therefore), and four more so badly damaged that they only just reached England. It was hardly surprising that this period became known by the Americans as the 'Bloody Summer of 1943'.

The 29th of July was a bright and virtually cloudless day, perfect conditions for the Eighth Air Force's purposes. The target for today was the Arado plant at Warnemünde, another works producing the Fw190. For the RAF's 2 Group, the task of providing diversionary attacks continued. The Kenley Wing was first to fly Ramrod 112, providing top cover to American B-26 Marauders attacking Schipol aerodrome. The complexity of planning such an operation is evident from the details of 12 Group's Order No 12G/6:

Bombers: 18 Marauders of No 3 Wing, No 323 Group USAAF.

Fighters:	Close Escort Cover	402 Sqn (LR Spitfires) (Digby)
		416 Sqn (LR Spitfires) (Digby)
		611 Sqn (LR Spitfires) (Coltishall)
		118 Sqn (LR Spitfires) (Coltishall)
	Escort Cover	302 Sqn (LR Spitfires) (Portreath)
		317 Sqn (LR Spitfires) (Portreath)
	Top Cover	303 Sqn (Spitfires IX) (Northolt)
		316 Sqn (Spitfires IX) (Northolt)
		403 Sqn (Spitfires IX) (Kenley)
		421 Sqn (Spitfires IX) (Kenley)

The Close Escort Spitfires took off from Ludham and Matlask at 0935 hours, and rendezvoused with the Marauders fourteen miles north of Southwold at 11,000 feet. The bombers, however, set off for the target a minute early and their formation became scattered. Some twenty miles off Ijmuiden, the Marauders turned south and flew parallel to the Dutch coast until reaching the Hook of Holland. Bombs were then jettisoned, after which the Americans turned west and headed home. The two wing leaders of the close cover escort wings, Digby and Coltishall, were perplexed as no enemy aircraft were in sight and visibility was unlimited, but tried in vain to contact the bombers over the R/T. The bombers had aborted due to a navigational error, having made landfall eighteen miles further north than intended. The Kenley

Wing continued to the target, crossing the Dutch coast at 22,000 feet over Zandvoort and sweeping between Ijmuiden and Schipol. Johnnie: 'Enemy aircraft were seen below and I instructed various Sections of 421 Squadron to engage, leaving 403 Squadron as high cover. I attacked the last aircraft of a pair of Me109s with cannon and machine-gun from 450-200 yards range, firing several short bursts from astern. Enemy aircraft gave off stream of black smoke and two de Wilde [incendiary ammunition] strikes were seen on the cockpit. As there were other enemy aircraft about I broke off this combat and last saw the 109 diving slowly down to 10,000 feet with a steady stream of black smoke coming away from the aircraft.' Johnnie had fired 134 rounds of 20mm and 270 of .303. The 109 was claimed as damaged. His wingman was more successful. Pilot Officer K.R. Linton: 'I was flying Black Two on 12 Group Ramrod Twenty-two, behind Wing Commander Johnson. After crossing the Dutch coast I saw an Me109 which Wing Commander Johnson immediately turned in and attacked. He could not get close enough, so pulled up and soon after this we saw one Fw190 chasing two 109s. Wing Commander Johnson's ammunition was getting low, so he told me to attack it while he covered me. It was 2,000 feet below and at two o'clock to me. I dived on him and when within 250 yards I gave several short squirts from dead astern. The top of his rudder was shot away and I could see strikes on the fuselage and wings, then he turned slightly to port and I got in a three second burst from 20 degrees. The whole of the Fw190 seemed to burst into flames and he half-rolled and dived straight into the deck just SW of Schipol aerodrome. At least four other pilots saw this. I claim this Fw190 as destroyed.'

While 403 Squadron provided top cover, 421 Squadron got stuck in, as the pilots' combat reports testify.

Flying Officer W.E. Harten:

'On 12 Group Ramrod 22 I was flying Green One. About 1035 hours I was about ten to twelve miles west of Schipol when three Me109s flew about 500 – 600 feet below me going north-east. They were turning to starboard, I followed them around and when we were about 500 yards away the centre one and the extreme starboard one half-rolled and went straight down. The third one continued on. I closed in and fired from about 250-300 yards, 30° off. He then turned slightly to port which brought me in line astern. I fired from 100-50 yards, observing strikes on cockpit and starboard wing. He turned over to left and went straight down, smoking. I circled the area then returned home.'

Flying Officer L.R. Thorne:

'I was flying Green Two to F/O Harten. About ten miles west of Schipol we sighted three Me109s. F/O Harten led the Section around, closing in on them. Two of them half-rolled straight down but a third continued straight on and seemed to be turning slightly to starboard. F/O Harten fired and the a/c streamed white smoke. F/O Harten then pulled away and I was in a position to see the enemy aircraft burst into flames on the starboard side. He (E/A) turned to the left and went straight down. I saw him fall 2-3,000 feet then we did a turn to starboard and on looking back I saw him burning on the ground, south of the lake just north of Leiden, about five miles. The E/A fired at by F/O Harten is definitely destroyed.'

Flight Lieutenant N.R. Fowlow:

'I was flying White One at 15,000 feet south-west of Amsterdam when I saw two Me109s flying west in echelon port, 5,000 feet below. I turned and dived down to attack the Number One in the formation, followed by my Number Two who attacked the port aircraft in the formation. The aircraft I attacked took violent evasive action, doing a quarter roll to starboard. I followed firing intermittingly and closing from 300 yards to 200 yards. The aircraft rolled on its back at about 5,000 feet with smoke pouring from it and I saw it dive straight down into the deck. I claim this Me109 as destroyed.'

Sergeant N.B. Dixon:

'I was flying as White Two to F/Lt Fowlow. When south of Amsterdam he sighted 2 Me109s crossing to port at 18,000 feet. Turning sharply port he cut in behind as one Me109 rolled over. He chased it down steeply and as the other Me turned starboard down after him, I gave him 3 squirts ranging from 300-50 yards, from 60° down to dead astern and above. With no reflector sight I hosepiped him and saw hits on the starboard wing. When he dived away he was turning and going down fast at a 70° angle. I pulled up and headed home, chased by one Me109. I observed three fires caused by burning aircraft south of Amsterdam. Near a lake I saw another small fire caused by burning aircraft.'

On this sortie, Pilot Officer J.E. Abbotts and Flight Lieutenant Golberg of 403 Squadron were flying White Three and Four respectively with 421 Squadron. South-west of Amsterdam, White Section was bounced and Abbotts simply disappeared. Fortunately the young pilot survived being shot down, but became a prisoner of war. 403 Squadron was about to attack three enemy fighters which appeared below, but then sighted a whole gaggle of bandits above. Upon climbing to investigate, Squadron Leader Godefroy confirmed these aircraft to be Spitfires before turning home. The wing, fragmented after 421 Squadron's hectic and successful combat, crossed out over Noordwijkerhout at various heights and times, pancaking back at Coltishall at 1115.

The 421 Squadron claims were as follows:

Wing Commander Johnson:	One Me109 damaged.
Pilot Officer Linton:	One Fw190 destroyed.
Flying Officer Harten:	One Me109 destroyed.
Flight Lieutenant Fowlow:	One Me109 destroyed.
Sergeant Dixon:	One Me109 damaged.

For one missing Spitfire pilot, it was an excellent result. Amongst the German losses was at least one experienced fighter pilot and leader, Hauptmann Karl Anton Waldemar, the Staffelkapitän of 7/JG54 *Grun Herz*. The IIIrd Gruppe of this famous Jagdgeschwader had been brought to the west from Russia and was now based at Oldenburg and Nordholtz on Heligoland Bight. JG3 *Udet* was also moved from Russia to the west, and JG26 was pulled away from the Channel coast to operate on a daily basis from bases on the lower Rhine and Holland, right on the American approach routes. The Me109s of 2/JG27 were withdrawn from North Africa, these augmenting the strength of JG11 at Jever, which had been formed in April 1943 out of JG1. Hitler, however, had yet to consider that the Reich defence force was top priority, and still sent the bulk of fighters to both the Eastern and Mediterranean fronts. In the first eight months of 1943 the output of Me109s and Fw190s soared to 7,477, but those available to the home defence force rose but slowly: 162 in May, 255 in June, and 300 in July.

After 421 Squadron's successful fight, Greycap led his Spitfires from Coltishall back to Kenley. At 1748 hours, the wing was up again, on Ramrod 171, a sweep of Dieppe, Neufchâtel and the Somme Estuary in support of No 2 Group bombers attacking the airfield at Yainville. The sortie passed without incident however, and the Spitfires were safely home by 1920 hours. But the day did not end there, as after refuelling the Kenley Wing flew back to Coltishall, where the pilots again stayed overnight, this being necessary for another early start.

On 30 July, 186 B-17s struck out and again attacked Kassel. The resulting interception by German fighters signified the fiercest clash so far between the 'Mighty Eighth' and the Luftwaffe: seventeen Fortresses were lost, eighty-two more damaged, and two Thunderbolts also failed to return. After this trip, the Eighth Air Force were in no position to fly another major mission to Germany without first making good losses in both men and machines. At the start of 'Blitz Week', the Americans had 330 aircraft and crews ready to go. Within a week that figure had been reduced to around 170. Over a hundred B-17s had been lost, and around ninety crews were either missing, killed or wounded. As Johnnie said, 'They took some hard knocks.'

At Coltishall, the Kenley Wing's Canadians were amongst a number of fighter pilots briefed for 12 Group Ramrod Twenty-three, a raid by thirteen Bostons of 2 Group's 107 Squadron, on Schipol aerodrome. Close escort cover was to be provided by the Digby and Coltishall Wings, top cover by the Kenley Mk IXs, and rear cover by 609 Squadron's Typhoons (based at Coltishall). The Kenley Wing was up at 1005 hours, Greycap leading. Rendezvous was made with the Beehive over Coltishall at 1009 hours, and a direct course was set for the target. At 1036 hours, the Kenley Wing started to climb and crossed in over Ijmuiden with squadrons stepped up to 23,000 feet. The beehive thence proceeded inland to Schipol, the Bostons dropping their bombs on target. As the bombers crossed out over Noordwijkerhout, two aircraft were seen 6,000 feet below and about seven miles behind. Suspecting the presence of more bandits, Wing Commander Johnson took the whole of 403 Squadron down, leaving 421 as top cover. Johnnie: 'There were some six E/A in this area, and I attacked the starboard 109 of the original pair. I opened fire from 400 yards with cannon and machine-guns, but E/A turned to port and dived down. As he dived away, I gave him a burst from 450 yards. I watched E/A and was surprised to see him pull out and climb steeply up. I closed in and saw that both wheels were down. I gave him another burst but did not observe any results. The 109 was then stalling and I broke away to see Flying Officer Lambert destroy the second 109. I orbited and saw a parachute descending from the combat area. This enemy aircraft is claimed as destroyed, shared with Flight Sergeant Shouldice (403 Squadron).'

Flight Sergeant G.M. Shouldice was Greycap's wingman, Red Two:

'Red One led our Section down to attack in a very steep dive from approximately out of the sun. When we were about 600 yards from these two E/As the port a/c veered off to port while the starboard one turned and dived to the right. Red One attacked the E/A which turned to starboard and I followed Red One. Red One took a squirt at the E/A and his wheels dropped down, and some black smoke was emitted. I took a short burst at about 400 yards after Red One broke off his attack. In the course of the scrap I had about four short bursts at the E/A but cannot definitely say that I saw strikes. At about 7,000 feet I took one short burst when the E/A had wheels and flaps down and was almost stalled – no results observed. After this Red 1 observed the pilot in his parachute from this aircraft. Since it is not clear whose fire caused this, we claim one Me109 destroyed (shared).

Flying Officer J.F. Lambert was Red Three in Greycap's Section:

'Red One and Red Two dived on the starboard E/A while I led Red Four on the other which climbed inland to starboard. As I went after it, it dived steeply and rolled and then straightened out again. I was closing on it. At about 7,000 feet and at very high speed, it began to pull out. I shot a two to three second burst at about ten to fifteen degrees deflection at about 500 yards range and then since I was very low I pulled back hard out of the dive. Levelling out at about 2,000 feet I then climbed back up to the Squadron. I last saw the enemy aircraft at about 5,000 feet, diving away very steeply and at high speed, but I did not see the result of my shooting since I had to pull out very quickly. Because of what Wing Commander saw, however, I claim this aircraft as destroyed.'

Flight Lieutenant H.J. Southwood was Yellow Two of 403 Squadron:

'I was following Yellow One down when at about 12,000 feet the windscreen fluid tank discharged nearly all its contents over the cockpit and myself. At first, I presumed there was an engine glycol leak and by the time I had organized myself and cleaned off my windscreen I had somehow managed to lose the rest of my Section. My height was about 10,000 feet and I was flying north when I recognised an Me109 coming towards me, slightly below and about 500 yards ahead. The enemy aircraft turned in on my starboard and I turned in towards and dived straight down on him, at the same time taking a very short vertical burst at about 300–400 yards, but there were no results. The enemy then turned starboard and I got astern of him. He then continued diving at 300-400 mph. I took a long burst at about 300 yards, then a much longer one closing to about 50 yards. I used up the cannon first and ended up using machine-guns. After the first long burst from astern the wheels fell down, and I saw black smoke over the tailplane but due to the fact that I was firing into the sun and the haze, I am not sure of seeing any strikes. My windscreen was still clouded up from the windscreen tank blowing up. I broke off my attack at about 4,000 feet, last seeing the E/A spiralling down to starboard with his wheels down and black smoke trailing. I claim this 109 as damaged.'

After the combat, 403 Squadron re-formed and re-joined 421 Squadron. The Kenley Wing left Holland via Zandvoort, where two Fw190s were seen but were out of range. The wing was safely back at Coltishall by 1140 hours, refuelled and returned to Kenley at 1320 hours. It had been another successful day for the Canadians, 403 Squadron's score being as follows:

> Wing Commander Johnson & Flight Sergeant Shouldice: One Me109 destroyed.
> Flying Officer Lambert: One Me109 destroyed.
> Flight Lieutenant Southwood: One Me109 damaged.

By now Johnnie was attracting an increasing amount of publicity, being hailed as 'Finucane's successor'. The following article appeared in the *Yorkshire Post*, headlined 'Hunts Huns in Foxes' Head Scarf':

> Wing Commander JE Johnson DSO DFC & bar, the Melton Mowbray fighter ace, now has 19 German planes to his credit.
>
> I met Johnson a year ago when he was a Flight Lieutenant at a fighter station on the East Coast. In private life he was an assistant in the office of the Borough Surveyor at Melton Mowbray.
>
> And appropriately enough for a man from hunting country, he never flies without a yellow scarf dotted with brown foxes' heads round his neck.
>
> At that time he had shot down about seven Germans, and the Air Ministry would not then pass his name for publication. Today he has reached the amazing total of 19. It is amazing because nowadays fighter pilots have to go out and chase Huns. That is why sweeps are organized. In the Battle of Britain the Germans came here.
>
> When I met Johnson he spoke confidently.
>
> On the door of his little office was painted the words 'Flight Lieutenant Johnson and Pusher'. Pusher was the most peculiar

> looking mongrel I have ever seen. He waved a long tail and looked like a spaniel with a setter's legs. He was a strange puce colour. But he adored his master, and 'Johnnie', as the riggers of his Spitfire called him amongst themselves, seemed to return the worship.
>
> When he went out to his plane to take part in a sweep over France that sunny April morning, Pusher followed.
>
> Some six months later I met him again. He looked older and harder. He had a bar on his DFC. We talked about the previous meeting. Pusher was dead, he said, killed by a lorry. He changed the conversation.

On 31 July, although the Eighth Air Force's bombers were stood down, the B-26 Marauders of Eighth Air Service Command were still active, and it was in support of twenty-one such bombers that the Kenley Wing took off at 1045 hours (Ramrod 179). The target was the aerodrome at Merville, and the Canadian Spitfires provided cover as the Marauders withdrew amidst the black puff-balls of a heavy flak barrage. South of Bergues a dozen Me109s were seen orbiting 6,000 feet below, so Greycap took 421 Squadron down to attack. Although Johnnie later wrote in his log book 'Me109s bounced but E/A ducked!', Pilot Officer Linton fired at a 109, on which strikes were seen around the cockpit area. The enemy fighter was last seen trailing a plume of black smoke at 3,000 feet. After this inconclusive combat (in respect of which Linton was awarded one Me109 damaged), the wing flew to Guines and Montreuil, between 22 and 29,000 feet. The remainder of the sortie was uneventful however, and by 1225 hrs the wing was back at Kenley. The day's second operation was Ramrod 181, forward target support to Marauders bombing Abbeville. The mission went according to plan but no enemy aircraft were seen, the sortie therefore passing without incident. At the end of the month, the score of the Kenley Wing squadrons was as follows:

403 'Wolf' Squadron:	One Fw190 destroyed.
	Six-and-a-half Me109s destroyed.
	One Me109 damaged.
421 'Red Indian' Squadron:	Four Me109s destroyed.
	Four Me109s damaged.
	One Me109 probably destroyed.
	One Fw190 destroyed.
	One Fw190 damaged.

In total, the Kenley Wing had flown an impressive 935.53 hours on operations; as Dan Browne says, 'We were a keen bunch.'

On 4 August Squadron Leader Godefroy briefed the pilots on the impending move to 126 Airfield at Lashenden, near Headcorn. Needless to say, Johnnie organized one last 'glorious thrash' in the Mess at Kenley before the wing moved into tented accommodation in Kent. Invitations were sent to all the wing leaders, the 'top brass' at RCAF HQ, and 2nd TAF. Suffice to say, the 'Big Wing Ding' was a huge success! Fortunately there was no flying the following day, which was spent drawing tents and other equipment in preparation for the imminent move to Lashenden. In the afternoon the ground crews erected their tents around the airfield perimeter. These were later taken down and all slept in the crew rooms and at dispersal, ready to go early in the morning. At 1000 hours the next morning, pilots not flying aircraft joined ground crews and left Kenley in a motor convoy for Lashenden. The ground crews were formally posted to '127 Airfield HQ', only the aircrew being assigned to 403 and 421 Squadrons. The convoy reached its destination at 1430, at which time tents had to be erected and the whole wing unpacked. At 1000 hours on 7 August 1943, Wing Commander Johnson led his Spitfires off from Kenley for the last time, bound for 127 Airfield. It was the end of another highly successful era. As the Canadians landed at Lashenden fifteen minutes later, a new and even more exciting time was about to begin: *The Great Adventure*.

Chapter 2

A long affair

We had a long affair, you and I. You, the most beautiful fighter ever built, and me the happy, proud, pilot. We grew up together – in combat over England, the Channel, France, Belgium, Holland and Germany. We said farewell to each other after a six-year love affair.

We were introduced at Hawarden during that shining summer of 1940, when the obedient and disciplined Germans had already proved their new concept of war – *Blitzkrieg* (Lightning War). France had surrendered and we, in Britain, were bereft of Allies. Our Army, driven into the sea at Dunkirk, was virtually disarmed. The Royal Air Force was severely weakened. We faced invasion by the strongest military power in the world.

Our fate now depended on whether or not a thousand fighter pilots, the majority flying your cousin, the older yet sturdier Hurricane, could hold the ring against the all-conquering Luftwaffe until the gales of October.

You stood on the stained grass at dispersal, lean and drab in your war coat of grey and green paint. My instructor – if he had any qualities of leadership I never spotted them – walked round you and I noticed a patch on your wing root where you had been hit by your main adversary – an Me109 – over Dunkirk. I climbed into your narrow cockpit: 'Bit tight across the shoulders for me,' I remarked.

'You'll soon get used to it,' he replied. 'Surprising how small you can get when a yellow-nosed 109 is on your tail. You'll keep your head down then! Otherwise you won't last long!'

I will pass gently over our first *pas à deux* over the Welsh mountains, but I got you down in one piece, which is more than I did a few days later when, trying to get into a short airfield, I completely stalled you and wrote-off your undercarriage. I gave my shoulder a nasty wrench, but that landing hurt you more than me.

Flying with 616 Squadron I found that your fabric ailerons produced such high stick pressures in a steep drive that they aggravated an old rugby injury to my shoulder. So, for a few weeks we parted company when I went into hospital to get my shoulder fixed.

Then we flew south and joined the Tangmere Wing led by the fearless, indomitable, Douglas Bader. You were fitted with metal ailerons and the previous high stick pressures were greatly reduced, which was good for my shoulder. In the high summer of 1941, we flew almost every day, and we fought 'Dolpho' Galland and his gallant pilots of JG26 over the chill waters of the Channel and above the *Pas de Calais*. We won our spurs that season, and when in the autumn we returned to the north, we had half-a-dozen victories.

The next year, 1942, we were outclassed by the formidable Fw190 and we nearly came to grief when we were supporting Canadian troops on their hopeless Dieppe raid. We became separated from the rest of 610 Squadron and an aggressive Fw190 came at us over the town. Unlike most German fighters he stayed with us in the tightest of turns. In the dogfight I asked you for all you had, but still the Kraut hung on. Eventually, we threw him off by flying straight at one of our destroyers who, of course, always fired at friend and foe.

In the spring of 1943, I led the Kenley (Canadian) Wing and we flew your beautiful high altitude Mark IX with its splendid new Rolls-Royce engine. The engine was mounted in your old airframe so that our great tactical advantage was that apart from your longer nose, and more exhaust stacks, you looked just the same as your slower sister.

We had a good season with the Canadians. We were better than any Me109 or Fw190 and we roamed far and wide and helped the 'Mighty Eighth' on their daylight missions over north-west Europe and Germany. After our three-year affair we parted company, but not before we had arranged to meet again for the 'Great Adventure'.

We met each other again in the spring of 1944 at Digby in Lincolnshire. Another Canadian Wing had arrived for the Normandy invasion and on that momentous day we flew four times over the beaches. A few days later, on 10 June 1944, we had the honour, you and I, of leading the first Allied fighters to land in France since 1940.

We fought a lot over the bocage and eventually flung the invaders out of Normandy. In late August we heard that large German fighter formations were protecting the remnants of their Seventh Army withdrawing across the Seine, and we led the wing to intercept. I made a big and nearly fatal mistake on that day.

My wingman turned back with a rough engine and Larry Robillard asked if he should detach a wingman from his section. I declined, swept over Paris and down the Seine and saw sixty-plus German fighters ahead and slightly below.

We bounced the Krauts and shot down two – the last at ground level. Then, alone, we climbed over the Seine to try and find some friends. Larry called and said he was over the Seine at 15,000 feet. I said I would climb up and join him. At 15,000 feet I saw six fighters behind, and told Larry to join me. Seconds later tracer flashed over your canopy. The six fighters were lean 109s, two behind and two on either side. I flung you into the tightest of turns and thought .... 'You stupid clot' ... to get yourself into such a mess after four years of air fighting.

We, my beauty, turn and turn and turn. And because we can turn inside the 109s we survive. But we cannot turn over the Seine for ever. I figure that if we can somehow reach 19,000 feet your second stage supercharger will cut in and then we can outclimb the opposition.

The sun is at its zenith. I slam the throttle through the gate to give full emergency power and we climb steeply into the sun's blinding glare. The 109 leader hangs on and I feel you shudder as a cannon shell slams into your starboard wing root. We turn and turn to get inside him. Climb into the sun again. The second supercharger cuts in and we run away ... to fight again another day.

In our caravans and tents we trekked across Europe to be halted at Arnhem – a bridge too far. Soon after that gallant failure we were leading 443 Squadron down the Rhine looking for trouble. The Squadron Commander himself, Wally McLeod, was in the formation, but this great fighter pilot and outstanding shot had one flaw – he, unlike me, never knew when to break-off a fight. Flying just below a thick, heavy cloud base we bounced nine 109s and as we climbed away from our victim I saw Wally, leech-like, behind a steeply climbing 109. Both disappeared into the cloud. We never saw Wally McLeod again.

In the spring of 1945 we crossed the Rhine and from Celle, once a Luftwaffe stronghold, we flew over a stricken, burning Berlin – symbolic of the evil empire.

After the war we flew home together. The jet age had arrived and it was time to end our long affair of nearly six years. We crossed the Channel as we had done a thousand and more times before with never a break in your Merlin's song. Over the south coast the high sky was blue and clear – just as it was in that long, hot summer of 1940. The contrails that marked the air battles have long been swept away. The grass is long on some of the graves of those who fell; but as long as men fly, you, my beautiful Spitfire, will be remembered.

Air Vice-Marshal James Edgar 'Johnnie' Johnson CB CBE DSO** DFC*

Chapter 3

The Commander

Johnnie:

During the winter of 1943, I spent a few months on the planning staff of 11 Group, and, knowing that Operation Overlord would take place in the following summer, I, like many others, made quite certain that I was included in the Great Adventure. Already the victorious top brass from the Desert, Sicily and Italy – Eisenhower, Montgomery, Tedder and Coningham – were in the UK making sure that experienced fighter commanders, at the lower echelons, joined their team. Our own AOC of 83 Group, 'Dicky' Dickson, who had fought in the First War, was charming, enthusiastic, straight as a gun barrel, of the highest integrity, and very proud of his command. Dicky was a father figure; we all admired him and knew he was of the right stuff to take us through the storms of north-west Europe but, much to his dismay, he was replaced, at Montgomery's insistence, by the more experienced Harry Broadhurst.

Dickson had a tremendously loyal staff headed by Air Commodore Dermot Boyle, a Cranwell man, who organized a splendid party to say goodbye to the little man. Boyle made an emotional speech, but when Dickson responded he simply said that the decision to replace him was correct because Harry Broadhurst, universally known as 'Broady', had for the past year commanded the Western Desert Air Force where he had supported Montgomery's Eighth Army and gained the respect of its commander.

Harry Broadhurst always wanted to fly and used to watch old biplanes flying 'circuits and bumps' at Gosport, the home of the Central Flying School. His father, however, had a poor opinion of the junior Service and Broady began his military career with a short stint in the Royal Artillery, but in 1928 transferred to the Royal Air Force.

Like most young flyers he wanted to be a fighter pilot and was disappointed when, after flying training, he was posted to 11 Squadron, equipped with Fairey Fawns. These were old, wooden, two-seater biplanes, with the observer sitting behind the pilot. He had been on the squadron about two months, when 'I lost a pot (a rotary engine cylinder) and had to force-land on the polo ground of the 8th Hussars at Tidworth Camp. I bounced over a couple of jumps, but the aircraft was all right and I started to walk across the grass to the Sister's quarters to telephone my CO. However, John Elton, who was flying at the same time, saw the incident and started to beat me up. He was busy making rude signs with his fingers when he hit one of the jumps, went arse-over-tit, and wrote-off his Fawn.

In accordance with regulations, they telephoned their CO to report the incident. Broady spoke first and explained his mishap.

"Are you alright?" asked the CO.

"Yes Sir, I'm fine."

"What about the aeroplane?"

"No damage, Sir!"

"That's alright then, there is nothing to worry about."

"I think", replied Broady, "You'd better have a word with Flying Officer Elton!"'

Broady continued:

Just after the 8th Hussars incident, my HRD motor-bike was banned from the camp because they did not like the noise. So, my father bought me a three-wheeler racing Morgan for my birthday, which I could not use very much because I was doing a month's Orderly Officer for some misdemeanour or other.

I had driven the Morgan up to the Flight Office and was fiddling about with it, when John Whitworth walked up and said: "Broadhurst, I've been looking all over the place for you. There's an aeroplane waiting to take you to Andover." So, I hurried into the Flight Office to get my stick, gloves and cap, and off we went to Andover in a Fawn.

At their destination the weather clamped down and the last thing Broady remembered, before he awoke in hospital, was his pilot groping about in the murk. Eventually the pilot flew the Fawn into a hillside, where the wooden aeroplane broke up. The heavy metal ring came away from its mounting and nearly decapitated the passenger. Unfortunately the first thing his father knew about the crash was when he read in a local newspaper that his son had 'pranged' into the side of a hill. This incident did not improve Broadhurst senior's already low opinion of the Royal Air Force.

'Broady' Broadhurst:

'The best time of my life was between 1933 and 1939 when I achieved my great ambition of flying fighters. In those days we had the Siskin, followed by the Bulldog, the Gauntlet and the Gladiator.'

Indeed, this was the golden age of flying. In their small, stubby, gaily-painted biplanes Broady and his contemporaries, Teddy Donaldson and Dick Atcherley, looped, rolled and gambolled over their airfields to their heart's delight. Broady had a gift for aerobatics and gave individual shows at the annual Hendon Air Displays. He was an outstanding shot and he and Teddy Donaldson fought out the annual firing competition for the Sassoon Trophy, which he won on three successive years. He was selected to perform in several pre-war Hendon Air Displays which perhaps expressed the junior Service's cheerful approach to life.

The Prince of Wales arrived in his private aeroplane to join the vast crowd that watched air refuelling, autogiros for Army co-operation, bombers from some of the auxiliary squadrons trailing smoke across the sky, teams of dumpy, chequered fighters led by Broady, tied together with coloured rope, looping and stunting over the airfield and landing in immaculate formation with the ropes unbroken, parachute dropping, flying boats, bombers bowling over giant skittles with small practice bombs, dogfights with blank ammunition, and the shooting down of a balloon.

Imperialism was unfortunately portrayed when the fighter boys beat-up with flour bags a native fort, whose coloured occupants were about to commit some dastardly crime. After the natives had abandoned the fort it was destroyed with a small quantity of explosive which went off with a large bang. Unfortunately on one occasion the timing of the various events went astray. The fort was demolished just as Dick Atcherley was flying upside-down a few feet overhead. The blast blew him the right way up and Atcherley, and the display, proceeded.

In the late thirties Fighter Command changed its old wooden biplanes for Spitfires and Hurricanes, and when in early September 1939 the Second War began, Squadron Leader Broadhurst was commanding 111 Squadron based at Northolt. He had the squadron well trained for the contest but there was little Luftwaffe activity over our island home, except for their reconnaissance aeroplanes coming in at night over the Firth of Forth. An auxiliary squadron, based at Acklington in Northumberland was not having much success against these raiders and when the Commander-in-Chief visited 111 Squadron, Broadhurst said to the great man: 'Why not send a decent squadron to Scotland and we will shoot down all these Huns for you?' 'Stuffy' Dowding stared at Broadhurst, looked displeased, and soon left. Broady thought he had 'dropped a clanger' but the next morning 'Treble-One' received orders to move up to Acklington. Soon after, it was perhaps fitting that the CO should have his squadron's first success when, on 29 November 1939, he brought down a Heinkel 111 bomber in foul weather.

At the beginning of 1940, that fateful year, Broady was promoted and posted as Wing Commander Training to 11 Group Headquarters at Uxbridge, and soon after it was announced that Keith Park was coming to Uxbridge as Air Officer Commanding. Park, a New Zealander, was efficient but unpopular. Broady had served under him before and did not relish another stint under the teetotal AOC. He saw a senior officer about a posting who, amused, told him that he was by no means the first to make such a request.

Thus, in the late spring, the Wing Commander was posted to the new fighter airfield of Coltishall, in Norfolk. There were as yet no aircraft based there, for it was his task to get the station ready for the fighter squadrons, the first of which were due to arrive in June. But on 10 May the 'Phoney War' ended when Hitler launched the most successful military campaign since Alexander the Great's invasion of the Persian empire – the *Blitzkrieg* in the west.

Broadhurst wanted to get to the air fighting in France, and when he saw a signal asking for experienced Hurricane squadron commanders in France, he immediately volunteered, despite having to revert to squadron leader rank. His AOC, Leigh-Mallory, expressed his displeasure – losing an experienced station commander, dropping a rank to go to France, which would soon be finished anyway – but Broady stuck to his guns and was posted to command 85 Squadron at Vitry.

He arrived on 18 May, just as German aeroplanes and armour were blasting their way through the Low Countries and France. Fighter pilots from four countries took on the Messerschmitts as best they could, but the French were poorly placed in their old Moranes, and their younger Dewoitine D.520s and Bloch 152s were too few to make any difference. Any sting in the fighter arms of Holland and Belgium had been much reduced by the bombing, and although our Hurricanes were reinforced by more squadrons and part-squadrons from Fighter Command, most of these pilots had never fired a shot in anger. More than one hundred Hurricanes had already been lost in combat.

Apart from their lack of combat experience, RAF fighter pilots were at a very serious disadvantage because of their appalling tactical training which was based on *vics* of three fighters flying in tight formation, wing-tip to wing-tip. Their 'bible' was a remarkable document called *Fighter Command Attacks 1939* which described, with excellent diagrams, six rigid attacks against formations of enemy bombers.

The 'bible' assumed that the air threat to Britain would be hordes of German bombers flying in close formation, not escorted by fighters, since the Messerschmitt 109 could not reach our shores from airfields in Germany. Apparently those who assessed the threat did not take into account either the possibility of more adjacent airfields becoming available to the Luftwaffe, or that Willi Messerschmitt might double the range of his formidable fighter by fitting long-range tanks. Dogfighting was assumed to be a thing of the past.

I remember flying with 616 (South Yorkshire) Squadron on 15 September 1940 – Fighter Command's greatest day. We were at 20,000 feet when Yellow Leader called me on the R/T and said I was too far out and to get in closer. I edged in so that my wing-tip was only a few feet from his cockpit. All my concentration was on keeping formation. There was no opportunity to look either sideways or behind.

Flying in those criminal formations a lot of RAF pilots were killed because they were completely blind to astern and quarter attacks from the roving 109s. Many pilots never knew of their extreme peril, and never knew what killed them until enemy cannon shells smashed into their cockpits, engines and wings, ripping open fuel tanks and exploding oxygen bottles so that they were incinerated when their fighters blew-up like bombs.

'He's a cheery old card' grunted Harry to Jack
As they slogged up to Arras with rifle and pack.
But he did for them both with his plan of attack.

Siegfried Sassoon, The General (1919)'

Both the British and Germans had learned all about open fighter formations in the First War when scout pilots flying about fifty yards apart guarded each other. Later, in Spain, the Germans began flying their new Messerschmitts in a close wing-tip to wing-tip formation but in 1937 adopted a far better style of air fighting.

This perfect fighter formation – for it is still flown today – was based on the *rotte*, that is the element of two fighters. Some two hundred yards separated a pair of fighters, and the chief responsibility of number two, or wingman, was to guard his leader from attack; meanwhile the leader navigated and covered his wingman. The *schwarme*, of four fighters, consisted of two pairs and was exactly the same abreast pattern as that devised by Oswald Boelcke, a great fighter pilot and leader of the First War, except that the spacing between aeroplanes had increased from about fifty yards, the turning radius of Boelcke's Albatross, to three hundred yards, the turning radius of a Messerschmitt 109.

Flying in this fashion, a Messerschmitt squadron of three *schwarmen* arced across some one and a half miles of sky. Each *schwarme* flew at varying heights so that the down-sun *schwarme* could search into the sun and guard the rest from surprise attack. These staggered heights gave cross-cover in all directions, and the fighters in this open, fluid formation were able to hunt and exploit their qualities of speed and surprise. Meanwhile RAF fighter formations, despite appalling losses, pressed on in their rigid patterns.

Long after the Second World War, Johnnie, who learned about tactics the hard way, said to Broadhurst:

'Why had we got ourselves into such a mess in 1940? You commanded the Air Fighting Development Unit and the "bible" says the six Fighter Attacks were based on the results of experiments carried out by your AFDU. Were you responsible for that dreadful document?'

'No, I bloody well was not!' retorted Broadhurst. 'The AFDU only reported on new aeroplanes like the Defiant and the Lysander. We had nothing to do with tactics and that report was written by the staff at Fighter Command. The Me109 did not have the range to escort their bombers from Germany and no-one thought about 109s operating from airfields in France!'

'There were many Messerschmitts and few Hurricanes, so the dive-bombers had a splendid time. The screaming Stukas seemed to have a personal antagonism for everyone on the ground. It seemed to civilian and soldier alike that disaster came with the Stukas; after the noise, the bombing and the strafing, came the tanks, rolling through France. The Stukas meant death, confusion and terror. To the French, the Stuka was not part of the Blitzkrieg, it *was* the Blitzkrieg.'

Johnnie:

Broady found Vitry 'an absolute shambles'. He saw a burning Hurricane crash and saw Fred Rosier, a Flight Commander with 229 Squadron, parachuting safely down. The wrecked Hurricane of another Flight Commander lay in the back garden of the officers' mess and more pranged fighters littered the airfield, which was pock-marked with bomb craters. He soon discovered that the sustained bombing had wrecked communications, isolated headquarters, and left 60 Wing ignorant of the battle situation in the forward zones and of the whereabouts of the nearest German armour. He was told that retreating units of the French army were demoralised, with soldiers abandoning their arms and deserting. To make matters worse, the local people, terrified by the Stukas, wanted peace at any price. They were sometimes quite hostile and often tried to block the grass airfields with carts and tree trunks. Perhaps, thought Broady, he should have stayed at Coltishall after all!

He went to report to Wing Commander Jack Boret, found that he was out of action with a nervous breakdown, and was ordered to assume command of what remained of 60 Wing.

The new CO soon found that our light bomber squadrons had been cut to pieces. Battles and Blenheims operated in daylight against the enemy columns, sometimes attacking from tree-top height to evade the Messerschmitts. During these desperate first days of the German advance it was the *flak* that inflicted the heaviest toll. Enemy rapid-firing automatic weapons were accurate up to 5,000 feet, while lower down the hordes of machine guns added to the hazards faced by the crews. The theory of low-level attack was sound enough. In theory, gunners would have insufficient time to traverse and aim their weapons; but the Fairey Battle was so slow and vulnerable that, of thirty-two sent out on 10 May, eighteen were lost and all the rest damaged. Next day only one returned from eight attacking armour in the Ardennes. On the day following, 12 May, five of 12 Squadron were sent to attack two bridges near Maastricht. None returned.

Light bombers from England fared little better. On one mission on 12 May, seven Blenheims of 139 Squadron, six of 15 Squadron and four from 40 Squadron were lost while attacking the Maastricht bridges, mostly shot down by 109s. Broady heard that his lifelong friend Wing Commander the Earl of Brandon, who was to become a legendary and deeply admired leader in the Royal Air Force, had survived a disastrous mission on 17 May when he led 82 Squadron against German columns near Gembloux. The twelve Blenheims were set on by fifteen Messerschmitts of 1 Staffel, Jagdgeschwader 3, and eleven of the bombers were shot down. 'Paddy' survived and only his great determination prevented the temporary disbandment of the squadron. Within forty-eight hours Paddy had scraped together enough crews and new Blenheims to lead six bombers on another mission.

Bomber losses were hard, but worse was to come. Four days after the Blitzkrieg began, a strong enemy spearhead, supported by clouds of Stukas, crossed the River Meuse at Sedan – the ominous name that had featured in three wars against Germany and now filled all Frenchmen with despair. On this day all Allied bombers were ordered to attack the enemy bridgehead, but some French formations suffered so badly that their remaining missions were cancelled. Then came the turn of the Advanced Air Striking Force. Seventy-one light bombers, operating in small formations, made concentrated attacks against five bridges and enemy columns near Sedan. Hurricanes were sent to patrol the area, but most of these were engaged some way from the target area. When the light bombers approached, they were set upon by hordes of Messerschmitts and many were destroyed. Others fell to flak and yet more were shot out of the sky on their way home. To illustrate the sheer carnage of this day, one German pilot, Hauptmann Hans-Karl Mayer of 1 Staffel, Jagdgeschwader 53, was credited with destroying two Blenheims, two Battles and a Hurricane in the space of sixteen minutes. Of the seventy-one light bombers sent out, only thirty-one returned. Five days of daylight operations had cost about half the RAF's bomber strength in France, causing some squadrons to be taken out of the line.

The Lysanders, used for army co-operation, were finished. A year before, when Broady was at the Air Fighting Development Unit, he had written a 'stinking report' on their shortcomings. This had been refuted by Wing Commander 'Fatty' Grant who commanded the Lysander units. Grant told Broady that his aircraft could survive by turning inside the 109s. Now, after a few days of fighting, they had all been shot out of the skies and Grant was making his way home on foot.

The depleted Hurricane squadrons did their best. Lacking positive information about the ground battle, they patrolled where wing and squadron commanders thought best. Whenever they encountered escorted German bomber formations, they were always outnumbered. Many Hurricanes were shot down. The marauding enemy formations should have been opposed by Hurricanes in wing and squadron strength, but the losses meant that each squadron could only put four or five fighters into the air. Every pilot was flying four or five missions a day and they were becoming very tired. They fell back to Lille where they were joined by another Hurricane Wing, or rather what was left of it, led by Wing Commander Finch.

Broadhurst:

'It was here, on 22 May, that we received orders to destroy everything and withdraw to Northolt. Finch was able to take the airmen to Boulogne and I was to take the Hurricanes back to England. I arranged for ground crews, two for each fighter, to see us off, and they would be collected by transport aeroplanes of 24 Squadron later that day.

'I set about assembling dumps of valuable equipment, from wrecked and unserviceable Hurricanes, that I knew to be in short supply in the UK – radios, guns and tool kits. A distraught and overworked Warrant Officer violently disagreed with this order, thinking that they should try to make some of the Hurricanes airworthy. And for the first and last time during the war, I pulled my gun and ordered him to get on with it.'

Broady was the last to leave Lille:

'When I took off, the Harrows and the escorting Hurricanes were mere specks in the sky, so I chased after them, completely forgetting that the sky was full of German aeroplanes. Very soon four Me110s – fortunately not 109s – jumped me, and I was hit in the wing and the oil tank in the root of the port wing. I was turning steeply with oil squirting all over the place and a bottle bouncing all round the bloody cockpit. But I managed to get away and back to Northolt.

'I have already recorded, in another work, *Winged Victory* [see bibliography], how, soon after his return from France, Broadhurst was summonsed to Bentley Priory where he gave Dowding a blow by blow account of his momentous five days in France, and how Dowding told him that he was to take command of the well-established fighter station at Wittering. His AOC there was Trafford Leigh-Mallory whose background was with Army co-operation rather than fighters, and whose somewhat pompous manner concealed a quick and questioning mind; to his junior commanders 'L-M', as we called him, was a respected father figure.

'In France, Broadhurst had realised that there was something wrong with our wretched 'vics', but during the desperate retreat there was no time to experiment with obsolete formations. At Wittering, however, there was time and he began training his squadrons to fly in a line-astern formation.'

One day Broadhurst was leading the Wittering Wing, under Hornchurch control, at about 18,000 feet near the Thames estuary, when he saw, through the broken clouds, large numbers of Italian bombers. Broadhurst asked the Hornchurch controller for permission to send two squadrons to attack the bombers, but was told: 'The situation is being dealt with.'

On returning to Wittering however, he learned that the Italians had not been attacked and so telephoned the Chief Controller at 11 Group,

Group Captain Lord Willoughby de Broke, and asked him whether or not the Italians had been intercepted. After a pause de Broke said that he was handing Broadhurst over to his AOC, Keith Park. Broady thought quickly because he did not want to get involved with Park and he knew that L-M would be furious if he knew that one of his station commanders was talking direct to Park. However, he briefly told Park about the Italians and when he had not attacked on instructions from the Hornchurch Controller, Park said he would investigate, and that was the last Broadhurst heard of the incident.

He had been at Wittering but a short time when that momentous luncheon took place with Dowding and Leigh-Mallory. Dowding, being pressed by Churchill to send more fighters to a stricken France, asked Broadhurst what he thought about taking a wing to France – and got the answer he needed when the Wing Commander said they would not last a week; Dowding returned to Stanmore to fight his private battle to maintain his force for the coming onslaught.

The Battle of Britain, as it unfolded through July, August and September 1940, has been told from many different angles, including two accounts by this author, and it is perhaps sufficient to say here that it was won by a very narrow margin, and our salvation was Göring's change of strategy on 7 September 1940, when he switched his bombers from our battered sector stations to London.

Towards the end of the Battle of Britain, with shortening days and autumn weather, the Luftwaffe paid more attention to night bombing. Harry Broadhurst now had his hands full trying, with his small force of night fighters, to oppose German raiders heading for our industrial cities in the Midlands. Our American friends too were keenly interested in our attempts, including airborne radar, to stem the invaders. Broadhurst found himself host to Colonels 'Tooey' Spaatz and Frank Hunter, both of the US Army Air Corps. The Station Commander showed them his operations room and how his Beaufighters, Blenheims and Hurricanes were controlled and later the visitors were entertained in the officers' mess, where they met a lot of our fighter pilots. These associations were soon to bear fruit.

As this fateful year closed, Dowding, the victor of the great battle, was replaced by the ambitious Sholto Douglas, and Park, the gifted tactician, after a mere eight months, by the likeable Leigh-Mallory. Whenever the top brass moved, their protégés soon followed, and Group Captain Harry Broadhurst went to Hornchurch in south Essex. This important sector station was the home of 41, 64 and 611 (Spitfire) Squadrons and had a well-established operations room from which the station commander could, if he so desired, direct the Hornchurch Wing.

In the spring of 1941, Fighter Command was expanding, since it was thought that the Battle of Britain would be resumed; but Hitler had his sights on the East and, there being no day fighting over our island home, we began 'reaching out' to France in squadron or wing strength. At first the enemy ignored our high-level sweeps so Sholto Douglas introduced Circus operations when we escorted a few Blenheims to attack targets in France. The Luftwaffe responded and some stern air battles took place.

It was clear that fighting in wing strength was here to stay and wing commanders (flying), soon to be known as wing leaders, were appointed to lead the various wings; Douglas Bader went to Tangmere, the fearless 'Sailor' Malan to Biggin Hill, and Andrew Farquhar, an auxiliary officer, to Hornchurch. Broadhurst, as we have seen, had a low opinion of auxiliaries, and Farquhar had already made himself the laughing stock of Fighter Command when he shot down a German bomber which crash-landed in Berwickshire, and for some reason Farquhar landed on the soft ground beside the bomber, turned his Spitfire upside-down and had to be freed by the Germans! After a few weeks at Hornchurch he was replaced by Joe Kayll, a highly experienced and well-decorated leader.

Johnnie:

The 'season', as we called it, was in full swing and on most fine days there were Circus operations over France. We were mainly opposed by Jagdgeschwader 51, led by Werner Mölders, a fighter leader of great distinction who will be remembered for his tactical thinking and for his development of the *schwarme* formation in the Spanish Civil War. In mid-summer, however, JG51 left for Germany and eventually went to the Eastern Front. Mölders stayed in Germany to become the first General of Fighter Forces but was killed in a flying accident. JG51 was replaced by JG26 led by the redoubtable Adolf ('Dolfo') Galland, an outstanding fighter leader, a master tactician and a deadly shot.

Joe Kayll was supposed to lead the Hornchurch Wing and Harry Broadhurst administer a fairly complex fighter station, and to keep his hand in by flying occasionally as Kayll's wingman or leading a section of four Spitfires. The Station Commander, however, had other ideas and the records show that during the 1941 season he led the Hornchurch Wing on more missions than his various wing leaders. Sometimes there were harsh words between Kayll and Broadhurst about who would lead the wing, and indeed on 25 June 1941 Broadhurst led Circus 22 with Kayll as his wingman. Over Gravelines they were badly bounced by a gaggle of 109s and Joe Kayll baled out of his blazing Spitfire to become a prisoner. Soon after, on 4 July, the Group Captain, having destroyed two 109s, was badly shot-up and crash-landed back at Hornchurch.

In August the *London Gazette* announced that Acting Group Captain Broadhurst DFC AFC had been 'almost continuously employed on active operations since the war began' and was appointed a Companion of the Distinguished Service Order.

Johnnie:

The Air Officer Commanding, 11 Group, Trafford Leigh-Mallory, was a frequent visitor to his sector stations – Biggin Hill, Hornchurch, Kenley, North Weald, Northolt and Tangmere. Since, like most group commanders of his day, he did not fly operationally and had never flown a Spitfire, he usually arrived in an ancient two-seater Proctor. He kept abreast of fighter tactics by talking to his pilots; thumbs in his chest pockets and leaning slightly backwards, he was a good listener, always keen to hear our views about the air fighting in France.

During one of these visits to Hornchurch, towards the end of the season, he had a quiet word with his station commander, suggesting that he should fly less often and leave the job of leading the wing to his wing leader, Eric Stapleton. Broady muttered something about 'keeping his hand in' and a few days later claimed an Me109E damaged over the Channel.

L-M had other means of curbing Broady's enthusiasm for the game and he was selected, together with other notable airmen, to visit the United States on a goodwill tour and talk to their senior airmen about the French Campaign, the Battle of Britain and our 1941 offensive. The party consisted of Broady, Bob Tuck, 'Sailor' Malan and three bomber men – John Boothman of Schneider Trophy fame, Hughie Edwards VC, and Charlie Whitworth.

The 'prima-donnas', as they were called, arrived in Washington to be met by a battery of photographers and reporters, and soon after were taken to the Pentagon to meet General 'Hap' Arnold, head of the US Army Air Force. The impressive, silver-haired general said: 'Glad to welcome you gentlemen. You can help us and I hope we can help you. You're going on manoeuvres now. You'll see everything we've got, and the things we haven't got. The time for us to talk will be when you get back.

'While I was waiting to see "Hap" Arnold', related Broady, 'one of my colonel friends, now a general, emerged from his office. This was "Tooey" Spaatz, who took me to see and fly all the latest American fighters and then to see some big manoeuvres in South Carolina, where I met General Ira Eaker and renewed my acquaintance with Frank Hunter, also a general.'

Broady, impressed by these keen, highly professional generals, told them all he knew, and some of the 'bull' sessions lasted well into the night. In later years these contacts proved invaluable, as they all came to England, Spaatz commanding the Eighth Air Force, Eaker the Eighth Bomber Command, and Hunter the Eighth Fighter Command.

On his return from the US, Broadhurst reported to the Air Ministry and then returned to Hornchurch to find the Messerschmitt-hunting season over. The last big show of 1941 had been flown on 8 November when, in a savage action against Fw190s and Me109s, no less than seventeen escort fighters had been lost, including three squadron commanders and a wing leader for claims of five enemy aircraft destroyed plus damage to several others.

As the new year approached, Broady and Victor Beamish of Kenley were the only two station commanders flying regular operations, the fighting Irishman now with eight confirmed victories and Broady with a round dozen. Broady's worth was recognised by the *London Gazette* dated 19 December 1941, which announced the award of Bar to his DSO: 'This officer has organized and led his Wing with conspicuous gallantry and success... Since being awarded the Distinguished Service Order in June he has destroyed eight and probably, destroyed a further four enemy aircraft.'

Operation *Fuller*, issued in 1941, warned that the German battle cruisers *Gneisenau* and *Scharnhorst* and their heavy cruiser *Prinz Eugen* would, sooner or later, leave their well-defended harbour at Brest and attempt the narrow and dangerous passage through the Dover Strait to break out into the northern seas. They would have to sail the whole length of the English Channel which, since 1690 (when Tourville defeated the Anglo-Dutch fleet off the Isle of Wight) had never seen strong enemy naval forces.

Admiral Ciliax sailed four nights before the full moon which gave him a flood tide up the Channel. The German squadron rounded Ushant in the early hours of 12 February 1942, set course for the Channel, and at 1000 hrs, still undetected, the intrepid Ciliax and his sailors were off the mouth of the Somme. The first alarm was given by Group Captain Victor Beamish and

Wing Commander Finlay Boyd, from Kenley, who were flying a Channel reconnaissance patrol. Seeing some vessels below through thin cloud, they dived to investigate and instantly found themselves in a maelstrom of flak and fighters, with three huge capital vessels at the centre! Disengaging from the German fighter cover, they streaked northwards at sea level. They had been ordered to maintain radio silence and it was not until after they had landed that Beamish reported the enemy flotilla was entering the Dover Strait.

The Hornchurch Wing, for once without Broadhurst, took off shortly after noon to rendezvous with the Biggin Hill Wing over Manston, and there to escort Lieutenant Commander Eugene Esmonde's 825 Squadron's obsolete Swordfish against the German ships. The station commander, anxious to get in the act, followed minutes after but never saw his wing and headed, alone, towards Boulogne just below the 3,000-foot cloud base. There was nothing to be seen over the French coast so he headed to mid-Channel and, through broken cloud, caught glimpses of several E-boats heading towards Dunkirk.

Later, at 6,000 feet, the lone Spitfire pilot sighted a gaggle of Me109s, attacked 'arse-end Charlie' and shot it down into the Channel. Higher 109s came down on Broadhurst but he escaped into cloud and returned to Hornchurch to claim his victory.

During the remainder of this disgraceful day, some 242 bombers were dispatched in waves against the German squadron but only thirty-nine succeeded in bombing. No damage was done. A few torpedo boats and some ancient destroyers also failed to harm the ships which had breached the Channel.

All six Swordfish were shot down. Of the eighteen officers and men taking part, thirteen were killed and four seriously wounded. Esmonde, the Swordfish pilot, was awarded a posthumous Victoria Cross; the four surviving officers were given DSOs and the surviving gunner a Conspicuous Gallantry Medal.

A subsequent board of inquiry whitewashed the whole sordid affair, finding that no-one was to blame. In his memoir, *The First and the Last*, Galland, General of Fighters, recorded the truth when he wrote that the break-out was 'a great and impressive victory' and that the RAF had been sent into action 'with insufficient planning, without a clear concept…and without systematic tactics'.

The formidable 190s had now been giving Fighter Command a tough time for six months and it was high time the Spitfire Vs were either replaced with something better or given uprated engines to at least match the performance of the German fighter. Rolls-Royce had been developing a new version of their superb Merlin, the 61, which had a two-stage supercharger. Two Spitfire Mark Is had been modified to accept the new engine as 'test-beds' for what would eventually become the superlative Mk IX. In the early spring of 1942, Jeffrey Quill, Supermarine's Chief Test Pilot, decided (unofficially) to take Spitfire R6700 to Hornchurch to allow Broady to try it out. Clive Gosling, test-flying with Jeffrey Quill wrote:

'After seeing off the Hornchurch Wing, Jeffrey put Broady into R6700 and off he went, Jeffrey being taken to the Ops Room to see the wing in action. They went as far as Lille and, as they were coming out of Boulogne, he noticed a single plot following the wing. Jeffrey asked what it was and was told it was Broady at 35,000 feet in an aircraft without loaded guns and not stressed for aerobatics! Jeffrey thought about what he was going to say if a secret Spitfire belonging to the Central Research and Development Unit was lost over France or the Channel. Fortune smiled and Broady returned safely.'

Johnnie:

'In the spring of 1942 we began 'reaching out' again and Victor Beamish, the well-decorated, much admired Station Commander at Kenley, was lost. This prompted Leigh-Mallory to ground Harry Broadhurst who was posted to LM's own Headquarters as Group Captain Operations, where he was responsible for the daily operations of all fighter wings in 11 Group. On his departure from Hornchurch, in his memoir *Spitfire into Battle*, Duncan Smith wrote: "Harry Broadhurst did not understand the meaning of fear and the stickier the situation the better he liked it. We missed his leadership, his sparkling sense of fun and his companionship; above all, he was always one of us!"'

Acting Group Captain Harry Broadhurst, DSO and Bar, DFC, AFC, was now involved in the planning, in 1942, of the combined operations against Dieppe. Called Operation *Jubilee*, it was devised by Vice-Admiral Louis Mountbatten when he was Chief of Operations and a member of the Chiefs of Staff Committee. He was given two main functions – organization of raiding operations on the Continent with limited objectives, and development and technique for such amphibious operations. Mountbatten's imaginative and audacious personality was soon apparent in the successful, but costly, attack on the German-controlled port of St Nazaire on 28 March 1942.

On that occasion an old destroyer, HMS *Campbeltown*, packed with explosives, rammed and blew up the gates of the dry dock, one of the largest such installations in the world. This 'brilliant and heroic exploit', to use Churchill's tribute, made Mountbatten's planners cast around for another target. What better than the small coastal town of Dieppe, within easy reach of an assault from southern England? The beaches were suitable and well within the limited range of our fighters.

According to the Canadian Official History of the Dieppe raid, the troops were embarked on 2 and 3 July, briefed and sealed on board. However, the operation was cancelled because of the weather. The troops were disembarked, but not before German bombers had attacked the ships lying in the Solent. The Canadian historian says:

'As the troops had been fully informed of the objective of the proposed raid, and once they left the ships, it would no longer be possible to maintain complete secrecy, General Montgomery recommended that the operation should now "be off for all time".'

Now, six weeks later, Montgomery had left for the desert and Operation *Jubilee* was on again. Some 6,100 troops, of whom 4,963 were Canadian and about 1,075 were British, would attempt the assault. There were also fifty US Rangers, a few French Commandos and anti-Nazi nationalists. The Naval Force Commander had the difficult job of controlling a fleet of 237 ships and landing craft. Leigh-Mallory would control the air effort by seventy-four squadrons from his headquarters at Uxbridge and he had a representative abroad the headquarters ship, HMS *Calpe.*

It was arranged that the Group Captain Operations would fly over Dieppe and report directly to Leigh-Mallory, either by radio telephone from the battle area or by telephone after he had landed. The first units had been airborne for ninety minutes before Broadhurst took off and headed south. At this time the only German aircraft airborne were fighters, mainly Fw190s. The available German bombers, Do217s of Kampfgeschwader 2, required more preparation and would not be seen for another three hours. Almost as soon as he arrived he found the enemy. Broadhurst's combat report reads:

'I took off from Northolt at about 0600 hours on a reconnaissance patrol over Dieppe. While at 25,000 feet I noticed that the Huns were working their aircraft in pairs, some being Fw190 fighter bombers. The enemy aircraft were flying out about five miles north east of Le Tréport and getting well up into the sun and then diving straight down through our patrols, and towards the ships lying off Dieppe. Some would attack these ships and some would attack our Spitfires on patrol. I circled for about ten minutes, and gradually lost height down to 20,000 feet. Enemy aircraft were operating from 15,000 feet and about to commence their dive, and I dived on the rear one giving him a long burst of cannon and machine gun. This enemy aircraft gave off large clouds of black smoke, spun and hit the sea. After a short burst at his leader I broke off and climbed back into the sun.'

Johnnie:

His patrol convinced him that our standard wing tactics were far too cumbersome against the German fighters, operating in hard-hitting pairs and fours. He noticed that when our wings, each of three squadrons, reached the French coast they were immediately bounced by the higher, faster Focke-Wulfs. They were then spilt up and never re-formed. Broady reckoned that it would be far better to fly in the more flexible pairs and fours and, after landing at 0750 hours, he telephoned Leigh-Mallory and put his case. The AOC, very much the 'big wing' man, could not be persuaded to alter his tactics. His group captain persisted, but realised that he had lost his case when Leigh-Mallory suddenly became pompous, the familiar 'Broady' being replaced by 'Broadhurst'.

After refuelling and rearming, Broady took off again at 0915 hours and was again in the thick of things. On this sortie he engaged three separate Fw190s and was credited with damaging all three. When this bloody day was over, Broady had flown a further two combat sorties. L-M may have had second thoughts about his earlier attitude, for he recommended him for a Bar to his DFC; whether or not he was wise to fly alone for eight hours is another matter.

L-M hailed Dieppe as a great victory. His fighter squadrons had claimed no less than 271 enemy aeroplanes destroyed or damaged. As usual we had over-claimed, for the actual loss suffered by the Germans was seventy-two, while we lost 106, of which eighty-four were fighters.

The Dieppe raid was, and still is, a highly controversial affair. Tactically it must be regarded as a complete failure, for none of its stated objectives were achieved in full measure. It is a record of poor security, of faulty intelligence, of inadequate communications between air and ground, of a confused and bloody ground situation over which central coordination could not be exercised. It is a story of great gallantry and loss of life. The record of the (Canadian) Essex Scottish, who brought back fifty-two personnel, of whom twenty-eight were wounded, of a force of 553, gives some indication of the desperate situation on the ground. Perhaps Chester Wilmot made the best assessment on the operation when he wrote, '[the] Dieppe raid yielded bloody warning of the strength of the Atlantic Wall.'

After Dieppe, Harry Broadhurst flew to Old Sarum to talk to senior officers from all three services about the lessons of the air fighting. Afterwards there was a lively discussion on the ways and means of getting back into France. During lunch Broady sat between Montgomery and Air Chief Marshal 'Ugly' Barrett. Both these senior officers had been involved in the ill-fated French Campaign, Monty as commander of the Third Division and Barrett as commander of the British Air Forces in France. They discussed the bloody fiasco at Dieppe, the very heavy casualties of the Canadian Second Division, the devastating and unsubdued enemy crossfire on the beaches, the need for massive fire support, and the closer integration of air and land forces. Harry Broadhurst was deeply impressed with Monty's thinking and professional knowledge, and it is more than likely that Montgomery was impressed by this fighting airman, because soon after he took over the Eighth Army in the Western Desert, Broady was posted as Senior Air Staff Officer to the Desert Air Force, where the vain, highly-strung and temperamental New Zealander 'Mary' Coningham reigned as AOC. Harry Broadhurst was promoted to Air Commodore – always a big step in an airman's career – and was on his way.

Chapter 4

'Cab Rank' Broadhurst

Since 1940, when Italy declared herself against Britain, there had been continual war in that area of the world known as the Middle East – which is approximately one-third larger than the USA. Its boundaries had varied a great deal, stretching at different times from the western wadis of the Libyan desert to the left flank of the Red Army in Persia, and from the high snow mountains of the Balkans to the Central African jungles.

Small British forces had been driven from Crete and the northern area of Greece. A few dozen fighter pilots and the Royal Navy's convoys had held Malta in the face of great odds.

The Italians were no great problem in the Middle East, but following a serious reverse Mussolini appealed for assistance to his German master, Hitler, and in March 1941 the small (four divisions) but audacious Afrika Korps, and its brilliant general, Erwin Rommel, arrived on the scene with supporting elements of the Luftwaffe. Although their campaign in Libya was regarded by the German High Command as small beer – a sideshow – Rommel and his tough, truculent men were soon a painful thorn in the side of the Eighth Army with its unhappy recent record of failed generals and a surfeit of 'amateur' officers.

Rommel was one of that very rare breed – a 'soldiers' general'. Unlike his British counterparts – who still thought about the 'set piece battle' and trench warfare of a previous conflict – he understood and exploited the cut and thrust of armoured warfare. This confident, professional figure amidst the dust and confusion of the desert battle inspired his men – 'À la guerre les trois quarts sort des affaires morale,' said Napoleon.

Claude Auchinleck, the Commander-in-Chief Middle East Forces, found it necessary to write to his commanders: 'There exists a real danger that our friend Rommel is becoming a kind of magician or bogey-man to our troops who are talking far too much about him ... I wish you to dispel by all possible means the idea that Rommel represents something more than an ordinary German general. The important thing now is to see to it that we do not always talk of Rommel when we mean the enemy in Libya. We must refer to "the Germans" or "the Axis Powers" or "the enemy" and not always keep harping on Rommel.'

The principles of air support were thrashed out during the First War, and only their application had changed with the improvements in aeroplanes, weapons and communications. Fortunately, RAF leaders had stopped a determined attempt to make the service adopt the dive-bomber as a primary weapon for air support, for the Army and Navy had been so impressed by the Stuka that they had fallen into the trap of believing that such an aeroplane was itself a battle winner. In reality, it was capable of exploiting a battle that had already been won – the air battle. The legend of the Stuka was slow in dying, for the Germans used this dive-bomber in one way or another until almost the end of the Second War, but it was never successful in the face of strong fighter opposition.

Harry 'Broady' Broadhurst knew that the fighter-bomber was the only type of aeroplane suitable for bombing and strafing whenever enemy fighters were about. He knew that the battlefield must be isolated to stop the enemy from moving into, and within, the combat area. He knew that the fighting men on the ground wanted close air support at the right time and the right place, and that the whole thing depended on confidence between airman and soldier.

Unfortunately, so far in the Second War that confidence did not exist.

Johnnie:

After Dunkirk the Army was very suspicious, and rightly so, about both the RAF's intention and ability to provide tactical reconnaissance and air support, and although we had formed the so-called Army Co-operation Command it had few teeth, for the Air Staff awarded the highest priorities to our offensive capability, Bomber Command, and to the defence of our industrial base by Fighter Command. In 1942, I was the CO of 610 (County of Chester) Squadron, one of the hundred or so fighter squadrons in the UK, when all of our operational flying time was spent on fighter sweeps, bomber escorts and convoy patrols. Occasionally, perhaps once or twice each year, we fired our cannon and machine guns at static targets before an Army audience, and on one occasion their low opinion of our air-ground capability was not improved when some of their top brass were killed by a Polish Spitfire squadron. Nor was inter-service confidence helped by the

Dieppe fiasco, when throughout that long day fighter leaders, including me, were unable to contact the Headquarters Ship for information about the bloody ground situation.

Since the RAF was equally suspicious about the Army's will to come to grips with the crack Afrika Korps and to get on with the ground fighting, inter-service relations in the Middle East were at a low ebb, especially when the Army called for the control of all air forces in the field, including the specific allotment of aeroplanes down to divisional level. This was heresy to the air marshals who firmly believed that centralised control was the only method of achieving concentration and flexibility and dreaded the breakdown of the RAF into 'penny packets'. The situation worsened when the GOC Western Desert Force called for an 'air umbrella' for the defence of the ground forces during their approach to the battle area! Eventually the Prime Minister thought it opportune to state that the Royal Air Force was an independent Service and would remain so.

There was room for much improvement in Army/Air Force affairs as Air Chief Marshal Sir Kenneth Cross recalls: 'When in 1941 I started in the desert we had nothing. There was no understanding with the Army. No organization. No centralised control and no command structure. Nothing. We had so-called Army co-operation squadrons but you know what happened to them in France. No-one had any idea of Army-Air Force integration and because we did not have any command organization the Army told the Air Force what to do.'

Air Commodore Jimmy Fenton, another distinguished airman, said: 'In the early days there was a complete lack of co-operation with the Army, and when we were retreating I would sometimes get a hundred Army officers calling at my Wing headquarters asking if we knew what was going on, where were their headquarters, and so on. The British Army could fight alright but it was not centrally controlled as was the Afrika Korps under Rommel. It changed pretty radically after Alamein and that was one of Montgomery's major achievements.

When the New Zealander 'Mary' Coningham took over the Desert Air Force, in 1941, it was a semi-organized shambles which he sorted out and got a bit of morale and decent administration into it. The New Zealander was one of the first practical British airmen to comprehend the ebb and flow of the land battle and to understand the soldiers' constant requirements for reconnaissance and air support.

'The Army's scapegoat', said 'Bing' Cross, 'for all their failures was "lack of air support".' Senior Army officers had repeatedly said: 'If you can keep the enemy off our backs that's all we ask, we can cope with the rest!' So Coningham's job was to achieve air superiority so that the Army, hopefully, could get on with the ground battle – and in this he succeeded.

'Coningham,' continued Bing, 'like many of his contemporaries, was not a practical airman and had to rely on others for tactical advice. But he was a political airman and it was at his urging that the Desert Air Force and the Eighth Army formed a joint headquarters, and the GOC, Neil Ritchie, and Coningham, lived alongside each other, and for the first time we had an Army/Air Force organization to jointly process requests for air support. It was a big improvement.'

This long overdue and admirable system worked well for some time until, during a hasty retreat, Coningham was told that his forward airfields were in danger of being overrun by Rommel's columns, and he moved his squadrons and, for some reason, his own headquarters, inside the Egyptian border. Thus the precious link between the two commanders, and their staffs, was broken and was not re-established until the GOC, Ritchie, was sacked.

'We have,' said Winston Churchill in the House of Commons in 1942, 'a very daring and skilful opponent against us, and, may I say across the havoc of war, a great general, who struck with such speed and vigour that on 21 June 1942, our garrison at Tobruk surrendered, and three days later Rommel's Panzers entered Egypt.' As secret documents and staff papers were burned in Cairo, Auchinleck sacked his GOC Eighth Army and himself took over. He decided to make his stand on a narrow defence position between El Alamein and the impassable Qattara Depression.

The stoic nine-day defence of Bir Hakeim by General Koenig's First Free French Brigade drew the whole of the German dive bomber force, plus long-range bombers flying from Crete. Coningham's Desert Air Force flew some 1,500 sorties in support of the Fortress, some of which could be seen by the defenders who signalled Coningham: 'Bravo! Merci pour le RAF,' and the AOC courteously replied, 'Bravo à vous! Merci pour le sport!'

Retreating along the narrow coastal road the vehicles of the Eighth Army were helplessly bunched nose to tail for several days during the 400 mile withdrawal – and had the enemy fighter bombers been active, the retreat would undoubtedly have been turned into a rout. In the event, only six British soldiers were killed by enemy strafing. There were two reasons for this lucky escape. First, the Luftwaffe did not have the vehicles and the mobility (including the prepared landing grounds all the way back to Egypt) of the Desert Air Force, who only withdrew from their airfields when they could actually see our bombing some twenty miles distant against Rommel's squadrons, supply lines and airfields. Second, Arthur Tedder, Air Officer Commanding-in-Chief, Middle East Air Force, saw his chance and threw the considerable weight of all his squadrons against Rommel's squadrons, supply lines and airfields.

Tedder reinforced his subordinate, Coningham, with Spitfires from Malta, and Hurricanes from training units in the delta, and at this desperate hour the lack of a joint headquarters was of little consequence since the simple requirement was to stop Rommel. In one crucial week the DAF flew more than 5,500 sorties, and at the same time Tedder attacked with anything that could fly and drop a bomb – obsolete Bisleys, naval Albacores, Beaufighters, Baltimores, Bostons, Hudsons, Mitchells, Halifaxes, and Liberators and Fortresses from the newly arrived USAAF squadrons. Towards the end of this Battle of Alamein, Tedder could muster no less than ninety-six Allied squadrons and formations, and shuttle bombing, by night and day, was commonplace with big formations of up to 150 fighters and bombers.

The war diary of the Afrika Korps shows what they thought of our air attacks: 'Two bombing attacks on the 21st Panzers Division while the GOC is there … enemy Air Force very active today but there is no sign of the Luftwaffe … 15th Panzer Division reports that it is unable to continue its attacks owing to lack of fuel … bombing attacks are made every hour causing considerable losses. There is nothing to be seen of the Luftwaffe.'

In mid-August 1942, Montgomery took over the Eighth Army at, for him, an opportune time since Rommel had been stopped and more tanks, aeroplanes and Americans were arriving in the Middle East. 'Monty' was an able professional commander who knew the value of tactical air power and realised that the weapon the Germans had invented, *Blitzkreig*, could now be turned against them; on the debit side he was vain and boastful.

When, on 17 August 1942, ULTRA warned that Rommel would soon attack again, Tedder and Coningham, with swelling numbers of aeroplanes, began their offensive while the Eighth Army remained in its defensive position at El Alamein. Thousands of sorties were flown against the Germans and the Italians, and the war diary of the Afrika Korps reported that apart from colossal material damage, the morale of both officers and men was severely shaken by the incessant bombing. On 3 September our reconnaissance pilots saw the Axis forces in full retreat, and thus began the long trek which took the Eighth Army out of the Middle East and into Tunisia. The second battle of El Alamein was not the victory of the Eighth Army alone. Nor was it the victory of the Eighth Army and Coningham's Western Desert Air Force. It was the victory of the Eighth Army and all our air forces in the Middle East including the American squadrons. Rommel himself recorded what he thought: 'British air superiority threw to the winds all our tactical rules ... the strength of the Anglo-American Air Force was ... the deciding factor!'

The British people, hungry for success after years of humiliation and defeat, made much of the desert victory. At home the church bells were rung and Montgomery, hitherto largely unknown to the public, became overnight a national hero. According to Monty's Staff Officer Freddie de Guingand, 'He received a tremendous ovation wherever he went; in the theatre, stepping in or out of the War Office, crowds would shout, "Good old Monty!" or "God bless you, Monty!" Walking across the Horse Guards Parade to his club he would be followed by hundreds of his fellow countrymen, all pressing forward to shake his hand or at least get a glimpse of him. What this must have meant to a somewhat lonely man is easy to understand. Not to have enjoyed it would not have been human. He did, and sometimes asked for more. It was also a good thing for the Army, which had sunk so low in the public's esteem. It needed this favourable reaction – and it needed a successful General. The main changes which I noted were: firstly, Montgomery had, perhaps, lost a little of his simplicity, and, secondly, he now realised that he was a real power in the land and that there were few who would not heed his advice. In fact, he realised that in most cases he could be really tough to get his own way!'

Unfortunately the victorious General, unlike his Chief of Staff the admirable and talented Freddie de Guingard, scarcely mentioned the RAF's tremendous contribution at Alamein, without which Rommel would undoubtedly have entered Egypt. He only stressed what he and his Eighth Army had achieved. Thus the seeds of the rift between Montgomery and his senior airmen, Tedder and Coningham, were sown in the Desert, and became a bad harvest in Normandy.

Broadhurst paid a courtesy call on Tedder, who startled the Air Commodore by exclaiming: 'There's nothing for you out here! We don't want you!' Broadhurst beat a hasty retreat and wisely stayed in Cairo until after Alamein when, despite Tedder's threat, he took over from George Beamish, SASO to Coningham. A senior air staff officer is strictly a number two man who cannot make any headway as a commander simply because he is not in the chain of command which, usually, is jealously guarded by the commander.

Johnnie:

I once slipped into Monty's private Dakota and found some handwritten notes to his Chief of Staff, they were headed "Notes for the Chief of Staff" and number one was to the effect that only under the most exceptional circumstances was the Chief of Staff to visit operational units. The chain of command, wrote Monty, was from himself to his corps commanders, and then to the divisional commander and to the battalions and companies. A very simple, almost sacred, link of authority, and staff officers were not allowed to interfere with it. Staff officers were to "remain in the background and get on with their administrative duties".

Harry Broadhurst, essentially a leader himself, had to bide his time and keep his strong views to himself unless, of course, Coningham asked for them. He soon found that his AOC, like Monty, was a vain man, but the New Zealander could be agreeable and charming – and utterly ruthless. Indeed, the gallant highly-decorated, strong-willed Basil Embry, brought out at Tedder's express request as Coningham's SASO, lasted exactly six weeks. Fortunately for Broady, in February 1943 Coningham was promoted to air marshal to command the newly established Northwest African Air Force, and Broadhurst took over the Western Desert Air Force with the acting rank of air vice-marshal.

At 37, Harry Broadhurst was the youngest air vice-marshal in the RAF and unlike our previous high ranking commanders in the Fighter Arm (Leigh-Mallory, Park, Sholto Douglas and Coningham) he had flown operational tours and continued to fly operationally through the war. Later, we held that a man could not properly command a group (the equivalent of a division) unless he had completed an operational tour: Don Bennett of the Pathfinder Force and Basil Embry of 2 Group were prime examples of this policy and because they and their pilots spoke the same language they did not have to rely on second-hand opinions.

'When Broady took over the Desert Air Force,' Bing Cross recalled, 'it was more or less plain sailing, for our American friends had invaded the other end of North Africa and the Luftwaffe, always good on priorities, left a few 109s facing the Eighth Army while the remainder, reinforced by Fw190s, turned to their main tasks of protecting their essential bases at Tunis and Bizerta.'

Broady, always a practical airman, looked around for something to do with the Desert Air Force. The task of 'keeping the enemy off our back' was being well looked after by the 12th Air Support Command, the 15th Air Force and 242 Group, so he decided to give his chaps a much better close support capability – and who better to do it than him?

'I have talked with Broady about this', I said, 'and he wanted to give the soldiers more close and better support, for at this time, we could not bomb or strafe within 500 yards of our own troops, largely because of identification problems, and also it took about one hour between the origin of a request for air support and the time the fighter-bomber took to get to the target including about twenty minutes flying time. Also, he was far from happy about the big disparity between our claims of enemy transports, guns and tanks destroyed and the actual numbers counted when we arrived on the battlefield.'

One of the first things Broady did was to lay on a demonstration with about twenty fighter-bombers strafing an old truck and was not amused when no-one hit it. The boys were all convinced that they would all get killed by the accurate German flak, but by using his considerable experience in ordering difficult operations he convinced the squadrons that ground attack was not necessarily synonymous with sudden death. Broady gave the Desert Air Force far more flexibility by turning his fighters into fighter-bombers so that they could both fight in the air and provide the soldiers with close support. He had the situation, the equipment and the time to do it, and I used to call him "Cab-Rank Broadhurst". He did it well, becoming Monty's friend, and the soldiers' friend. But Mary Coningham did a great job with the Desert Air Force before Broady arrived.

He was called 'Cab-Rank Broadhurst' because to cut down the time from army request to target, his pilots, already in the air, were briefed by RAF controllers in armoured cars, situated with the forward troops and in radio contact with the fighter-bombers. Pilots and ground controller gave targets to the waiting 'cab-ranks' of fighter bombers.

This 'Rover David' system, linking the fighter-bombers with the armoured cars, later proved very successful especially in Italy. 'Rover' patrols were decided upon the day before, at a joint conference, and enemy targets, stationary or moving, were attacked within a few minutes of a request from those forward troops in contact with the enemy; with better marking techniques and better weapons, our fighter bombers were soon operating very close to our forward troops and on one occasion, in Italy, they attacked enemy troops dug in on the other side of a street from our own forward positions.

Thus Broadhurst began to develop new techniques of applying tactical air power to the battlefield. The new AOC showed his talents when, on 20 March 1943, Montgomery resumed his advance against the Mareth Line. The opening stages of the frontal attack did not go well because well-sited anti-tank guns knocked out a lot of British armour and a few days later Montgomery had little option but to withdraw his troops and attempt a flanking left hook across some very hilly and rough terrain.

The crucial obstacle before our troops was a high concentration of German armour deployed on a front of about four miles between two hills, and Broadhurst, remembering the Blitzkrieg devastation in France, concentrated all his aeroplanes against the target to stun and paralyse the enemy – as the BEF had been stunned and paralysed some three years before.

After two nights of heavy bombing, three formations of bombers, escorted by fighters, made low-level flights to the combat area and achieved complete surprise; immediately afterwards, Kittyhawk fighter-bombers were fed into the area at intervals of fifteen minutes, bombing and strafing at low heights, and Hurricane 'tank-busters' attacked and broke up enemy tank concentrations. Spitfires patrolled overhead to ward off 109s while other fighter-bombers attacked all known German airfields and landing grounds within one hundred miles. Thirty minutes after the first bomb fell our infantry advanced behind a heavy barrage slowly creeping forward at about one hundred feet per minute, and thus Broadhurst's pilots could see the bomb line and shot up every moving thing ahead of it.

The result of this concentrated activity by the Western Desert Air Force was that during the night Eighth Army armour passed through the bottleneck as the Mareth Line was turned. 'The outstanding feature of the battle,' recorded Montgomery, 'was the air action in co-operation with the outflanking forces.'

While Montgomery hammered away at the Mareth Line, the Allies launched Operation Torch, aimed at neutralising the Vichy regime in Morocco and Algeria, seizing Tunisia and trapping Rommel's army between the Torch forces and Monty's Eighth Army. Prominent amongst the Torch forces was the US West Task Force commanded by the bullshitting, controversial, Lieutenant-General George S. Patton, and after Rommel had mauled Patton's green troops, killing and wounding a few GIs and capturing some old tanks, Patton sent a signal copied 'to the world' (Broadhurst's description) that read: 'Forward troops have been continuously bombed all morning. Total lack of air cover for our units has allowed German Air Force to operate almost at will.'

In the 1960s, Wing Commander Johnnie Johnson and Spitfire EN398 were immortalised by Airfix's 1/72nd scale model. This is the original box art by artist Roy Cross – which so inspired the young Dilip Sarkar. (*Courtesy Arthur Ward*)

Greycap Leader: Kenley, 1943.

Wing Commander Johnson – a born leader able to relate and inspire all under his command, regardless of their status. Johnnie always paid tribute to the essential work carried out by his units' ground staff – another Kenley Wing snapshot.

Air Vice-Marshal Harry Broadhurst, AOC 83 Group, 2nd TAF, Johnnie's boss, and a guest enjoy a post invasion party in Brussels.

Air Marshal Coningham, Commander of the 2nd TAF, addresses a gathering of Allied troops in England before D-Day, 24 May 1944.

Wing Commander Johnnie Johnson in Normandy with his friend, the New Zealand fighter ace, Wing Commander 'Hawkeye' Wells, whom he held in high regard.

Above left: Johnnie's lifelong friend, the America, Squadron Leader Danforth 'Danny' Browne DFC.

Above right: Wing Commander Johnnie Johnson DSO** DFC*, leader of 144 Wing, 1944.

St Croix-sur-Mer, just inland of the invasion beaches and where Johnnie's Spitfires were the first to land in France after D-Day.

Johnnie in his Operations Caravan, Normandy 1944.

Wing Commander Johnnie Johnson in Normandy with 'Sally', 1944.

Air Vice-Marshal Johnnie Johnson at the IWM Duxford, 1996.

Group Captain 'Iron Bill' McBrien looks on whilst Johnnie and other officers of 144 Wing meet Churchill in Normandy.

Above left: The Prime Minister leaving Crepon as a passenger in Broady's captured *Storch*.

Above right: Johnnie on Sally on the 'Long Trek' into Germany.

Above left: Johnnie was always angry about the 'Arnhem fiasco', having enormous respect and sympathy for the airborne troops. He is pictured here with Colonel 'Dicky' Lonsdale of the Parachute Regiment, who famously led and organised the defencc around Oosterbeek church.

Above right: Wing Commander Johnson with his new boss, Group Captain Stan Turner in Holland; Johnnie was unhappy serving under Turner, whom he considered a 'poacher turned gamekeeper'.

A destroyed Allied aircraft at Eindhoven, New Year's Day, 1945: Operation BODENPLATTE.

Group Captain Johnson meeting Field Marshal Montgomery, whom he considered a gifted general but a vain and boastful man.

Air Vice-Marshal Johnnie Johnson with Dilip Sarkar at the launch of *Bader's Tangmere Spitfires* in 1996.

The strong-willed 'Mary' Coningham, always critical of army generals, signalled back, also copied 'to the world', stating the real problem was that II Corps was not battleworthy.

At this time Tedder was staying with Broadhurst – Tedder in Broadhurst's comfortable caravan and the latter reduced to a tent. Broadhurst was the first to see the two signals and thought them very amusing, but Tedder was not pleased and immediately took off, without breakfast, to 'sort it out with Ike!'

Coningham was ordered to apologise, in person, to Patton, and the two prima donnas met at Patton's headquarters where, after an uneasy start, they lunched together and, eventually, became good friends.

As the Axis forces were pressed into an ever-decreasing bridgehead, ULTRA warned of the enemy's intention to fly troop reinforcements from Sicily to Tunisia and AOC was able to stage one of the greatest air battles of the Mediterranean theatre. He selected experienced South African Spitfire and Tomahawk squadrons who, on the morning of 22 April 1943, fell upon a great gaggle of six-engine Me323s, each capable of carrying one hundred troops on their two decks, escorted by German and Italian fighters.

It was, as Laddie Lucus related, 'a rare battle in the annals of air fighting: thirty-six Kittyhawks and eight Spitfires in combat with the gunners of the huge transports and their escorts. The opaque mirror of the water below was broken by the splash of plunging, blazing machines; the air streaked with cannon and machine gun fire as the fighters wrote their destruction. As Lieutenant Gilson dashed towards the air fleet, four Macchis dropped their long-range tanks and dived away, leaving him to sweep over the great troop-carriers and down the first one, then another in a mass of flame!'

The South Africans claimed to have destroyed thirty 323s, which was later disputed by the Germans, but, whatever the score, it put an end to all the further daylight reinforcement flights, and some weeks later the Axis forces in North Africa surrendered.

In this desert war, tactical air power had played a decisive part. It had won the freedom of the skies, sometimes against fierce opposition. It had saved the Eighth Army in retreat, hastened its advance and, for the first time in the Second World War we had, at Mareth, used tactical air power for the close and integrated support of ground forces; the distinguished military historian Liddell Hart wrote it was a 'stunning adaption of the German *blitz* method' which worked very effectively – although frowned on by distant RAF superiors as a breach of Air Staff doctrine.

It was frowned upon because the Air Staff had backed 'Bomber' Harris's claim that if Bomber Commander received priority in the production of the Lancaster bombers, Germany would surrender in the spring of 1944. He got that priority but there still remained much fighting after the spring of 1944, and tactical air power not strategic bombing would play a major part. Indeed, the tremendous impact of tactical air power on the campaign in Europe has never been fully assessed.

After Dunkirk there was a complete lack of confidence between soldiers and airmen; 'Mary' Coningham helped to restore that confidence. Montgomery was the first British general to appreciate the significance of tactical air power and after his initial setback on the Mareth Line, when Broadhurst's squadrons were grounded by bad weather, he never again went into a set-piece battle without assured support from his trusted airman, Harry Broadhurst.

'During the retreat,' I said to Bing Cross, 'Coningham was anxious about his forward airfields and withdrew them, and his headquarters, inside the Egyptian border. The joint headquarters was lost, but immediately Montgomery arrived on the scene Coningham went to see him, and the general wholeheartedly agreed they must live alongside each other. How would you summarise Coningham's stewardship in the desert?'

'Bing' replied, 'Coningham, with Tedder's support, got the organization straight and goodness knows what we would have done without him. No-one had any idea of what the airmen at the top went through in those days. Tedder and Coningham together were simply splendid. They broke Rommel's last thrust and saved the Eighth Army at Alamein.'

The big difference between Coningham and Broadhurst was that the former always considered himself an 'equal' of the army commander because they occupied a joint headquarters and took joint decisions, whereas Broadhurst thought that because the army were doing the bulk of the fighting, and occupying the ground, they were the senior partner and the AOC's job was to provide the army with the best possible tactical air support; and he had the battlefield situation, the equipment and the time to do it. He did it well, but 'Mary' Coningham was the true architect of the Desert Air Force.

Montgomery soon realised that in Broadhurst he had an air commander and trusted him. Thus, despite the big difference in their ages (and their widely differing life-styles) they got on well together and their close relationship had an excellent effect on Army-Air Force cooperation down to battalion-squadron level.

For the airmen in the desert, it was fortunate that in mid-August 1942 Montgomery took over the Eighth Army from Auchinleck. I say 'fortunate' because this highly professional commander was the first soldier to fully understand the full potential of a strong tactical air force in support of an army. He remembered the devastating Blitzkrieg in the French campaign and realised that the very weapon the Germans had invented could now be turned against them. He had his bad points for he was vain and exceedingly boastful and later he failed to handle his Allied opposite numbers, but there is no doubt that he was an outstanding commander. No-one in the inter-war years had stretched the military art with such singleness of mind. He fought his battle according to sound and well-established principles, interpreted them into operation plans with great thoroughness and pressed these through to victory with unrelenting authority.

Chapter 5

144 Wing, RCAF

I was anxious to get back on ops and during my time at 11 Group headquarters I tried to keep up-to-date by flying, about once a month, with either the Kenley Wing or the Tangmere Wing. Looking back this was a big mistake, and indeed dangerous, because I had to fly in a subordinate role as wingman to a relatively inexperienced section leader and had no voice in the conduct of the operation. As a staff officer I should have ceased operational flying altogether and taken a short refresher course before returning to the fray.

Like many of my contemporaries I returned to the fray because the squadron, or wing, was our family, our home, and the very powerful force that – once we were taken off ops – called us back. For in the Royal Air Force, unlike the older Services, provided a man was genuine and could fly reasonably well, he was accepted into his squadron where, of course, he had to earn his keep. A man was not judged by any of the old standards of race, religion, birth, schooling or wealth, but according to his personal integrity and skill.

The Tangmere Wing had the Griffon-engined Spitfire XII whose best fighting height was about 12,000 feet and I was told that the Wing Leader, Ray Harries, flew at this height below enemy formations and then turned steeply into the German fighters once they had started their diving attack. I found this tactic very odd because my operational flying had taught me that the leader who has the height controls the air battle.

The following day found me in the Tangmere briefing room listening to their small but brilliant leader. We were to sweep the Rouen–Beauvais area under radar control and I would fly wingman to Ray: in other words, I was a pilot officer again for the duration of this mission. The Wing Leader concluded his briefing: 'We'll fly between 10 and 12,000 feet as usual. The 190s will be above us. So just report them quietly to me. We'll pretend we haven't seen them and when they're just out of range we'll break into them.'

Ray and I walked to our Spitfires. Before we climbed into our cockpits, I said: 'I always thought the chap with the height held all the cards, Ray.'

'Yes, he does,' replied the Wing Leader. 'But 12,000 feet is our best fighting height. Somehow, we've to pull down the Hun to our level. Once he's down, our Spits are so much better that we can break into him, out-turn him and soon get on top of him. One day we saw twenty-five or thirty Huns above us. We drew them down, broke into them and clobbered nine. I hope you'll see how it's done today.'

I could think of no suitable comment!

The Controller gave us various courses to steer and eventually we were flying immediately below a gaggle of 190s. The pilots reported them quietly enough, and for a few minutes we flew some 5,000 feet below the enemy aircraft. Ray followed every move the German leader made and held us below the Huns, and I sweated it out and felt like a live bait being dangled before the sharp teeth of a very hungry pike. But soon the 190s made off and Ray didn't have the opportunity to demonstrate his tactics to me.

Early in the new year a well-known Canadian night fighter pilot came to see me. This was Group Captain Paul Davoud, who before the war had been a bush pilot in Canada and possessed a great fund of amusing stories about his flying experiences in the North-West Territories.

Paul told me that the Canadians were about to send a further six fighter squadrons to England for the forthcoming invasion. They would be formed into two wings, one of Spitfires and the other of Typhoons. He had been selected to command the new unit and was looking for a wing leader for the Spitfire squadrons and had already suggested to the Canadian authorities that I should be offered the appointment. The Canadians were agreeable and so was my boss, Air Vice-Marshal 'Dingbat' Saunders, the wise and kindly AOC of 11 Group.

Thus, in the spring of 1944 I was appointed Wing Commander Flying of 144 Wing, Royal Canadian Air Force, and at RAF Digby, Lincolnshire, I began to lick the three Squadrons, (441, 442 and 443), into shape for the forthcoming Great Adventure. At twenty-eight I was a year or two older than the average wing leader in Fighter Command, but some of our outstanding leaders – Bader, Broadhurst, and Malan – were all over thirty. I had a total of some 1,500 flying hours with 1,300 on Spitfires, and the previous summer I had led the Kenley (Canadian) Wing on 127 missions. On the Fighter Command score sheet I was credited with twenty-five victories. I held the DSO and Bar and the DFC and Bar and was considered to be an above-average shot.

Wellingore, a Digby satellite airfield, was the place where John Gillespie Magee, author of the widely acclaimed poem *High Flight*, was killed in an unnecessary and stupid accident. He joined 412 RCAF Squadron at Digby in mid-September of 1941, three months after his nineteenth birthday. He was tall and slender, with a small moustache and was popular with his brother pilots. His father was an American and his mother was English; they were both missionaries and had met and married in China where John was born. John was sent to prep school and thence to Rugby, and in the summer of 1939 was on vacation in Washington when the war begun. For some reason the American government would not allow him and other American students to return to England. The following June he went to Canada, joined the RCAF, trained as a pilot and was sent to Britain. After completing his training, he was posted to 412, which had Mark II Spitfires with eight machine guns. 412 had only been formed a short time before John arrived; its commanding officer and its two flight commanders had little operational experience. During the closing months of 1941, the Squadron flew many convoy patrols over the North Sea, and occasionally journeyed south, with other squadrons, to form the 12 Group Wing on fighter sweeps over Northern Europe. Such a sweep was flown 8 November 1941, when I flew with 616 Squadron and John Magee with 412 Squadron in the 12 Group Wing.

I have already described this disastrous operation in *Wing Leader* when we patrolled just inside Dunkirk providing withdrawal cover for Blenheim bombers returning from Lille and were soon set upon by Me109Fs and fast radial-engined fighters the like of which we had not seen before; these proved to be the redoubtable Focke-Wulf 190s, which, together with the 109s, gave us such a hard time that we lost seventeen Spitfires, including our own inexperienced Wing Leader who was last heard to say: 'I think I am a little too old for this game, chaps!' But somehow John survived this shambles and actually fired at an enemy fighter.

On the morning of 11 December 1941, the Squadron was detailed to take part in a Wing formation practice with 616 from Kirton-in-Lindsey. Visibility was good with a cloud base of 1,500 feet and several thousand feet of overcast. After the exercise the Wing Leader told Squadron Leader Jack Morrison to take his squadron home to Wellingore. They were still above the cloud layer when Morrison saw a gap in the clouds and the ground below and decided to put the squadron into line astern and accordingly they formed into single file behind him at about a hundred yards apart and dived through the gap. Their speed soon exceeded 400 mph and each pilot, except their leader, would be concentrating on the Spitfire ahead. Unfortunately they were very near Cranwell, whose circuit held some twin-engined Airspeed Oxfords, and John Magee's Spitfire collided with an Anson – both aeroplanes crashed to the ground killing both pilots and a student pilot.

Jack Morrison wrote the customary letter to John's father and mother. Their reply contained a copy of *High Flight* and said he had written it about a week before he joined 412 Squadron.

'High Flight'

Oh! I have slipped the surly bonds of Earth
And danced the skies on laughter-silvered wings;
Sunward I've climbed, and joined the tumbling mirth
Of sun-split clouds, – and done a hundred things
You have not dreamed of – wheeled and soared and swung
High in the sunlit silence. Hov'ring there,
I've chased the shouting wind along, and flung
My eager craft through footless halls of air…

Up, up the long, delirious burning blue
I've topped the wind-swept heights with easy grace
Where never lark, or ever eagle flew –
And, while with silent, lifting mind I've trod
The high untrespassed sanctity of space,
Put out my hand, and touched the face of God.

Hitherto the three squadrons had been based in Canada, flying Hurricanes and Kittyhawks, and except for the squadron commanders, lacked combat experience, but the average 144 Wing pilot had plenty of flying hours and took to their Spitfire IXBs like ducks to water.

George Ulysses Hill, a wiry, pug-faced, tousle-haired veteran of twenty-six, from Nova Scotia, commanded 441 Squadron. He was one of the few holders of the DFC and two Bars and had shot down his first enemy aeroplane during the ill-fated Dieppe raid. Later, in North Africa, he commanded the famous 111 Squadron and had fourteen victories. George was a strong character who was outspoken and forthright – especially when he'd had a few beers. He would be a good man in a tight spot, and I could not have a better Squadron Commander.

The quietly-spoken 'Brad' Walker commanded 442 Squadron. He had already completed one tour of operations from the UK and had been with his squadron for some time in the Aleutians. His tour was nearly over and I would have to think about a suitable replacement.

The third squadron commander, Henry Wallace McLeod, was a tall, alert, cold-eyed man of almost thirty from Regina in Saskatchewan. Wally had fought with distinction over Malta destroying thirteen enemy aeroplanes and winning the DFC and Bar. He had the reputation of being very fast in the air and was, unlike most fighter pilots, a deadly shot.

We had been at Digby a few days when I briefed the inexperienced Canadian fighter pilots about our fighting tactics since we first took the offensive at the beginning of 1941. The ever-increasing speed of fighters and the coming introduction of faster, jet aircraft made it quite obvious that our large, unwieldy wing formations of up to thirty-six Spitfires would soon be a thing of the past, except for offensive operations which were planned well ahead and you had time to form up. While we continued to operate from England, we would usually fly in wing strength, but these formations were getting more and more difficult to hold together in the air.

Once based in France, our mobile radar system would not give us a lot of warning of the approach of enemy formations: if the Luftwaffe kept at low level, there would be no warning. Certainly, once on the Continent, the vital time factor would not permit the lengthy take-off and assembly procedures which we used today. When our ground troops found themselves in a tight spot they would want our support in the shortest possible time, and a flight, or at the most a squadron, would be occasional wing shows. But the experiences of the Desert Air Force clearly indicated that small, manoeuvrable formations would be the order of the day. The reign of the wing leader, which had lasted since early 1941, was drawing to a close, and squadron and flight commanders were emerging as the key figures in our changing pattern of fighting. From now it would largely be a squadron commanders' war. This trend of smaller fighting units was to continue, and later in Korea, when Sabre-jet met Mig 15, it became a flight commanders' war.

I was happy with my three squadron commanders but was desperately short of experienced flight commanders and section leaders. I telephoned 'Iron Bill' MacBrien who was commanding two Canadian Spitfire Wings and put my case: I suggested three or four good men and Bill said he would think about my proposal – but I could have Flight Lieutenant Larry Robillard immediately.

I accepted because I knew the small, wiry French-Canadian from our Tangmere Wing days with Douglas Bader, knew that he was difficult to handle, drank too much, chased the girls and was rarely out of trouble with 'Iron Bill'; he had actually missed an Investiture at Buckingham Palace because of an all-night party; but there are no greater loyalties than those founded in combat and I knew that he would stick with me when lesser men had fled.

Larry soon arrived at Digby, and one evening, over a few beers, he told me about his escape from France:

'I was just over twenty when, in the spring of 1941, I joined 145 Squadron, which was one of the three Squadrons in the great Tangmere Wing led by Douglas Bader. I was a sergeant-pilot and I well remember those early, exciting fighter sweeps over the Channel and the Pas de Calais.

'We knew that one of the outstanding German fighter pilots opposing us was Adolf Galland commanding JG26 at St Omer. At this time Galland had notched up some seventy victories and had just been awarded the Oak Leaves with Swords to the Knights Cross of the Iron Cross.

'On 2 July 1941, Galland and I (we subsequently learned) met in the air with pretty dire results for both of us. In his Me109F Galland attacked and destroyed a Blenheim bomber. When I saw him attacking a Spitfire, I got onto his tail and, after a steep dive and some steep turns, I got in close. I was about to finish him off when I saw a flash of other fighters in the sun and I had to break hard into four Me109s coming at me head-on. They approached very fast. Their leader was firing at me, and I fired and hit him. Somehow we missed colliding and I turned and dived for the ground, and safety. Suddenly I felt a great wallop in my back and part of my wing fell off. My Spitfire went into a vicious spin, completely out of control. The ground was spinning and turning in every direction and the "g" force was so great that I could not raise my hands to release the hood and bail out. Well, I thought, I've really had it, and I had a strange feeling of accepting the fact that I was going to die. I was not scared.

'Suddenly there was tremendous bang and I blacked out. The cockpit must have disintegrated because when I came to I was falling with a tremendous light behind me and the ground coming up at me at a great rate of knots. I grabbed wildly for the ripcord and could not feel it. I looked down, saw the D-ring, pulled and nothing happened and again I thought I'd had it. Suddenly the parachute opened with a great wallop and I was looking up into the canopy of white silk, polka-dotted red – my blood. Somehow I got my legs unhooked, and saw a couple of 109s coming right at me.

I hung limply, hoping that they would think I had been hit and not shoot at me. Then the ground came up with a rush and I landed at the bottom of a railway embankment.

'I sat there, barefooted, in a state of shock, trying to get rid of my parachute when a little boy ran up and told me in broken English that I had better hurry up as the Germans were coming. As I am French-Canadian I speak French fluently and I remember Jean being a bit disappointed because he could not practise his English. Then Jean pointed across the fields and I saw a German truck and soldiers getting out. This jerked me out of my stupor – I started to think clearly and realised that I could not get out of my parachute because the Sutton harness was still around my neck! I undid the harness release and got rid of both harness and parachute.

'Four or five Frenchmen arrived on the scene and I asked them to hide the parachute. Then the boy led me along the embankment which was hard on my bare feet. We crawled through a small tunnel to the other side of the railway line and the boy took me to a farmhouse where the people on seeing me were very worried because the Germans were all around. But they were brave people who gave me a glass of cognac, a long overcoat and a beret. I was in some pain with broken ribs and torn muscles and when I passed out the farmer got hold of the local doctor who patched me up, but I realised from their apprehension that they desperately wanted me out of the way before the farmhouse was searched. So the boy led me out of the house and we made our stealthy way through gardens and farm buildings to his home where his mother, Madame Coudert, a lovely, tall, strong lady, welcomed me, as did his father, Camille Coudert, who became a noted Resistance fighter.

'Soon a M. Rousseau, a brewer, arrived with his big truck and a blue smock for me so that I looked like a French worker. We drove through the German patrols, M. Rousseau and his helper, to the village of Lillères where I was taken to the house of the mayor, Mons Jules Godfrin. I was told that I was to stay with these wonderful French people until the arrangements had been made for my long journey. I was absorbed into the local community and, dressed as a Frenchman, I got around the small town, talked with the people and helped my host in his general store, selling food and groceries and sticking coupons in ration books.

'My friends were always concerned about informers and one day the mayor said, "We have caught a real German who is pretending to be a RAF pilot. We pretend to believe him, but we are going to kill him."

I replied, "How do you know he is not a RAF pilot?"

"He is too English and it is quite apparent that he is acting the part."

"Well," I replied, "tell him to write down who he is and where he is from and bring the paper to me."

'The next day he brought me back a scrap of paper on which was written: "Sergeant Douglas Crabtree, Baders Bus Company."

'I exclaimed, "Christ, I flew with this guy!" And so we got on our bicycles and found Doug Crabtree sitting in a village garden with his leg up because he had broken his ankle when he bailed out a few days after me. He had foolishly thrown away his identification tags and had nothing to prove he was RAF and my French friends thought that Crabtree was a German trying to find out who were helping people like me.

'I had a bicycle and I visited Crabtree fairly often while also cycling about the countryside. I remembered the sites of German headquarters, airfields, ammunition dumps and the like and made little maps of these places on cigarette papers which I had sewn behind the labels in my beret.

'Eventually it was time to leave our good friends who at the risk of their own lives had given us shelter, food and tended to our injuries. It was, for me, an emotional parting and I tried to assure them that one day I, and my friends, would be back.

'Crabtree and I were given fake identity papers, escorted to a nearly railway station and on the way met another evader, Hank Duval, who was a Canadian in the RAF. Then we were joined by three British soldiers who had been hiding since Dunkirk, the year before. The train took us to Abbeville, on the Somme, where we had to cross the bridges into what was known as the occupied zone from "La zone interdite" (the forbidden zone).

'We needed special papers to cross the bridge and these were provided by a most outstanding parish priest, Père Charpentier, who was in his early thirties and who, alas, was later executed by the Germans. It was arranged that when we had crossed the bridge we should hand these special papers to a young Boy Scout, in uniform, who would be waiting on a certain bench on the other side.

'Crabtree and Duval went on one bridge while the three soldiers and I went to another. I told the soldiers that they should behave like Frenchmen and appear annoyed that they had to provide the special papers to cross over one of their bridges and they should be quite stern about the procedure. The three went ahead of me but when they were about fifty yards from the guard they hesitated to see who was going to go first. I saw the German guard was looking at them so I did what I should have done in the first place – I walked in front of them, produced the special papers, and went straight through and they followed without any incident.

'We could see Crabtree and Duval crossing the other bridge. They passed the first guard all right but when they got to the guard at the other end they were stopped at the guardhouse where we saw them standing at attention. There was a big German staff car nearby and we thought the game was up, but eventually they were let through and we all got together in a restaurant in the *Hotel de la Gare* near the railway station since we had to wait for several hours for the train to Paris. We never did know what caused the hold up by the German sentries.

'When we arrived the restaurant was empty, but soon the place filled with German soldiers. None of the other chaps spoke French so I recited all the French poetry I knew while the others said *'oui, oui'* or *'non, non'* and waved their hands as if in animated conversation. We two Canadians and four Englishmen were completely surrounded by Germans as I recited the *Fables of La Fontaine*!

'Eventually we were taken to Paris where we spent six or seven days with our hosts from the Resistance, but we had to be careful where we went because Paris was full of Germans and informers.

'We took the train to Tours, walked throughout the night into Vichy France, and went on to Marseilles. On this leg of our journey we did not have an escorting Frenchman, but we had the name and address of a contact and eventually found him. We were separated and I stayed with the head of the Resistance in that area and the lady of the house helped me to learn a little Spanish for the journey ahead.

'We were taken to Perpignan where we met our guide, a Spanish smuggler and a Republican, who took us for a long walk across the Pyrenees in rotten weather. This journey lasted almost two days until we arrived at a remote Spanish farmhouse where we rested. The following morning our guide took our party of six to the local railway station where we thanked him as we got on the train for Barcelona.

'Looking back, I suppose this was the most vulnerable stage of our journey. Six young, fit men travelling, unescorted, across Spain, with no Spanish papers whatsoever and hardly a word of Spanish between us. Spanish police were indeed on the train and when it stopped at a remote station the police got off with a couple of prisoners. After this incident the train was not searched and we reached Barcelona where we contacted the British Consul who told us we were the first group to escape from occupied France.

'After a few pleasant days in Barcelona we were driven to Madrid where the British Ambassador, Sir Samuel Hoare, was delighted to see us and hear our stories. After a week in Madrid we were driven in an Embassy Rolls Royce to Gibraltar and then on to England in a Sunderland flying boat. The date was 9 September 1941, and it had taken us ten weeks to make the round trip.

'Before returning to operations, Doug Crabtree and I toured the fighter squadrons and talked to the pilots about our escape. We said that if they were brought down, without serious injury, they could count on much support from the ordinary French people and that once in the hands of the Resistance they would always be lodged in a safe house or a safe hotel.'

Back to Johnnie:

Our ground equipment was brought to Digby by road convoys and our brand-new Spitfire IXBs were flown in from the maintenance units. I flew several from the grass airfield, and selected MK392, which handled well and had a sweet-sounding engine. Once again, my initials and wing commander's pennant were painted on the engine cowling, and as with her predecessor (EN398) of a year ago, I never had occasion to regret the choice.

During my tour with the Kenley Wing we had operated at 24,000 feet, or above, escorting the 'Mighty Eighth', or on free-lance fighter sweeps, and rarely attacked a ground target. However, 144 Wing was now classed as a fighter-bomber unit and we would have to support the Second British Army in Europe just as the Desert Air Force had so brilliantly supported the Eighth Army in North Africa.

Dive-bombing was an important part of our training. Our Spitfires were fitted with racks under each wing and the aeroplane was stressed to carry two 500-pound bombs. The theory of dive-bombing was to put your aeroplane into a steep dive, aim it at the target and release your bombs about the same time as you pulled out of the dive. Unfortunately, the bombs did not possess the same line of flight as our Spitfires and if you aimed directly at the target then the bombs fell short. You also had to make the necessary allowance for the prevailing wind on any particular day. Our latest gyroscopic gunsights automatically computed the amount of deflection you should allow when attacking an enemy aircraft, but we had no such assistance to determine the distance or time you should allow before releasing your bombs. Some leaders counted 'one, two, three' and then released their bombs. Others counted to four, and some devised a system whereby the bombs were released when the target passed through a certain portion of the gunsight.

The first time I saw my lean Spitfire with two bombs hanging on its slender wings, I decided that I was never going to be crazy about this phase of our work. The Spitfire seemed to be intolerably burdened with her load, and the ugly, blunt bombs were a basic contradiction of all the beauty and symmetry of the aeroplane. Perhaps I was unduly sensitive about flying Spitfires for a long time. It was one thing to dive-bomb with a heavier type of fighter-bomber strapped to your back, which weighed almost seven tons and literally descended like a bomb, but it was quite another matter to force this relatively light, sensitive aircraft into a screaming dive against a ground target.

'What do you think of it, Wally?' I said to McLeod as we stood together inspecting a bombed-up Spitfire.

'Not much, Sir,' replied the veteran from Malta. 'If we'd got two decent long-range tanks to hang under the wings, instead of those things' – pointing to the bombs – 'we could go to Berlin with the Yanks and get stuck into some real fighting.'

After two weeks of hard training at Digby we moved south to Holmsley South, an airfield near Bournemouth, and took the opportunity to rehearse the operational procedure for the move of a tactical wing. First of all, the advance party, which consisted of about half our ground crews and vehicles, left Digby and drove in small, well-camouflaged convoys to the new base. Immediately they arrived they set up a skeleton wing headquarters, including flying control, and prepared to receive the Spitfires. Meanwhile we continued to fly from Digby and carried on with our training. Immediately we received word that the advance party was ready to operate the squadron, we flew to our new airfield and within a few minutes of landing were refuelled and ready for the air again. The rear party, back at Digby, rounded up all our equipment, loaded their three-tonners, set course for the south and within two days had joined up with their comrades of the advance party.

It was arranged that my good friend 'Hawk-Eye' Wells would be attached to my wing and fly a few missions before getting a wing of his own. Before the war he had won several clay-pigeon competitions in New Zealand and became that country's leading marksman with a twelve bore shotgun. Aptly dubbed 'Hawk-Eye' during the Battle of Britain, because of his amazing eyesight, he had a dozen enemy aeroplanes to his credit and held the DSO and DFC with Bar. Hawk had done more than his share of operations but, like other good men, he wanted to return to the comradeship.

On 28 March 1944, we flew our first mission when it was planned that we would cross the French coast at Fécamp and sweep south of Paris, hoping to find a few Krauts in the air and blood my new Canadians. 443 Squadron was away on an air firing course so I led 441 Squadron with 442 Squadron as top cover. We crossed the Channel at low-level – to avoid radar detection – and when I saw the French coast I climbed the wing to 10,000 feet and headed for Paris. At this point, however, my radio failed and, as briefed, I waggled my wings to Hawk, who was flying as my number three, he drew alongside and when I tapped my microphone he immediately understood and took the lead.

It was a spanking day with good visibility, and as we flew near to Dreux airfield, west of Paris, we could see about thirty German aeroplanes parked in their dispersals. Hawk, I later discovered, instructed 442 Squadron to remain as top cover, hopefully to draw the flak, and led 441 Squadron into the sun, echeloned them to starboard and dived at top speed for the airfield to make his strafing run. For me, without a radio, it was an uncomfortable feeling, but I knew that I had to keep the correct spacing from Hawk and when I saw him open fire I turned my attention to a twin-engined machine and set it ablaze. Other pilots attacked gun sites, the control tower, the headquarters building and a flak tower and then, suddenly, we had left the airfield behind and after a few miles at ground level – to clear the defences – Hawk climbed us to 20,000 feet and brought us home.

I was well pleased with 144 Wing's first mission. We had destroyed half a dozen enemy aeroplanes without loss and within three weeks of receiving their Spitfires, the newcomers from Canada had flown like veterans and kept cool heads under fire.

In the Pas de Calais the Germans had constructed hundreds of V1 launching sites from which they would send flying bombs against targets in southern England, and for some weeks before D-Day these 'ski-sites' were attacked by heavy bombers, medium and light bombers and our own Typhoon and Spitfire fighter-bombers. These ski-sites were very difficult to hit because they were well camouflaged and heavily defended by flak. My Canadians came through all these operations without loss, but on one mission we had to pull young Johnnie Marriott out of the drink.

When we made our run-up to the launching site we were bracketed by many bursts of heavy flak. On a fighter sweep I would have climbed the squadron a few thousand feet, changed direction once or twice, and so confused the enemy predictors on the ground below. But this time I had to make a steady approach to the target at a constant height, wait until the launching site appeared under my port wing, then half roll, ease out into a steep dive, and release our bombs from about 4,000 feet when we pulled out of the dive.

Near the target the flak increased, and so did my respect for the bomber boys who had to put up with this sort of thing on all their missions. At last the target passed under the wing of my Spitfire. When it appeared again I half-rolled. We plunged down and the light flak came into his own. I released the bombs, braced myself to take the 'g' and zoomed up. The flak followed suit. I was not surprised when Marriott piped up:

'Greycap from Red 2. I've been hit! Temperature's going up.'

We were almost over the French coast. Marriott had little chance of escaping if he baled out over this thickly defended area. I decided to get him as far across the Channel as possible.

'OK, Johnnie,' I replied. 'Stay with her as long as you can. I'll get the Walrus to meet us. Red 3, transmit for Mayday.'

I circled round Marriott's Spitfire as it gradually lost height. He was flying very slowly with low revolutions to keep down the critical oil and coolant temperatures. Every few seconds a puff of white smoke belched from his exhaust stacks.

'How's it going, Johnnie?' I asked him.

'OK, Sir. Temperature's off the gauges. But she's still ticking over.'

The Spitfire was down to about 2,000 feet. Marriott would want this height to bale out and there was always the danger that the aeroplane would start to burn.

'Step out, Johnnie,' I ordered, 'We'll pick you up in no time.'

'OK, Sir,' he cheerfully replied.

We saw his parachute spill out. Then he clambered into his dinghy and waved when I passed a few feet above him. I left a section of Spitfires to circle his dinghy, but these were soon released. After landing, the controller told me that Marriott was already in the Walrus and heading for a coastal airfield. It was a perfect rescue operation.

Later that day, Johnnie Marriott returned, none the worse for his ducking. He was a likeable lad, possessed a good voice and liked to sing. We celebrated his return with a party, and he burst into song after his first pint. He was still singing when the party broke up, and was attempting another ditty when he was not un-gently eased into bed.

The highly successful Allied team of top brass who had chased Rommel out of North Africa and invaded Sicily and Italy now came to England to direct the Normandy invasion and liberation of Europe. The team was headed by the American, Eisenhower, who had the knack of getting high ranking officers to work together in harmony. The senior army general was the dedicated, austere Montgomery who had won battles in the desert and was the first British general to realise the importance of air superiority; he had learned the hard way for on one occasion, when the Desert Air Force was grounded because of bad weather, he advanced against Rommel without air cover and the brilliant German general turned and struck so hard that Montgomery rarely moved again unless he had plenty of air support.

Three outstanding airmen accompanied Eisenhower and Montgomery. They were the learned, yet brittle, four-star Tedder who was the senior airman and Ike's deputy. The vain three-star 'Mary' Coningham, who had done well in the desert, commanded the Second Tactical Air Force which would support the British and Canadian Armies. The shrewd Harry 'Broady' Broadhurst, who had developed the Desert Air Force into a highly mobile striking power at the right place and the right time and, above all, gained the army's confidence. Broadhurst commanded 83 Group which would control the first wings based in France.

Johnnie:

It was just before D-Day when I led a finger-four, including Dan Browne, on a low-level Ranger as far as the German border and back. It was another spanking day with excellent visibility of some twenty-five miles. We were looking for enemy aeroplanes in the air, taking special care to avoid the very well defended enemy airfields where the excellent German gunners always seemed to be ready and waiting. Indeed, Coningham's Headquarters had issued instructions that because of heavy losses single-engined fighters were not to attack enemy airfields. On the way home we flew over some rising ground, and there, on the other side and only a few hundred yards away, lay – like a huge octopus – a big airfield with hangars, runways, a bunch of fighters at the end of one runway about to take off, and the flak.

'There was flak, flak, bags of bloody flak,' as the old song goes, above, below, in front and behind us. The boys, all very experienced, knew exactly what to do. Straight ahead. Hugging the ground at twenty feet. Over the perimeter track and out of the danger area. I climbed our little band to 20,000 feet, checked each other's Spitfires as best we could, and headed for Westhampnett.

After landing we were standing discussing our fruitless and dangerous mission when a gaggle of top brass swept up including Eisenhower,

Leigh-Mallory, Coningham, Ira Eaker of the Eighth Air Force and Broady. Our Group Captain, 'Iron Bill' MacBrien, who seldom flew operationally, made the introductions, and Eisenhower, with all the responsibility of the imminent invasion on his shoulders, was particularly interested in what we had seen and done. I had to tell the likeable American general that we had not fired our guns, but soon after, Broady drew me aside, looked at me with his cold penetrating brown eyes, and said:

'You must have seen something worth attacking?'

'Yes Sir, we did,' I replied, 'We saw a bunch of fighters about to take-off from, I think, Louvain.'

'Why didn't you attack?'

'Not allowed to. There's a Second TAF Op Order forbidding single-engined fighters from attacking enemy airfields.'

'Tell Ike, and ask him what he is going to do about it!'

I was in deep trouble. Coningham probably knew nothing about the order but as Commander-in-Chief, Second TAF, he was responsible for it and I certainly should not have bypassed him.

'Tell Ike, now,' ordered my AOC. 'Now.'

I walked up to Ike and related my sorry tale. The Supreme Commander was incredulous:

'For Christ's sake, Mary,' he shouted, 'What the hell is going on?' And he got into his car and drove off.

Coningham followed, but not before he snarled that I should be hearing from him. The AOC left too, but he had time for a grin and a broad wink.

Deep in thought, we walked across the grass, puzzled by this unsavoury episode. Dan said, 'We've heard a lot of bullshit about this great united team, but there's no love lost between Broadhurst and Coningham.'

We had walked another few yards when he added, 'I suppose you'll be leaving anytime now. You might recommend me for your job!'

Chapter 6

'Fair stood the wind for France'

'Magnitude, simultaneity and violence' were, said Winston Churchill, 'the prime requisites for the successful invasion of Europe', and we heard the details when, on 5 June 1944 the group captains and wing leaders of 83 Group were briefed by Harry Broadhurst about the following day's invasion. Standing before a large map of the Normandy coast he painted the big picture when he said the Overlord plan was for a five-division landing over eighty miles of coastline. The British divisions and one Canadian division would land east of Colleville-sur-Mer on beaches codenamed Gold, Juno and Sword, would take Caen, the ancient capital of Normandy and press on to the Caen–Falaise plain.

To the west, two American divisions would land on a 6,000 yard beach codenamed Omaha, and a third US division would land on Utah beach to secure the Cotentin Peninsula and capture the port of Cherbourg.

The sea landings would be preceded seven hours earlier by airborne and glider landings. The British 6th Airborne would land by parachute and glider to protect the British sectors from any possible counter-attack from east of the Orne. In the US sector two airborne divisions would drop to protect Utah beach and to assist the link-up with Omaha beach.

These beaches were guarded by steel palings sited in depth along the rim of the tide and armed with shells and mines. Ashore, enemy coastal batteries covered all the beaches in support of the German infantry defending the coast. About every thousand yards there were enemy strong points consisting of fortified houses, concrete pill boxes and linking trenches, and enemy positions were guarded by barbed wire minefields and protected by machine guns, anti-tank guns and field artillery; between the strong points the country was traversed with tank obstacles, and all likely beach exits were blocked. The minor ports were strongly defended and some thirteen German infantry battalions held the coastal defences facing our Second Army.

The fighters and fighter bombers of his Group, continued Broady, would be controlled by Fighter Direction Tenders for fighters, and Headquarters Ships for fighter-bombers and reconnaissance aeroplanes. These control vessels would be moored in the shipping lane and approximately in the centre of the beach area. The forward echelon of his Group Control Centre, under Group Captain Jimmie Fenton, would be ashore and operating on the evening of D-Day.

If all went well, by nightfall on D-Day the American and British armies would have a firm bridgehead running from the Orne in the east, to the Contentin Peninsula in the west; and within this bridgehead the Royal Engineers would have five Airfield Construction Groups to build an emergency landing strip at Asnelles (B1) and advanced landing grounds at Bazenville (B2), St Croix-sur-Mer (B3), Bény-sur-Mer (B4) and Camilly (B5). The emergency landing strip would be ready late on D-Day and hopefully the ALGs would be ready on the evening of D + 1 – but this would depend on how long it took to offload the bulldozers and graders. Until such time as our own ground crews arrived in Normandy our fighters would be maintained by our own Servicing Commandos.

Broadhurst said we had a very good understanding with the Army; for example when his staff came to plan the landing of the ships for D-Day the army naturally wanted to land the earliest ships ashore with tanks and fighting vehicles. We, however, wanted some of our important communication and radar trucks ashore, or the army would not get proper air support. Boyle was unable to win his case with his opposite (Army) number and therefore insisted on it being referred to Montgomery's headquarters who signalled back: *83 Group know what they want, give it to them.*

Harry Broadhurst, the soldier's friend, concluded his excellent and comprehensive briefing when he said that the army had a very tough job ahead and asked us to give them the utmost support. He wished us well and as we repaired to our airfields to brief our own pilots. I was thankful that I had a place in this great endeavour.

Throughout that critical night more than one thousand Lancaster, Halifax and Mosquito aeroplanes attacked the enemy coastal batteries, and as it was growing light the last of the night bombers left for home. Meanwhile, the British naval bombardment squadrons, preceded by minesweepers, closed the shore and took up their positions; the eastern squadron, which included *Warspite, Ramillies* and *Roberts,* mounting fifteen-inch guns, opened fire soon after 0530 hrs on the vulnerable flank east of the Orne. With the light down, a vast shield of fighter aeroplanes fanned out over the beaches, while the Fleet, shepherding the convoys through the swept channels, received continuous air cover. Along the entire front, the enemy fortifications were blasted from the sea and from the air.

We were called well before dawn and after a light breakfast our groundcrews strapped us into the cockpits of our Spitfires. 441 Squadron took off first, followed by 442, and when they were both on the downwind leg I led 443 into the grey dawn. The cloud base was about 1,500 feet and held 443 at that height, with the other squadrons on either side, and as I watched the mighty armada, I was very conscious that we were making history just as William of Normandy did, in the opposite direction, some 900 years before. William was accompanied by his half-brother, Odo, Bishop of Bayeux, who in turn was escorted by two 'wives' to cater for his sexual requirements. Nine centuries later alas, alas, we were not provided with such comforts!

I made an accurate landfall on the Normandy coast where the flying conditions were better than the gloomy forecast, with a cloud base of 2,000 feet and visibility between five and six miles. Later I learned that the wind was south-westerly force five, the sea moderate, with a slight swell; severe conditions heavily laden landing craft.

I called the wing leader of the formation we were about to relieve and told him that we were already on our appointed patrol line. Had he seen anything of enemy fighters? 'Not a bloody thing,' he replied, 'although the flak is pretty hot if you fly a few hundred yards inland.'

Amongst the mass of shipping below us was a fighter direction ship. I called the RAF controller on my radio and asked if he had any plots of enemy formations on his table. The controller came back with the guarded reply that for the moment he had no positive information for me.

We swept parallel to the coast beneath a leaden grey sky, and I positioned the wing two or three hundred yards off-shore so that we should not present easy targets to the enemy gunners. Our patrol line ended over the fishing village of Port-en-Bessin, while further to the west, beyond our area of responsibility, lay the two American assault beaches Omaha and Utah. When we carried out a wide, easy turn to retrace our flight path, a wing of American Thunderbolts harried our progress and for a few uneasy moments we circled warily round each other. Formations of different types of Allied aircraft had attacked each other during the preceding months, but on this occasion recognition was soon effected and we continued our flight to the south of Orne. For the present there was little doubt that we were the undisputed masters of this portion of Normandy sky, so for the first time that morning I was able to turn some of my attention to the scene below.

Off-shore the sea was littered with ships of all sizes and descriptions, and small landing-craft ploughed their way through the breakers to discharge their contents at the water's edge. We could see a fair number of capsized vessels, and afterwards learnt that the various obstacles erected by the Germans below the high-water mark were considerably more formidable that had been expected. Further out in the bay, cruisers and destroyers manoeuvred to line broadside on to the assault beaches: we could see the flashes from their guns as they engaged the enemy defences well inland. As I watched the naval gunners and their targets, no doubt the shells were well above our heights of 2,000 feet, but I made quite certain that we did not exceed this altitude.

Swimming tanks, a recent innovation, were launched from their parent ships well out to sea. From the air it seemed as if these amphibious tanks had a fairly long and rough sea journey before they reached the beaches. During the last lap of their journey the tanks opened fire against adjacent enemy positions, and this must have come as a considerable surprise to the defenders. Here and there the enemy appeared to be putting up a stiff resistance: we saw frequent bursts of mortar and machine-gun fire directed against our troops and equipment on the beaches. Small parties of men could be seen making their way to the beach huts and houses on the sea front, many of which were on fire. But the greatest danger to us pilots lay from the mass of Allied aircraft which roamed restlessly to and fro over the assault areas. Medium bombers, light bombers, fighter-bombers, fighters, reconnaissance, artillery and naval aircraft swamped the limited air space below the cloud and on two occasions we had to swerve violently to avoid head-on collisions. Towards the end of our allotted patrol the controller asked me to investigate bogey aircraft flying down the Orne from Caen, but these turned out to be a formation of Typhoons, so we resumed our cruise above the beaches.

We flew four patrols on D-Day and never a sign of the Luftwaffe! We could see that despite the rough seas the British and Canadian troops had made good progress and Arromanches, Meuvaines and Ryes were occupied. The leading Canadians, despite some shelling and considerable mortar fire had cleared the beaches by mid-morning and were heading towards Caen. In the British sector the Normandy landing had succeeded, but to the west the Americans were having a hard time on Omaha beach.

Somehow it had escaped Allied intelligence that an experienced German infantry division had moved into the Omaha sector and thus there were two enemy divisions to defend the most formidable beach in

Normandy – for Omaha was overlooked for nearly four miles by steep bluffs reaching to 200 feet.

The rough seas and the long distance from ships to the shore swamped many swimming tanks, ducks and amphibious vehicles. The experienced defenders held their fire until the soaked Americans struggled to the beaches. Then heavy fire from automatic weapons raked the beaches cutting down the badly exposed troops. Tanks and armoured vehicles never reached the shore and for six hours the GIs held only a few yards of beach, which remained under heavy enemy fire.

According to Carlo D'Est in his *Decision in Normandy*:

'It rapidly became evident to the US commanders that remaining in their exposed positions was tantamount to suicide, and they began to rally their troops. Some extraordinary acts of heroism followed. The Assistant Commander of the 29th Infantry Division, Brigadier General Norman D. Cota, deliberately exposed himself to enemy fire by striding up and down the beach exhorting his men to get moving. In the 1st Division sector the Commander of the 16th Infantry Regiment, Colonel George A. Taylor, performed a similar feat; he led his troops in an attack against German machine-gun positions declaring: "Two kinds of people are staying on this beach, the dead and those about to die. Now let's get the hell out of here!" Throughout D-Day the situation on Omaha was so perilous that General Bradley seriously considered evacuating the beachhead and switching the follow-up units to the British sector or to Utah beach.'

Precarious as the position was some progress was made and at the end of this bloody day Omaha was carried by the slimmest of margins at a cost of 2,000 Americans killed, wounded or missing.

On the evening of that great day Air Commodore Dermot Boyle, accompanied by a few staff officers, went by destroyer to Normandy and, off the coast, transferred to a landing craft. The sea was rough and about 300 yards off-shore the naval officer in command announced that he could go no further. The sea looked deep and forbidding so Boyle ordered his smallest officer, Peter Homes, to act as his dip-stick and sent him down the sloping ramp of the craft. When Holmes touched bottom the water was up to his armpits which was good enough for Boyle who was much taller.

Chapter 7

Normandy

During the early morning of 8 June 1944, before we had begun the day's work, I was called to the telephone and heard the familiar voice of 'Dingbat' Saunders, AOC, 11 Group. He had just received word that the first ALG in Normandy, St Croix-sur-Mer, was completed and would I send over a section of good pilots as soon as possible to see if the strip was fully operational and whether the Servicing Commandos could cope with rapid rearming and refuelling? I selected the experienced Dal Russel, and his wingman, who were soon back with the splendid news that all was well. I passed the good news to 'Dingbat', who then asked me to take the wing and refuel at St Croix-sur-Mer, from where we were to carry out a further patrol before returning to Ford.

I was very anxious to sweep as far south as the Loire river, since we knew that the Luftwaffe possessed some airfields in this locality and I felt quite certain that they had reinforced the sector. But once more the weather was against us and low cloud prevented the execution of our planned route. When our fuel ran low we swept across St Croix at 1,000 feet to have a look at the general layout before landing. We had to make a fairly tight circuit to avoid the barrage balloons hoisted over vulnerable concentrations on the beaches. It was a most curious sensation, preparing to land on territory from which we had been accustomed to receiving all types of shot and shell during the previous four years. Keen and energetic Servicing Commandos guided our Spitfires to their various dispersals and began refuelling our fighters. Two commandos climbed on my Spitfire, opened the fuel tank and placed a large steel funnel, lined with chamois leather, in the neck of the filler. The jerry cans, each containing four and a half gallons of 100 octane fuel, were lifted six of seven feet to the men on the wing who opened the cans and poured in the fuel. It was hard work but thirty-six Spitfires were fuelled in less than one hour and I found time to thank the commandos for their splendid work.

We gathered together and lit the inevitable cigarettes. Keith Hodson, who was in charge of the airfield, drove alongside in his jeep and advised us not to stray far from the strip. One or two enemy snipers were still at large and they could make life unpleasant. There were several minefields scattered about the locality and a country stroll could end in disaster. Only that morning an airman had walked into an abandoned enemy strongpoint and had found some discarded German uniforms. To impress his colleagues, he donned one of these garments and shouted to them as he stepped out of his pillbox. His gestures were unfortunately misinterpreted and he was shot stone dead.

I walked into a nearby orchard, where a control organization had already been established.

A few days ago the best of von Kluge's Panzers were here – the Panzers that four years ago had terrorised Europe: at that time we had nothing to match the German tanks with their deadly 75mm guns, but today we had the Typhoons with their equally deadly 60lb rockets, and in this Normandy orchard, with a few dead waxen faced Germans lying here and there, we could sense the end of that evil empire. Soon we were greeted by a deputation from the nearby village of St Croix. The local country folk had seen our Spitfires land, and since it was something of an occasion they brought with them gifts of fruit, flowers and wine. Occasionally enemy shells thumped into adjacent fields, but the peasants paid little heed and stolidly continued to till their ground. I noticed several strong coveys of partridge scuttling about and was thankful for the foresight which had induced me to pack a twelve bore in the caravan. Come September a few plump partridges would make a welcome change from compo rations.

I had a beer and a snack with some of the Royal Engineer officers who had built the airfield. They told me that at 1800 hrs on 6 June they were anchored off the beach but could not get ashore because of the stormy sea. Major Mitchell, the CO of 693 Artisan Works Company, RE, explained that to get his earthmoving equipment and men ashore, shallow draught rectangular floating platforms with a freeboard of about two feet, and with an outboard motor at each corner, had been constructed in Britain and towed across to the beaches. The plan was to manoeuvre these platforms to the bow of the Landing Ship Tank whose bow ramp was to be lowered onto the floating platform. Men and equipment would go down the ramp to the platform which, using its outboard motors, would take them ashore.

The next day, 7 June, the sea worsened, so Mitchell and some of his men transferred to a smaller landing craft, brought alongside with great skill by a young American naval officer. They were soon ashore where they were checked in by the Beach Master and at 1410 hrs had reached their rendezvous at St Croix-sur-Mer where the proposed airfield was under enemy fire.

Mitchell walked through the deserted village and wondered if there were any German snipers at large since a fellow sapper had already been shot on the same street. There was no-one to be seen and he made his way to some farm buildings which was the rendezvous point for his company.

At 2000 hrs some mechanical equipment arrived and his sappers and men of the Pioneer Corps began work on the end of the airfield furthest from the enemy and continued until it was dark. The next day work began at dawn, more equipment arrived and the ALG with its taxi tracks and aircraft dispersals was completed by noon on 10 June. For no apparent reason a Spitfire flown by a Scot was the first to land at St Croix. He was followed by a damaged Typhoon, and soon after, Dal Russel and his wingman made their survey.

St Croix was totally different from our well-established airfields in England where our quarters were spacious, warm and comfortable and where if you were lucky enough to be a young pilot stationed at Tangmere you could, after the day's work, bath and change into a clean uniform and, when funds permitted, dine well with your girlfriend under the cool rafters of the Old Ship at Bosham. But here at windswept St Croix, a few small sleeping tents were pitched in a nearby orchard, a marquee served for messing and some crude latrines where half a dozen men crouching side by side could exchange a few pleasantries. Shells crumpled into nearby fields and a great cacophony of sound came from the mass of shipping offshore who fired at friend and foe alike. A section of Typhoons, rearmed and refuelled by the Commandos, taxied along the perimeter track raising clouds of dust from their powerful engines. There was grit everywhere because the soil on which our airfield was constructed was found to contain a high proportion of abrasive silica dust, which lowered the life of our engines.

Lunch in the marquee, supposedly Irish stew, consisted of dehydrated potatoes and tiny pieces of bully beef floating on top of some lukewarm gravy. This was followed by ships' biscuits, evil-smelling processed cheese, and the sort of foul sweet tea that only the British can produce. Definitely, as my old headmaster would say, room for improvement.

After our snack I walked to the edge of the orchard, which was flanked by two narrow roads, and at the intersection stood Montgomery, seeing and being seen, as a continuous nose-to-tail procession of trucks, tanks and armoured vehicles made their way to the front line. For some time I watched the General, who waved and shouted encouragement to his soldiers, and marvelled at the organization which had brought us back to France almost four years since our ignominious departure at Dunkirk.

In accordance with Montgomery's doctrine of Army and Air Force Headquarters being 'welded together', the location of 83 Group headquarters had been decided months before D-Day, alongside Second Army Headquarters. But soon after they had settled down in Normandy, Boyle learned that Montgomery wanted the 83 Group site for his staff. Boyle was incensed but later had the chance to explain his case to the great man when they met on a narrow road. Boyle pulled over to let Monty and his large escort of military motor cyclists pass but the General also stopped and said:

> 'Hello, you are Harry Broadhurst's Chief of Staff aren't you? How are things going?'
>
> 'Very well thank you Sir,' replied Boyle, 'but we are having some trouble over the location of your Headquarters.'
>
> 'What trouble?' asked the General; and Boyle told him, giving his reasons, and Monty said his headquarters had to go on the 83 Group site.
>
> Boyle, somewhat unwisely, said there was another site nearby which would be quite suitable for the General's Headquarters.
>
> 'Underneath your washing line,' retorted Monty. 'You don't understand. I fight big battles and must have room. Goodbye!'

Soon we took off from Ford for the last time. Our ground crews had arrived safely at St Croix and were ready to operate the wing. We stuffed our overnight kit into various odd corners of our Spitfires, thanked the ground crews and thirty minutes later were at St Croix. I was very pleased to see Fred Varley again, who had brought my Labrador, Sally. Fred had sited my caravan alongside the clutch of operations vehicles in the orchard, and he greeted me with a good cup of tea.

I spent the rest of the day checking the small group of vehicles which formed the operations centre of the wing. Two Canadian Army liaison officers were marking up the various friendly and enemy ground positions on large-scale maps. Our own intelligence officers were sifting through reports about the Luftwaffe, and I was pleased to learn that their expected reinforcements had arrived and some 300 enemy fighters were based on airfields to the south and south-east. We had the honour to be the first wing based in Normandy: as such we had a far greater range than those Spitfires operating from southern England. We should be able to strike deep into enemy territory.

Varley had already spent two or three nights in Normandy and repeatedly told me that the customary evening barrage was quite unpleasant. According to him, a few enemy reconnaissance and bomber aircraft put in an appearance immediately it was dark and every gun on the beachhead opened up at the intruders. Varley suggested that perhaps the safest place for my bed would be in a narrow slit trench, but I am afraid that I paid little heed to his advice and was determined to sleep in the caravan – a decision I was to regret before many hours had elapsed.

I turned in quite early, as it had been a strenuous day and I wanted the benefit of a good sleep for the activities of the morrow. I was rudely awakened by the loud staccato chatter of a Bofors gun situated some twenty yards from my caravan. Faintly I could hear the typical unsynchronised drone of a few enemy aircraft, and so great was the clamour of our barrage that sleep was quite impossible. I might as well get dressed and see what it was all about. To the south-east the sky was bright from the large fires, but the enemy pilots were directing their attentions against the mass of shipping lying off-shore. The naval gunners opened up with everything they possessed, and orange tracer ripped across the sky in fantastic criss-cross patterns. Pieces of hot shrapnel fell on my caravan, and the thousands of anti-aircraft guns concentrated in the relatively small area made the general din almost unbearable. Searchlights swept the sky but were hampered by the low cloud base, and occasionally the earth reverberated to the impact of the bombs. Deciding that the tin roof of my caravan offered little protection against this sort of thing, I went in search of Varley, so that together we could move my bed to a more secure position; but the wise fellow had long since gone to earth, and the Labrador with him.

I dragged my sleeping bag from the bed and struggled into it underneath the rear axle of the caravan. This would at least afford me some protection from the shrapnel. But sleep was quite out of the question, as the Luftwaffe sent over sporadic raids until the small hours and, to my regret, our gunners did not appear to suffer from any lack of ammunition! The dawn found me cold and miserable – I crept out of my damp sleeping bag and walked across the soaking grass to the mess tent for a hot drink. I wondered how my three squadron commanders, Browne, Russel and McLeod, had fared during the firework display, and went in search of them. I had some difficulty in tracking them down, but eventually I found them, warm and snug, in a stoutly constructed underground dugout which had been built in the orchard by the Germans. I watched them for a few seconds as they lay in deep slumber and resolved that the coming night would find me alongside.

Twelve of us were sitting at readiness in the cockpits of our Spitfires prepared for a quick scramble. I had decided to fly with Wally McLeod's squadron and he was leading the other flight of six aircraft. Should the enemy show any activity in the air, his movements would be picked up by 83 Group's radar and plotted on the operations table at the group control centre. 'Kenway', the codename for the centre, would then telephone through to our operations caravan and order the readiness squadron into the air. The signal to take off would be a Very light fired from the operations caravan. Once we were airborne we should receive our instructions over the radio direct from Kenway. After half an hour in the cockpit, gloved and masked ready for an immediate take-off, I was rather drowsy as a result of my lack of sleep, but my cramped uncomfortable position sufficed to keep me awake. Suddenly a red Very light soared into the air from the orchard. Switches on, my fingers pressed the starting button and the Merlin roared into life. Then I was travelling down the narrow taxi-track and made the right-angled turn onto the steel-planked runway at too high a speed, for a starboard wing tilted down at a dangerous angle. A few seconds later and the twelve of us were airborne in a ragged, straggling gaggle, but the boys were already picking up their battle formation.

'Greycap to Kenway. Airborne with twelve Spits. What's the form?'

'Kenway to Greycap. Bandits active five miles south of Caen at low level. Please investigate.'

'Greycap to Kenway. Roger. Any definite height on bandits?'

'Kenway to Greycap. No, but they're below 5000 feet. Out.'

There was scattered cloud between five and six thousand feet, and above the sun blazed from a clear sky. If Kenway's information was correct, they were probably a raiding party of fighter-bombers. I eased the Spitfires through a gap and flew immediately below the cloud base.

'Stay down sun, Wally, and keep as near to the cloud base as you can. I'll drop down a few hundred feet.'

'Greycap from Blue 3. Bandits at nine o'clock, 2,000 feet below.'

'Roger, Blue 3, I have them. They're heading toward us. Turning port.'

The bandits were a mixed gaggle of Focke-Wulfs and Messerschmitts. About a dozen all told. Now they were immediately below me, heading towards Caen. They were not higher than 2,000 feet, and the sun was behind us. We had all the makings of a perfect bounce.

'I'm going in, Wally!' I explained. 'Cover my section. Take any of the bastards who climb above me.'

My section was streaking down but still well out of range when the Huns saw us, probably because of the white cumulus cloud. They broke round into our attack in an experienced manner and I realised they were led by a veteran.

'Get in, Wally. These brutes are staying to fight.'

Now twenty-four fighter aircraft twisted and jockeyed for an advantageous position. My number two called up:

'Greycap! Keep turning. There's a 190 behind!'

I kept turning and saw the ugly snout of the 190 over my shoulder. But he couldn't draw a bead on me and soon he was driven off by a Spitfire. I made a mental note to buy my number two a drink back at St Croix.

The enemy leader must have given the order to withdraw, for his aircraft dived towards the ground and set course for the south. Then I spotted four 190s flying in a wide, evenly spaced finger formation, but the starboard aircraft was lagging badly and, in this position, could not be covered by his colleagues.

'Red 2. Cover my tail. I'm going to have a crack at the starboard 190.'

'OK, Greycap. You're clear. Nothing behind.'

Flying a few feet above the bocage country, I narrowed the gap between my Spitfire and the 190. His three comrades were still well ahead of him and he was an easy target. I slid out to one side so that I would not have a low line-astern shot and pulled slightly above him to avoid some high trees as I concentrated on firing. I hit him with the first burst on his engine cowling. More cannon shells ripped into his cockpit and the 190 plunged into the ground only a few feet below. We were over a strongly defended area, for as I pulled up into a steep climb we were engaged by a considerable amount of light flak. Gaining altitude, I spiralled my Spitfire and caught a last glimpse of the remaining three 190s. Oblivious of the fate of their comrade, they continued to streak away at low level, and after making quite certain that they were not going to return, the two us flew back to St Croix in a wide abreast formation.

Back at our airfield I learnt that Wally had smacked down a 190 and that Don Walz had accounted for a third victim. It was a pity the Huns had seen us launch the initial attack: if we had achieved complete surprise, we could have knocked down half a dozen. Still, three victories were better than none, and the engagement marked our first success from St Croix. My own personal score now stood at twenty-eight.

Most unfortunately Walz, together with three other pilots was shot down later that day. At the time we knew nothing of the circumstances, only the bare fact that a complete section of four aircraft failed to return from a scramble. The four aircraft had taken off late in the evening and eventually located a force of Focke-Wulfs, which then attacked. In the fading light they were not aware that they had engaged a far superior force. The Germans, realising their advantageous position, stayed to fight, and all four Spitfires were shot down. Walz's own aircraft was hit in the engine and the petrol tanks exploded. He lost little time in baling out and landed safely in a field. After some adventures on the ground he was eventually assisted by the local peasants and returned with the tragic story. The incident was especially grievous for Dal Russel, whose young brother, Hugh, was one of the three pilots killed on this mission.

Several times each day we flew over the bocage country, lying between the Orne and Vire rivers, whose forest, wooded hills, apple orchards, shaded vales and earthen banks – sometimes four feet high and surmounted by hedgerows – on either side of the small winding roads, made it difficult, if not impossible, to see camouflaged and well-dispersed German armour from a Spitfire flying at 230 mph. This lush countryside, in its summer finery, was of natural advantage to the defenders who had learned to fight without air support and whose small mobile units fought hard and were always reluctant to give ground. Man for man, Rommel's experienced troops were more than a match for their Allied counterparts who had not been trained for the vicious, close-in fighting in the bocage, and we fighter-bomber pilots, since we could not see the enemy, could not help in this stern contest.

The German Tiger tanks with their outstanding 88mm guns which could kill a British tank at 2,000 yards, were infinitely better than our Shermans and Cromwells. Their superiority was well illustrated to me when we landed after a fight against a mixed bunch of Me109s and FW109s. Thanks to some excellent ground controlling, I had been able to 'jump' an enemy gaggle, and as we drew on our cigarettes we found we had destroyed seven enemy aeroplanes without loss. We were still talking about the encounter when the AOC drove up in a jeep with none other than General Montgomery in the passenger seat. After the introductions Broady said:

> 'Tell the General what you've done today.'
>
> 'Well Sir, thanks to some excellent controlling we bounced a bunch of enemy fighters and destroyed seven without loss.'

> 'I wish,' commented Montgomery, 'that you could have told me that instead you had destroyed seven Tiger tanks!'

We could well understand Monty's unguarded and spontaneous remarks because already he was talking about his 'master plan' which envisaged the British pinning down German armour in the east while the Americans 'hinged' on the British and broke out on the west flank. However, I attended several briefings, before and after D-Day, when the aim was to take Caen on D-Day and to press on to the open plain between Argentan and Falaise: this was 'airfield country' which Tedder and Coningham badly wanted and they were angered by the General's failure to take this area.

Hitherto the Army Commander and the Air Force Commander had their headquarters alongside each other in the manner evolved by General Eisenhower, Air Chief Marshal Tedder, General Alexander and Coningham, in the Mediterranean. The 'responsible Soldier' and the 'responsible Airman' would thus meet for 'morning prayers', make decisions and leave it to their respective staffs to get on with the details. Also, they often met in the early evening to discuss the day's events and make some plans for the morrow. However, when in early August Coningham moved his headquarters to Normandy, he found that Montgomery had established a small tactical headquarters some distance away from his main 21 Army Group Headquarters, where he was near to his army commanders, had time to think, and could be seen by his troops. Thus the close Mediterranean relationship was gone and Coningham had to be content with infrequent visits to Monty's Tactical Headquarters and to dealing on a day-to-day basis with Montgomery's admirable Chief of Staff, General Freddie de Guingand.

Montgomery's move was soon followed by Broadhurst's opposite number, General Miles Dempsey, commanding the Second British Army, but this did not worry the airman who often saw Dempsey and sometimes flew him over the battle area in his captured Fieseler Storch. Coningham, however, was much perturbed by the split because, despite the fact that Montgomery was senior in rank, he considered he was the general's equal and did not relish having to deal with his subordinate.

Now we met and fought the Luftwaffe daily over the Normandy countryside. Whenever the weather permitted, they were active over the battle area, and we flew far to the south so as to cut them off before they could attack our ground tanks. They generally flew in small formations of no more than a dozen fighters. Consequently we flew in squadron strength, and 144 Wing seldom flew as a complete formation. I flew once or twice each day, leading the various squadrons in turn so that I did not lose my knowledge of all the pilots. The wing's total score of confirmed victories now stood at a pleasing figure, and my own personal score at twenty-nine, all of which were single-engined fighters. There was widespread speculation about how long it would be before I equalled 'Sailor' Malan's long-standing record of thirty-two victories, but I avoided discussion on the subject and tried to get on with my job. On 23 June 1944 I missed a golden opportunity of adding to my score.

It was a spanking day; the sun blazed down from a blue sky and there was a great deal of white cumulus cloud at 6,000 feet. I was leading McLeod's squadron and he led a section of two Spitfires on my starboard side. After we had left Alençon on our port side I spotted a gaggle of bandits at three o'clock. They were flying just below the base of the cloud, but five or six miles ahead the cloud ceased, and if they continued on the same course they would be sitting ducks.

Obligingly, the enemy leader held his course, and telling Blue Leader to attack the 190s on the port side, I led my six Spitfires down in a fast dive on the starboard fighters. As the range closed I automatically looked over my shoulder, to clear my tail, and then saw that the 190s were turning to starboard. Thus the 190s were now closer to McLeod than me and he hit a Focke-Wulf with his first few cannon shells. Flames poured from the cockpit; the enemy fighter turned over onto its back and fell vertically into the ground.

The Germans seemed confused by our sudden attack and remained twisting and turning. I selected a 190 just ahead of me. He was turning to port – an easy shot – and once again I cleared my tail as Douglas Bader had taught me long ago in the Tangmere Wing. All clear. I focus on the 190 but already cannon shells are tearing into his engine and wing root. Mortally hit, the flaming 190 crashes into the ground. I gave the order to re-form and set course for St Croix. I was angry, for I had spotted the bandits and brought them to battle and although several had been destroyed I, the leader, had not fired a single shot.

Back at St Croix I walked over to McLeod's Spitfire. The armourers were already busy and I tried to be nonchalant when I said,

'That 190 of yours was a piece of good shooting, Wally. I suppose you clobbered the second?'

'Yes, I got a couple of them. Did you see the second one, Chief?'

'I not only saw it Wally, I was about to shoot the bugger down,' I retorted.

'Hard luck, Sir! I saw a Spitfire behind the 190, but thought I'd better make sure of it. Of course, I didn't know it was you!'

You lying bastard, I thought. But I controlled my resentment and even managed a few words of praise when we learnt that Wally had only fired thirteen rounds of each of his two cannon: a remarkable feat of shooting which has never been equalled.

Back in my caravan I thought about the school teacher from Regina and his remarkable shooting. He could not have spared two or three seconds to clear his tail but simply went balls out against the 190s. I would, I decided, have a word with him about his lack of judgement at the kill, but this would have to be done informally at the right time and at the right place.

One of the German fighter leaders was easily identified in the air as he always flew a long-nosed Focke-Wulf 190, and our spies thought he was a well-known veteran named Matoni. Once or twice I saw him in the air, but he was cunning, elusive and hard to bring to combat unless he chose the venue.

Once airborne, I got into the habit of calling Ops and asking whether there was any news of Matoni today, and the story of my quest came to numerous press reporters in Normandy who were always on the lookout for a personal story. Several reporters came to see me and I gave them the facts, but some of the tabloid men garnished my account and wrote that I had challenged the German ace to a personal combat over Normandy. Thus I was subjected to a great deal of chaffing by my comrades, and the top brass, Broadhurst and Coningham, were displeased.

Matoni and I never fought each other because some Allied pilot in Normandy shot him down and he was wounded and sent into hospital. But soon after the end of the war he wrote to me from an address in the Ruhr and regretted that he had been unable to accept the challenge. But perhaps it was not too late for him to pay his respects? In my reply I asked him to dine with us at Lübeck, but he never turned up.

This incident had an interesting sequel. In 1985 I was strolling across Trafalgar Square, supposedly being photographed by my publishers. Unbeknown to me (but not my family) Eamonn Andrews was crouching beside a Landseer lion and intercepted me with his red book. Having participated in Eamonn's *This is Your Life* TV series, a popular biographical show, I knew that I should meet some old friends and acquaintances, amongst whom was none other than Walter Matoni. In those days the first rehearsal took place at 10 am and the participants were not allowed out of the Royal Theatre until the show finished at 9 pm;

but the bar was open all day and Walter had taken a few drams and was somewhat the worse for wear.

Each day I flew once or twice with the various squadrons and we had several sharp encounters with Me109s and Fw190s. I was a good shot, had excellent long-range eyesight, and my contemporaries said I was fast in the air. Also, I was always in the lead which meant that whenever we found enemy formations I was in the prime position. Thus the wing's score and my personal score steadily increased so that towards the end of June 1944 I drew level with the Sailor's score of thirty-two enemy aeroplanes.

On the last days of June, I was leading 441 Squadron when Ops told me that some Spitfires were having a hard time with enemy fighters six or seven miles away, and could we lend a hand?

I opened the throttle to 16lbs of boost and as we sped to the south I saw the dogfight silhouetted against a background of towering white cumulus cloud. Focke-Wulfs, Messerschmitts and Spitfires twisted and turned, and leaving six Spitfires as top cover I took the other six over to the jousting. My two section leaders, Red 3 and Red 5, soon reported suitable targets, and with their wingmen I sent them down to attack. My wingman, Bill Draper, and I were thus alone, with six Spitfires well above. I spotted a solitary Focke-Wulf and tried to stalk him from above and behind but we, in turn, were being hunted and Bill called: 'Greycap from Red Two. Two 190s turning in behind us. They're quite a way behind.'

'How far, Bill?'

'Well over a thousand yards. You have a crack. I'll tell you when to break.'

I tried to concentrate on the 109 ahead but the threat from the two yellow-nosed fighters made this impossible. My life depended on Bill's ability to assess the range of the German fighters.

'What's the form, Bill?'

'They're gaining. Break port. NOW!'

When I was a pilot officer in the Tangmere Wing, Douglas Bader had taught me that you could get on the tail of an Me109 in three steep turns, but this time after only two steep climbing turns we closed within firing range. But the enemy leader knew the form and half-rolled and dived for the deck. In such a manoeuvre they held a decided tactical advantage since their Daimler-Benz fuel injected engines continued running whereas the carburettors on our Merlin engines coughed and spluttered. So I gave up the chase.

Our tussle had drawn us further south and we flew over an unbroken layer of white cloud – a perfect backcloth on which to spot enemy aeroplanes.

A 109 sprang out of the cloud and levelled out some 2,000 feet below. We were ideally poised for a surprise attack, well hidden in the strong sun.

'One 109 at ten o'clock, Bill. Going down. All clear!'

'All clear, Greycap. I'm covering you.'

This was good teamwork. I could concentrate on the 109 and I hit his bright yellow nose with a long, steady burst of cannon. Thick black smoke poured from his engine and he dived for the protection of the cloud. We followed, which was not a wise move as I did not know the depth of the cloud and it could reach the ground. But I was under some pressure to pass Sailor's long-standing score and, perhaps subconsciously, wanted to get the 'league table', and the press, out of the way.

The cloud layer, however, was very thin and I soon saw the green and gold patchwork fields of Normandy. The badly damaged 109, trailing its banner of black smoke, was half a mile ahead and I closed in for the *coup de grace.* But the Messerschmitt was out of control, struck the ground and careered across the meadow. Then it hit a dyke, crashed into a thick hedge and pitched into the air for the last time. The wings and tail were torn apart. The fuselage twisted as it fell to the ground, where it disintegrated into hundreds of pieces.

Back at St Croix, there was much hand-shaking and back-slapping since the Messerschmitt brought my total to thirty-three victories and I was the RAF's top scorer. But I was none too pleased with this victory: McLeod summed it up when he said that it was a good thing the cloud base was high, otherwise…

The news soon spread, and within an hour a score of Allied press and radio reporters arrived at St Croix for their stories. How did I feel, they asked, about topping Malan's score of thirty-two? I was, of course, well prepared for this question and told them that there was a great deal of difference between the Sailor's defensive fighting of 1940 and our offensive fighting of 1944. He had fought with his back to the wall, at great odds, and his handful of Spitfires often tackled hundreds of Luftwaffe fighters and bombers. He was often at a tactical disadvantage, but had continued to fight until the Battle of Britain was decided and then had led the Biggin Hill Wing into 1941. On the other hand, I explained, I had only flown a few missions in 1940. I had usually fought on the offensive and after 1941 always had a squadron or a wing behind me. It was a different type of fighting. The main disadvantage was the two-way Channel crossing, sometimes several times a day, when a single bullet in the glycol tank could bring you down in the drink.

The news had spread to the village and a small deputation arrived, led by M. Raymond Turgis, the owner of our airfield, bearing gifts of flowers and, alas, the fiery Calvados apple brandy; this could only be consumed with equal quantities of cream, and several fighter pilots, including the Wing Commander (Flying), did not take to the air again on that day.

At the beginning of July we bogged down. We had only advanced about 32km into Normandy. A storm in the Channel had severely damaged the two Mulberries and that in the US sector had to be abandoned. The petrol situation was serious and some weeks later wings were grounded because of lack of fuel. Some 800,000 men were in Normandy and found it difficult to obtain space, for the beachhead was only one-fifth the size estimated by the planners. Our airfields were crowded, dangerously close to each other, and already there had been some fatal accidents.

Caen, a D-Day objective, was still held by the Germans and we could not capture the great plain stretching some thirty km south of Caen to Falaise – containing some excellent airfield country which Coningham desperately needed to reduce congestion in the beachhead. On 25 June, Montgomery said to Eisenhower: 'Blitz attack of 8 Corps goes in tomorrow, and once it starts I will continue battling on the eastern front until one of us cracks, and it will not be us.' Brave words, but after three days with high casualties and none of its objectives achieved, Operation Epsom was called off.

Montgomery called for the 'heavies' in Normandy because he and the other generals had underestimated the will and tenacity of the German army, devoid of air power, to resist in the face of overwhelming odds. However, L-M continually emphasised that bombing was not decisive but could drive a wedge into the German defences through which our own troops could not advance.

At this time the big difference between tactical and strategic bombing was that the former in good weather was accurate and precise whereas the latter was not. I have already described how the Stuka, handled by a good pilot, could plant a bomb within a circle of thirty-five yards diameter. Our Lancasters, because of their inaccurate bombing had to turn to the destruction of large cities, although the Americans with their Norden bombsight could hit a large factory or a big railway terminus. Neither the American or British heavy bombers were suitable for tactical targets, as we had seen at Cassino in Italy where the bombing attacks had created impossible obstacles to our own advance.

We had been in Normandy well over three weeks, but Caen, which should have been taken on D-Day, still held firm and barred our way to the airfield country south of the old city. Our fighter-bombers and light bombers had attacked enemy strongpoints on the outskirts of Caen many times, but the well-disciplined, tough, German troops had learned to fight without air cover and continued their stubborn resistance. It was therefore decided to reduce enemy opposition by saturating them with a heavy attack by Bomber Command.

Late one fine July evening the attack began and although my wing was providing target cover for the hundreds of Lancasters and Halifaxes, our presence was unnecessary as there was not an enemy fighter to be seen. But, as usual, there was plenty of flak and we saw a Pathfinder Mosquito shot down just short of the target.

As the bombers made their run-in from the sea, I circled to the west of the town so that I could watch the bombers from a down-sun position. We had been briefed that all the targets were contained in an area approximately two miles in length and a mile in depth, but it was soon quite apparent that a number of bombs had fallen well outside the target area, and as I watched the terrible destruction wrought on this ancient Norman city, I could not help but wonder whether we were using a sledge-hammer to crack a nut. The large *Hotel de Ville* where thousands of children were sheltering was unscathed.

During his stint with the Desert Air Force, Broady had acquired a captured Fieseler Storch. He brought the aeroplane to England and was often seen over the beachhead. The Storch carried one passenger and at this time was the best little aeroplane in the world. It could land and take off in a much shorter distance than any contemporary Allied aircraft, and was ideally suited for the AOC to hedge-hop between his airfields and army headquarters. Usually the Storch carried a VIP passenger and on one notable occasion we were delighted to see our Prime Minister, complete with cigar, in the back seat.

General Miles Dempsey, Commander of the Second British Army, had asked Broadhurst to show him the attack and they were flying together in the Fieseler Storch.

'Suddenly Dempsey said to me,' related Broadhurst, "Harry, Harry for Christsake put her down, we're being fired at!"

'I looked back and even though we were doing eighty miles per hour, the guns were all behind, and puff-puff. Well, you try and put a Storch down and it's not easy because of the high lift. So, I dived for the ground and by the time we got down to the ground there were all these chaps machine-gunning as well. Everybody was shooting at us… We landed in a cornfield.

Troops came rushing across headed by a captain and I said to Dempsey, for heaven's sake, get out and wave your red hat! If they see me in my blue uniform they'll shoot us. Well, he got out and waved his hat, looking the bloody fool. This Canadian came up and he realised something had gone wrong somewhere. He said: "I demand your identity card!" "Bimbo" Dempsey said: "Don't be a bloody fool, I'm your commanding general." We had been hit eleven times and I said to Bimbo, "Look, I can get it out of here, if you like, and push for home. We can keep it low down." He said: "I'm going with this chap!" After I got back he rang me up and said: "I can assure you no ack-ack is going to fire a bloody gun other than horizontally in my sector!"'

In mid-July we had still made little progress, and to try and break through the German defences, two operations, Goodwood and Cobra, were attempted. Goodwood began on 18 July, when Bomber Command and the Eighth and Ninth (US) Air Forces attacked the positions of Panzer Group West, south-east of Caen. By the end of that day some 4,500 Allied aeroplanes had taken part in the most awesome air attack against ground troops. After the bombing, Dempsey's Second Army with some 750 tanks would force a way through the demoralised Germans to the Caen–Falaise open plain, but two days later the attack floundered and was called off. Montgomery had previously told Eisenhower that if he could have the heavy bombers 'my whole eastern front will burst into flames', and the Supreme Commander commented: 'It had taken 7,000 tons of bombs to gain seven miles and the Allies could hardly hope to go through France paying a price of 1,000 tons of bombs per mile.'

In his report on 2nd TAF, written in 1945, Coningham tersely recorded: 'In spite of the assistance of the strategic air forces, which blew up large areas of Normandy… It was not found possible to force a breakthrough.'

Cobra, devised by General Omar Bradley to free the Americans from the dreadful bocage, got off to a bad start when carpet bombing by the Eighth Air Force killed and wounded hundreds of US soldiers through bombing errors on 24 and 25 July. The German troops, however, were demoralised, and, compared to Caen, thin on the ground and began to give way. Bradley felt that this was his opportunity and on 29 July launched four armoured divisions towards Avranches, the 'corner town' between Normandy and Brittany. At long last they were out of the hedgerow country and as the armour rolled at high speed into the enemy's rear areas the talented Brigadier General Weyland, heeding all lessons of tactical air power learned in North Africa, unleashed his fighter-bombers of the XIX Tactical Air Force:

each command tank carried an Air Force officer who was in constant touch with prowling P47s and P51s who, in open country and good weather, fell upon anything German that moved so that long straight roads were soon lined with wrecked and burned guns, tanks, armoured cars, command cars and here and there horse-drawn vehicles. This was the first time since D-Day that German defences had yielded to an Allied attack. Bradley's break-out was becoming a break-through, and waiting to fulfil his destiny was the flamboyant, pistol-packing, mercurial, aggressive, controversial Texan, Lieutenant-General George S. Patton, fighting Commander of the Third Army, anxious to make amends after the humiliation of being sacked in Sicily.

Only a generation separated him from the sixteen members of his Virginian family who had fought for the South in the Civil War. Brought up amidst the pride and traditions of his clan's military background, Patton entered West Point in 1903 – studied the tactics of Genghis Khan, the Roman Legions, Alexander, Caesar, Napoleon and Lee, and devoted himself to the military career which, he believed, was preordained for him.

In North Africa and Sicily, Patton, always straining at the leash, was highly critical of his superiors who, in turn, did not completely trust him; and after he had face-slapped two hospitalised soldiers in Sicily he was still very much on probation both with Eisenhower and General George C. Marshall, the Army Chief of Staff in Washington. The only reason Patton was in Normandy was because his superiors knew that once they broke out from the bocage, George would be leading the field.

Chapter 8

Breakout

On 7 August 1944, 200,000 men and 40,000 vehicles of the Third US Army, under the command of Lieutenant General George Patton, had passed through the left flank of the enemy south of Granville and reached the area of Lorient to the west and Brûlon halfway between Laval and Le Mans to the east.

Moving such vast nose-to-tail Allied columns would not have been possible without the complete air superiority we had established in Normandy and without the splendid relationship between Patton and Weyland. 'Opie', as the airman was known, was on excellent terms with Patton and admired his thrusting tactics. Patton too was a great exponent of joint air-ground operations and knew that, weather permitting, Weyland's aggressive fighter-bombers would support his armoured columns.

After he had taken Avranches, the Texan immediately saw the value of a long thrust east to the Seine, and when General 'Hap' Arnold, commanding the USAAF, asked him who would protect his southern flank, Patton replied, 'The Air Force takes care of my flanks!'

The Germans, however, soon appreciated that if Patton's armoured thrust could be cut off from its beachhead supplies, it could be defeated. And so it was that on the night of 6/7 August four Panzer divisions were clattering towards Mortain.

'The enemy mounted,' reported Coningham, 'an all-out attack supported by the best of his Panzer formations to cut the main American supply artery feeding the whole of Brittany and the south campaigns at the narrow Avranches gap. It was a desperate bid which, if successful, would have had a serious effect on the whole of the American sector and on the strategy of the entire Western Campaign. It was soon obvious that this German attack was a full scale effort, since five Panzer divisions were engaged, consisting of an estimated front-line strength of 250 tanks. Obviously, the enemy had drawn upon all available armour to launch a last effort counter-attack in the

Normandy sector. The relatively thin American ground strength of the First Army, which had borne the brunt of the fighting round Cherbourg, required the assistance of the maximum tactical air effort to blunt the cutting edge of the German attack.'

Fortunately for the Allies, ULTRA had intercepted the enemy messages and on the night of 6/7 August our senior commanders knew that the Panzers were about to attack. Coningham arranged with General Hoyt Vandenberg, commanding the USAAF Ninth Air Force, that P-47 Thunderbolts and P-51 Mustangs would sweep well to the south to keep enemy fighters off the backs of our Typhoons. Broadhurst had alerted his 'Tiffy' Wings, but the early morning of 7 August brought mists and low fog, ideal for the attackers, whose 2nd SS Panzer Division, 'Das Reich', had by noon recaptured Mortain from the US 30th Infantry Division; meanwhile the 2nd Panzer Division had advanced to Le Mesnil Adlée. The ground situation was critical.

Wing Commander Charles Green, 121 Wing, leading a pair of Tiffies from B5, Le Fresne-Camilly, on a weather reconnaissance paid particular attention to the Mortain area and spotted a large number of tanks. He radioed this information to his airfield, and 174 Squadron, followed by other squadrons, were soon in action.

Over Mortain, their leader, Squadron Leader Willy Pitt-Brown, spotted some sixty German tanks and about 200 vehicles lining the road between Cherénce and Saint-Barthélemy. The Tiffies were flying in pairs, number twos on the starboard of their leaders, when Willy, flying at 2,000 feet, half-rolled to port and plunged down at 450 mph towards the head of the compact column of armour. At a range of about 400 yards he and his number two fired all their anti-tank rockets, followed by bursts of cannon fire for good measure. They were followed, at ten-second intervals, by the remaining pairs. The leading enemy vehicles were set on fire and others were overturned and knocked sideways by the force of the rocket salvoes. Using classic fighter-bomber tactics, other Tiffies attacked the rear vehicles, thus sealing both exits of the German columns so that they could set about those between. Meanwhile other squadrons were getting airborne, and by the early afternoon a 'shuttle' service had developed over the stricken legion.

Squadron Leader Michael Ingle-Finch, an experienced Typhoon pilot who led 175 Squadron against the column, said: 'We could see Tiger tanks and armour on a track through the woods. We attacked with our rockets and then strafed with our cannon and did a fair amount of damage. We knew that some of our rockets had not exploded on impact, and after the battle we drove to

Mortain to see the damage. We found that although some of our rocks had not exploded when they hit the gun turret, the impact knocked a big hole in the turret, the metal inside the tank flaked and pieces of hot metal flew all over the place and killed the crew. We met officers of the US 30th Division who were loud in their praise of our Tiffies and some told us how they actually saw German crews jumping from their tanks before we opened fire.'

Geoffrey Murphy, 245 Squadron, wrote:

'During the first sortie... two aircraft, flown by Flying Officer Temple and Flight Lieutenant Lee, were shot down. Temple was killed ... Lee was wounded and, with his engine put out of action, force-landed in open country between the German and Allied fronts. After touching down, his aircraft turned over on its back and he was trapped inside, hanging from his safety straps, with a broken leg as well as minor wounds. With some difficulty, he managed to turn himself in the cockpit so that he was eventually sitting upright. Unable to get out of the aircraft because the cockpit sides were flush on the ground, he banged on the sides of the fuselage to try to attract the attention of possible rescuers. German troops in the vicinity fired on the wreckage and Lee sustained further slight wounds. Some five days later, having managed to exist on the emergency and survival rations carried at that time by pilots, he heard voices speaking English, and once more, although very weak, managed to bang on the sides of the cockpit loudly enough to attract the attention of some advancing American troops who dug a hole under the cockpit and managed to extricate him. In desperate need of medical attention, he was in very poor shape, and after being taken to a field hospital, was evacuated by air to England where he made a satisfactory recovery, having been awarded the Distinguished Flying Cross for his exploit.'

Usually the Typhoons flew in squadron strength of twelve fighter-bombers, but Broadhurst did not want his squadrons to waste time on the ground while all twelve aeroplanes were being rearmed and refuelled. He therefore ordered the Tiffies to operate in pairs and fours, keeping a 'shuttle service' over the enemy armour.

As the tempo of the attacks increased, 'The fighter bombers of the 2nd Tactical Air Force', wrote Coningham, 'adopted a "shuttle service" of attacking formations, and as the day developed it was obvious that air history was being made. As the tempo of the attacks increased so did the morale of the tank crews diminish, and at the height of the battle... the enemy were not waiting to stand our fire.'

Murphy, flying on another sortie in the late afternoon, wrote:

'I remember the sky being almost black, the haze of the lowering sun being intensified by the smoke from the burning oil and fuel of tanks and trucks and appearing to press down on the earth all around, like a dark shroud. On this sortie, eleven large trucks, trapped between others burning at either end of a convoy, were either badly damaged or set on fire.'

After hours of repeated Tiffy attacks, Charles Green reported that the battle area was so covered in dust and smoke that their targets were almost invisible. However, at about the same time, Broady heard that a control car near Vire was asking for immediate air support against a German attack. He immediately switched some Typhoons to Vire. The tanks were destroyed and the attack petered out.

In the late afternoon the Mortain countryside was punctuated with black columns of smoke rising into the blue sky. It was the first occasion in Normandy when the Typhoons had the opportunity of attacking a German column. It was also a situation requiring flexibility and concentration of firepower, and the Typhoons were equal to the task.

For the opposition, Generalmajor Rudolf von Gersdorff, Seventh Army Chief of Staff, reported: 'The air situation in the afternoon of 7 August stopped the whole counter-attack.'

Eisenhower and Bradley saw that Hitler's blunder at Mortain had left the German Seventh Army in a very dangerous situation because they could be encircled by the First Canadian Army, the Second British Army (who, at last, were making some progress south of Caen) and Haislip's XV Corps at Le Mans. Thus, on 8 August, Bradley, seizing his opportunity, instructed Patton to head north to close the 'pocket' between his Third Army and the Canadians.

The Germans, as usual, fought savagely against the Canadians, and on 12 August they were stalled at Falaise while Haislip's XV Corps was at Argentan and prepared to join up with the Canadians at Falaise, thus closing the gap. Haislip asked Patton for further instructions and was told to 'push on slowly in the direction of Falaise... upon arrival... push on slowly until you contact our Allies'. But when Bradley learned of Patton's intentions he made the most controversial decision of the campaign when he ordered the Texan not to proceed north of Argentan.

The Canadians did not capture Falaise until 16 August, which left some fifteen miles between the American and Canadian Armies – the now famous Argentan–Falaise gap, through which the Germans began a massive withdrawal, until, on 19 August, the gap was finally sealed by the Allies.

Harry Broadhurst, closely monitoring the drama from his headquarters, began to get reports from his tactical reconnaissance Mustangs that Germans armour was retreating eastwards in the Chambois area. However, the ground situation was uncertain because leading elements of the Polish Armoured Division also reported their position near Chambois when they were, in fact, some distance away at a place with a very similar name, and when Broadhurst telephoned General Crerar, commanding the First Canadian Army, the latter would not agree that the Typhoons should be let loose. Crerar's decision was perhaps understandable because his Canadians had been bombed, suffering heavy casualties, by both Bomber Command and the Eighth Air Force, bringing into doubt, and not for the first time, the wisdom of employing heavy bombers, with their imperfect bombing techniques, in close support of land forces.

The identity of the east-bound columns had to be established beyond all doubt, so Broadhurst immediately dispatched his most experienced ground-attack leader, Charles Green, who soon reported that the retreating columns were German and on being pressed by his AOC said, 'I saw their black crosses – and the square heads of their drivers.'

Broadhurst immediately telephoned Montgomery and said, 'The Germans are breaking out at Chambois and this is a great opportunity for the fighter-bombers, but the bomb-line is confused and some of our troops may get hurt. Do you want me to go ahead?'

Montgomery said he could call back in fifteen minutes, which he did, and trusting Broadhurst, said: 'Go, there will be no recriminations.'

On 19 August the pocket was finally closed by the junction of the Second British Army and the US First Army between Chambois and the Forêt de Gouffern. As the pocket decreased in size, we pilots had difficulty in differentiating between friend and foe, both in the air and on the ground; it was therefore decided that American fighter pilots would concentrate against targets in the pocket while we British prevented movement through the gap.

When we arrived over that small triangle of Normandy bounded by Falaise, Trun and Chambois, the Typhoons were already hard at work. As at Mortain, they used the tactic of sealing off the front and rear of a column by accurately dropping a few bombs thus imprisoning the desperate enemy on the narrow dusty lanes, and since the transports were sometimes jammed together four abreast, it made the subsequent rocket and cannon attacks comparatively easy. Some of the armoured cars and tanks attempted to escape their fate by making detours across the fields and wooded country, but these were soon spotted by the Typhoon pilots and were accorded the same treatment as their comrades on the highways and lanes.

Immediately the Typhoons withdrew from the killing-ground the Spitfires raced into the attack. The tactics of the day were low-level strafing attacks with cannon shells and machine guns against soft-skinned transports, including all types of trucks, staff cars and light armoured vehicles. Here and there amongst the shambles on the ground were a few of the deadly Tiger tanks, and although the cannon shells would have little effect against their tough armour plate, a few rounds were blasted against them for good measure. As soon as the Spitfires had fired all their ammunition, they flew back at high speed to their airfields, where the ground crews worked flat-out in the hot sunshine to rearm and refuel the aircraft in the shortest possible time. The Typhoons with their rockets did far more damage than our Spitfires.

Throughout the day and on all subsequent operations in the 'Falaise Gap' the Luftwaffe failed to provide any degree of assistance to their sorely pressed ground forces. Faced with the threat of losing their forward airfields to our advance, they were busily occupied with withdrawing to suitable bases in the Paris area, so our fighter-bombers enjoyed complete air supremacy over the battle area. Quick to exploit such a great tactical advantage, Broadhurst once again issued instructions that until such time as the Luftwaffe reappeared to contest our domination of the Normandy sky we would shuttle by operating in pairs and if necessary singly. Detailed briefings were unnecessary since all the pilots knew the area and the position of our own ground troops. Valuable time was saved, and it was possible to put the maximum number of missions into the air. Before Falaise an individual fighter pilot had rarely flown on more than three or four missions on any one day, but now it was not uncommon for a pilot to fly six times between dawn and dusk.

The bocage, in full foliage, afforded some cover to the Germans, who tied large green branches and shrubs on their trucks in an effort to conceal them from the eyes of our pilots. A gleam of reflected sunshine on metal here, a swirl or eddy of dust there, or fresh tracks leading across the fields were sufficient evidence to bring down the fighter-bombers with their assorted armoury of weapons. When darkness fell and brought some relief to the battered Germans there was time to take stock of the situation and to add up the score. The pilots turned in immediately after dinner, for they would require all their energy for the new day. As they settled down to sleep they heard the continuous drone of our light bombers making their flight across the beachhead to harry the enemy columns through the short night.

The pattern was much the same on the following day. We breakfasted well before the dawn, and the first pair of Spitfires retracted their wheels as the first hint of a lighter sky flushed the eastern horizon. The Germans were making strenuous efforts to salvage what equipment they could from the debacle and get it across the Seine. Broady had anticipated this move and some Typhoons were diverted to attacking barges and small craft as they ferried to and fro across the river. Once more our fighter-bomber pilots turned their attention to the killing-ground and attacked all manner of enemy transports wherever they were to be found. They were located on the highways and lanes, in the woods and copses, in small villages and hamlets, beneath the long shadows of tall hedges, in farmyards, and even camouflaged with newly mown grass to resemble haystacks. During the previous night many of the enemy had decided to abandon a great proportion of their transports: they could be seen continuing the retreat on foot and in hastily commandeered farm-carts. Sometimes the despairing enemy waved white sheets at the fighter-bombers as they hurtled down to attack; but these signs were ignored; our ground troops were still some distance away and there was no organization available to round up large numbers of prisoners.

On this day, 19 August, thousands of transports were destroyed or damaged, of which many were left burning. Afterwards our efforts in the Falaise gap gradually petered out, for the transports and personnel of the German Seventh Army had either been eliminated or had withdrawn across the Seine. The Falaise gap ranks as one of the greatest killing-grounds of the war, and is a classic example of the devastating effects of tactical air power when applied in concentrated form against targets of this nature.

In his report, Coningham said: 'One contribution of the Second Tactical Air Force to the two great victories of Mortain and the Falaise pocket, including the pursuit to the Seine during the month of August 1944, was the destruction of 10,500 of Germany's sorely needed transport and 850 of her first line armoured vehicles.'

Always there when it was wanted, whether in the thick of the ground fighting, facing the murderous flak, or seeking out and destroying reinforcements moving up to the front, the rocket-firing Typhoon was decisive in Normandy. Later, the wise, astute Harry Broadhurst said: 'I suppose that flying one of these aircraft was the most dangerous task the Royal Air Force has ever asked anybody to do.' We had some 400 Typhoons in Normandy; 130 pilots were killed and five are still missing to this day.

After the fighting had ebbed away from Falaise, some of us drove out to the killing grounds to see the results of our attacks at first hand.

The slaughter has been described over and over again in graphic detail, and no one who saw it will ever forget it. The Supreme Commander, Dwight Eisenhower, said it could only be described by Dante.

So ended the Battle of Normandy. A triumph for tactical air power, both British and American. A triumph for Patton and his Third Army, who could have closed the Falaise Gap had not Bradley stopped them.

The victory, however, was marred by the feuding air marshals and generals which, had it gone much further, could have adversely affected our operational capabilities.

Coningham was admired by all of his senior officers and they thought he was a very good AOC of the Desert Air Force. He was the first senior RAF officer to fully understand the Army's problems; but his weakness was that he always regarded Army/Air Force operations as a joint affair and therefore considered himself the equal of the Army Commander. The fallacy of his case was that the Army had to fight for and hold the ground and it was the Air Force's job to give them the utmost support. Thus, in these tactical matters, the Air Force was the junior partner. Coningham, unlike Broadhurst, simply would not accept that the Army was the senior partner; he lost Montgomery's confidence, and so the General turned to Harry Broadhurst. We noticed that whenever Montgomery visited our airfields he was always accompanied by our AOC, not our C-in-C.

The four-star, austere soldier – soon to become a Field Marshal – and the two-star *bon vivant* airman got on well together. They were of different generations – twenty years separated their ages. Neither smoked. The soldier rarely took a glass of wine, whereas Broady loved a good party. Montgomery knew Broadhurst from their desert days and trusted him.

This state of affairs did not please either Tedder or Coningham, both of whom had little regard for Montgomery, especially after his painfully slow progress in Normandy and his failure to take Caen. But Broadhurst thought he was the best general we had and always supported him. One day when all the brass were gathered together, the four-star Tedder turned to the two-star Broadhurst and said, 'How's your bloody little Army friend today?'

Broadhurst replied; 'Well, what do you expect him to be, my enemy?', and walked angrily away.

Montgomery was well aware that the two Air Marshals, Tedder and Coningham, were after his blood. He connived with the Secretary of State for War to get rid of Coningham, and, to make matters worse with the feuding top brass, another four-star character took a hand in the proceedings. This was none other than the cordial Leigh-Mallory who headed a completely unnecessary organization called the Allied Expeditionary Air Force which was superimposed on Coningham's Second Tactical Air Force. L-M, of course, had more authority than Coningham and, for example, could call on heavy bombers of both Bomber Command and the Eighth Army Air Force.

Later, Broady told me that Tedder and Coningham were conniving to get rid of both Montgomery and Leigh-Mallory. The two senior airmen would never forgive Montgomery for the lack of RAF recognition at Alamein, and Coningham is on record asking 'for a greater sense of urgency from the Army and a frank admission that their operations were not running according to plan!'

Montgomery initially disliked Leigh-Mallory, referring to him as a 'gutless bugger', but later on when Leigh-Mallory supported his request for help from Bomber Command he changed his tune and, apparently forgetting Broadhurst, recorded: 'We must definitely keep Leigh-Mallory. He is the only airman who is out to help us win the land battle and has no jealous reactions!' Montgomery, now already alienated from Coningham, dealt with Broadhurst on tactical matters and Leigh-Mallory on heavy bomber support. Not a very tidy arrangement and certainly not to the liking of Tedder and Coningham who plotted to get rid of L-M and his superfluous headquarters.'

Broady felt that Coningham's long-standing feud with Montgomery was bad for the whole of the Second Tactical Air Force, and he was not happy about being in the middle of the squabble. Coningham resented the good relationship between Broadhurst and Montgomery.

Coningham, excellent in the desert, failed in Normandy because his dislike of Montgomery clouded his better judgement, and also he could not realise that he was not Montgomery's 'equal'. His post-war report was so anti-Montgomery that it was never published.

Harry Broadhurst, 'the soldiers' friend', was the single airman who understood the army's problems in the bocage where his pilots could not get at the enemy, but he constantly assured Montgomery that once in open country his fighter-bombers would come into their own. Broadhurst's simple philosophy was that since the army was doing most of the fighting, his job, once they had made their plan, was to give them the fullest air support. He told me that Montgomery, with all his faults, was the best general we had.

After Normandy, L-M's superfluous AEAF was disbanded and he was posted to South East Asia. Some of us, at the fighting level, had known him since the Battle of Britain. We all had a soft spot for this kindly, shy man, and were very sad when we heard that he was killed, together with his wife and crew, when his aeroplane crashed in France en route to his new command.

Chapter 9

'A Bridge Too Far'

Two days after my stiff fight over the Seine, Paris was liberated, and in early September 1944 the Welsh Guards were the first to receive the spontaneous and tremendous welcome which awaited us in Brussels. The battle for France was won and it was time for the Wing to move.

Broady telephoned and said our new home was at Illiers L'Évêque, some four miles west of Paris, so Bill MacBrien and I flew to survey the airfield before we moved the squadrons: it had been heavily bombed and the runways were pitted with craters, but the Royal Engineers had filled some of the holes and made a narrow PSP runway across the grass, and so we left the dusty, crowded beachhead, which had been our home for nearly three months, and began our nomadic trek to Germany.

We were able to operate from Illiers for only two days before the vanguard of the British Army were well beyond the limited range of our Spitfires and we became non-operational until a suitable airfield could be found.

Illiers L'Évêque lay in some pleasant country with woods and streams and there was time to take stock and investigate the shooting and fishing prospects. Indeed, the first time I landed at Illiers I noticed several strong coveys of partridge scuttling over the stubbles and a fair number of pheasants were spotted near the woods: this game had not been shot for a long time and so we enjoyed some excellent walking-up sport when Sally came into her own. The cooks shook their heads in dismay whenever they saw us set out on these sorties, for they knew they would have to pluck and dress the game. One evening we returned with more than fifty brace, and two days later all the officers dined on roast partridge assisted by excellent champagne which had been given to us by a local Frenchman.

Two of our young doctors found a well-stocked trout stream and returned to our tented camp with baskets of brown trout some weighing up to two pounds (I have often wondered why most doctors seem to be able fly fisherman). There were good autumn vegetables available from the local farms and with all this excellent food we had to have some suitable wines, so Flight Lieutenant Larry Robillard was appointed Wines Officer, given a jeep and thousands of cigarettes (supplied free to the Canadians) and told to get on with it. He was highly successful and on his first sortie returned with a dozen cases of good champagne whose labels were stamped *Réserve pour le Wermacht*. I did not ask any questions about this particular transaction!

On another occasion he suggested visiting the Benedictine Monastery near Fécamp to try and get some of that excellent liqueur and this trip would give him the opportunity of visiting the villages of Lillères and St Pierre des Auxchelles where he could thank the courageous people who, in 1941, when he was brought down by 'Dolfo' Galland, had tended his wounds and helped him to evade capture and return to England. He wanted to be accompanied by Fred Kearns and Bob Fuller, both of 443 Squadron – a formidable trio indeed.

Larry had learned that the good monks were short of sugar – used in the making of the liquor – and a jeep was soon loaded with a couple of sacks of that commodity and other necessities. Wally McLeod and I saw them off with instructions to be back within a week as we were expecting an imminent move to Belgium.

During the air fighting over Normandy Wally had increased his score to twenty-one victories; he was a very taut man who, even at Illiers, found it hard to relax and continually badgered me for news of our next move so that he could have the opportunity of passing 'Screwball' Beurling's score of thirty-one victories and, doubtless, mine of thirty-seven.

Sometimes Wally would come with us when Sally and I walked the stubbles and I soon discovered that, as in the air, he was an excellent shot and very fast, but he was more interested in examining his cine films – trying to discover if he could have dispatched an opponent with less rounds. He checked and rechecked the harmonisation with his cannon and machine guns, and together with his ground crew polished and repolished his Spitfire because he thought he could get another five or six mph out of her.

The Luftwaffe were now in the process of making a most remarkable recovery after their defeat in Normandy and their hurried retreat to airfields east of the Rhine. The month of September witnessed a great effort by the German aircraft industry, and the production of single engined fighters attained record proportions. Fighter squadrons received ample supplies of aircraft: many of the units which had been decimated in France were re-equipped and able to return to the battle. A tremendous attempt was made to increase the size and efficiency of the fighter force even at the expense of the bomber and night fighter components. The German High Command was confident that their V weapons would be sufficient for offensive operations, and a proportion of bomber pilots were quickly converted to the fighter role. So the Luftwaffe was far from being a spent force: indeed, back at Illiers we heard ominous reports of the first appearances of fast, jet aircraft.

After two weeks of rest and relaxation at Illiers we were anxious to get back to the contest, so I flew to Brussels to try and see Broadhurst and tell him that our guns were rusting. I tracked down the great man who said that our airborne troops were in trouble at Arnhem, in the Netherlands, and we were to move to Le Culot, an ex-Luftwaffe airfield ten miles south of Louvain in Belgium, just as soon as the bomb craters were filled in. Thus, on 22 September 1944, five days after the big airborne drop at Arnhem, we established ourselves at Le Culot where we heard the grim news that the 1st Airborne Division had been dropped nearly eight miles west of their objective and were in grave danger.

From 127 Wing's operations staff, which included two Army officers, I soon learned that Operation *Market Garden*, conceived by Montgomery and backed by Eisenhower, was aimed at outflanking the German positions ahead by seizing the main bridges over the rivers Maas, Waal and the Lower Rhine by airborne assault, thus opening the way for Montgomery's armies to advance to the Ruhr and, hopefully, finish the war before the onset of winter.

MARKET, the airborne part of the operation, fell to the 101st US Airborne Division who were to capture the canal bridges north of Eindhoven, the 82nd US Airborne Division were to take the river bridges at Grave and Nijmegen, and the 1st British Airborne Division, with the 1st Polish Parachute Brigade, were to capture the most northern bridge at Arnhem.

GARDEN was the code name for the advance of Lieutenant General Brian Horrocks' 30 Corps from his start-line on the Meuse-Escaut Canal to Arnhem – and he had three days in which to cover those 59 miles. There was great optimism about this massive airlift and much talk about we British being in Berlin in a matter of weeks.

Due to insufficient aeroplanes, the 1st Airborne Division were to be landed in three lifts on dropping zones some eight miles to the west of Arnhem, and although Major General Roy Urquhart, commanding the division, had protested about this distance, he was told there were no other suitable sites. He had some excellent battalion commanders and senior officers, including Dickie Lonsdale, David Dobie and John Frost, all of whom I had met during their training at Melton Mowbray. Thus I had a personal interest in this operation.

Overall command was by the debonair Lieutenant General 'Boy' Browning, previously a Grenadier, whose Corps Headquarters would occupy no less than thirty gliders. Browning had received reports that the 9th and 10th Panzer Divisions were in the area but had dismissed these as being unreliable.

On the narrow road corridor, from Eindhoven to Arnhem, there were five major road bridges to capture. It was the fifth bridge over the Lower Rhine at Arnhem, sixty-four miles behind the enemy lines, that worried Browning and at a high-level briefing he pointed to the bridge and asked:

> 'How long will it take the armour to reach us?'
> 'Two days,' replied Montgomery.
> 'We can hold it for four,' said Browning, and then prophetically added:
> 'But, Sir, I think we might be going a bridge too far.'

On 22 September, six days after the first drop, I was up well before dawn, so that I could be briefed on the latest news from Arnhem. It was cold on that early morning and I was glad to be wearing my Irving fur-lined jacket. The cold heralded the on-coming winter and for the first time I realised that we would not be crossing the Rhine this year.

The situation at Arnhem, I heard, was bad. The initial drop on 17 September of 16,500 paratroopers and 3,500 troops in gliders was very accurate, but soon things went wrong. The plan had been made in the UK without consulting Coningham, despite that the drop was taking place in his area of responsibility and whose advice would certainly have included that since we did not have radars near Arnhem our fighters would have to rely on RT intercept, taking bearings from enemy radio telephone chatter. It would also have included that the Arnhem flak defences were formidable – as we found whenever we flew near the Dutch town. No proper arrangements had been made to enable our Typhoons to give close air support and the paratroopers had to send a request back to London which was then sent to 2nd TAF and then to 83 Group, and was always lacking in the precise details we requested and out of date.

Some airborne troops were dropped or landed in gliders far from their objectives, and their wireless sets did not work because they had the wrong crystals so, unlike Normandy, fighter-bomber leaders could not talk to the hard-pressed men on the ground. Thus the vital tools of tactical air support – reliable air-ground communications, good intelligence and RAF controllers with their airborne troops who could give instructions to the waiting 'cab ranks' of our fighter-bombers – were missing, making close air support, as we knew it in Normandy, almost impossible.

Two SS Panzer divisions were refitting in the area and, when the first landings occurred, an SS NCO training school was actually exercising at Oosterbeek, between the British landing and drop zones and Arnhem, in repelling an airborne assault – suddenly they had a real-life scenario and were perfectly-placed to deal with it. Our intelligence on their presence before the landings had been ignored, and to make matters worse, the capture of a US officer in improper possession of the operational order gravely endangered *Market Garden*.

The German counter-attack was swifter and fiercer than expected and the Luftwaffe had reinforced the area with fighters, including the formidable Messerschmitt 262 – the first jet fighter to be seen in this war. Also, the autumn weather was upon us bringing much cloud, rain and poor visibility. The NCO training school commander, Sepp Krafft, on exercise with his young Panzer Grenadiers, reacted rapidly and decisively: having guessed that the British objective was Arnhem Bridge, Krafft immediately established a blocking line, preventing the 1st and 3rd Parachute Battalions reaching Arnhem. (Only John Frost's 2nd Parachute Battalion was able to pass below Krafft's wall of steel, along the river road to Arnhem. Consequently, on that first day, only 500 or so British troops actually reached Arnhem Bridge, seizing the northern end, instead of a whole brigade of three battalions, as planned. Krafft's inspired reaction bought time for the Germans to pour reinforcements into the area, including armour, preventing subsequent landings reinforcing Frost at the all-important Bridge. Frost's small garrison was immediately cut off therefore, the Divisional battle becoming focussed around a thumb-shaped pocket at Oosterbeek, the base of which was the Rhine, in the hope of maintaining a bridgehead for 2nd Army to throw across Bailey bridges, and preserve what was left of the Urquhart's force. Ultimately, Frost held out at the Bridge far longer than was originally anticipated, but eventually, against overwhelming odds, the garrison was lost, and the rest of Urquhart's battered division evacuated across the Rhine.)

It seemed to us fighter pilots that the idea of pushing a vulnerable airborne force far out on a limb in doubtful weather and only approachable along the narrow exposed Dutch roads, with their countless bridges, was asking for trouble. There were still several pockets of well-armed Germans nearby; the road between Eindhoven and Nijmegen was still under intermittent shellfire.

On the day of the drop, the Guards Armoured Division were based on the Meuse-Escaut Canal, some fifty-nine miles from Arnhem. The plan was for the Guards to link up with the airborne forces, and at the same time the 101st US Airborne Division would land between Eindhoven and Veghel, and the 82nd US Airborne Division would drop around Grave and Groesbeek.

By the beginning of the third day, 19 September, the situation was bad both on the ground and in the air. The dropping zone, for resupply, was still in the hands of the Germans, and the radio frequency used by the Division clashed with another powerful frequency.

Those of us who flew at Arnhem were very much aware of the desperate situation on the ground, and because we shared an affinity with the airborne soldiers we pressed our attacks home closer than usual in the teeth of severe flak which, as usual, took a heavy toll.

On this day Flight Lieutenant Lord, captain of a Dakota from 271 Squadron, was briefed to drop supplies. When near Arnhem, flying at 1,500 feet, his aeroplane was the target for light flak, heavy flak, machine-gun fire and rifle fire. The starboard engine was set on fire, but with the dropping zone only three miles away the captain pressed on. With the engine burning fiercely he came down to 900 feet, where the flak was very fierce and highly dangerous. Undeterred the gallant crew dropped all but two of their containers and once again made their run-in. Their Dakota remained for another eight minutes under heavy and continuous fire. The captain ordered his crew to bale out but he himself made no effort to do so. The Dakota crashed in flames and there was only one survivor. Flight Lieutenant Lord was awarded a posthumous Victoria Cross.

Late in the afternoon of this fateful day a new supply dropping point was arranged, but after a drop by Stirlings it was captured by the enemy.

Meanwhile at the great Bridge, Lieutenant Colonel John Frost and his troops had seized the northern end and established his Battalion Headquarters. He had only to hold out for another forty-eight hours until the tanks of 30 Corps arrived.

The Guards left the start line at 1435 hours, drove up the straight highway, stopped for a brew-up, and at nightfall had only advanced seven miles; in the following days they managed another twenty-three miles, leaving them thirty-four miles short of the vital bridge.

The greatest mistake was the failure to coordinate the might of the 2nd TAF based on nearby airfields with the airborne effort. Here were numerous squadrons of pilots, highly trained in air-ground operations who, on the sunny Saturday afternoon of the first drop, did not even know that *Market Garden* was taking place. Indeed, we of the 2nd TAF were banned from the Arnhem area on the day of the first drop, and on all the seven subsequent reinforcement and resupply flights from the UK, because the planners, back in England, feared a clash between British and US fighters – despite that we had been fighting alongside each other for two years.

The historian Richard Lamb aptly describes this tragic affair: 'Montgomery's decision to take the Arnhem option, despite warnings from his staff and of evidence of enemy strength, resulted in resounding defeat. He wasted the Allies' strategic reserve, a force which could have brought victory in 1944 and sacrificed the cream of the British Army.'

We subsequently found it hard to understand how our own commander-in-chief, Coningham, accepted that all his squadrons would be barred from Arnhem during the drops until released from England, thus denying the paratroopers and glider soldiers of the very essence of successful air-ground operations – close air support. When I discussed the debacle with Broady, I said: 'I have often wondered why an organization that could cross the Channel and build airfields in twenty-four hours could not get the few miles to Arnhem.'

'I was dead against it,' replied my practical AOC: 'It was too late in the season to rely on good weather. We had no radar up there and had to rely on RT intercept. There was far more enthusiasm than judgement about the operation.'

It was from Le Culot on 27 September 1944 that we lost the fearless Wally McLeod over Nijmegen. There was a thick heavy cloud base at about 12,000 feet and I had no idea of the height of the tops and therefore decided to fly just below it. We were flying in two sixes – me leading the squadron and Wally the other six. The visibility was excellent and we could see a long way up the Rhine and over the rain-sodden flat landscapes of Holland and Germany. The controller broke the silence:

'Kenway to Greycap. Bandits active in the Emmerich area. They appear to be flying down the Rhine, towards you. Steer one three zero.'

'Greycap to Kenway. Roger. How many?'

'A small gaggle Greycap. Not more than a dozen. Out.'

I turned the Spitfires to the south-east and we flew up the Rhine, which was swollen by the recent heavy rains. To the east, Germany looked dark and foreboding. Suddenly Don Walz said:

'Greycap from Red Three. Nine 109s below.'

'OK Don. I have them. Wally, take the starboard gaggle. I'll take the buggers on the port.'

The enemy were flying on the same course as ourselves and were in two small line-abreast sections, one of five aircraft and the other of four. We were twelve Spitfires and had all the essentials of tactical success – speed, height and surprise. We tore down into a line-astern attack, and just before we closed to firing range I saw the leader of the enemy starboard section pull his Messerschmitt into a vertical climb. I knew this manoeuvre. The enemy pilot would half-roll at the top of his loop, having gained vital altitude. He would then aileron-turn his Messerschmitt and come down in a fast dive searching for a Spitfire. My own target was very close, but before I blasted him with my cannons I found time to cry:

> 'Watch that brute, Wally. He knows the form!'

I hit my opponent with a good heavy burst of cannons and machine guns. He started to burn immediately, but I was thinking of the danger from above and with throttle wide open I pulled my Spitfire into a near-vertical climb and got into the sanctuary of the cloud. It seemed as if I was upside down, so I eased the stick forward and fell out of the cloud into the clear sky. I went into a tight circle, cleared my tail and searched for either Messerschmitt or Spitfire, but there was no sign of other fighters. Wally did not answer to my repeated calls on the radio.

Since it was a dangerous place for a lone Spitfire I set course for Le Culot at high speed, leaving several burning wrecks on the ground; half an hour later ten pilots of 443 Squadron met me and we examined the fight in great detail. Wally's wingman had temporarily blacked out in the tight pull-out, and when he recovered he could not find his CO. Other pilots claimed victories and it seemed that our score was five for the loss of a very experienced Squadron Commander.

I told the downcast pilots that I would call the Duty Controller and keep them posted; he was an old friend from the Kenley Wing and would check all sources immediately. Soon after, he called back saying with regret that there was no information about Wally.

After the last patrol of the day I walked through the dusk to the mess tent. The ten pilots of 443 Squadron were very gloomy so I said to the senior Flight Commander:

> 'Don, get the CO's jeep and all of you change into decent uniforms. We will rendezvous here in half an hour and have a meal and a drink or two in Louvain. We could all get into two jeeps.'

They were spruced up well within the appointed time and we drove through the black night into Louvain. It was our first excursion into this old university town, and we knew nothing of the amenities of the place. After some reconnoitring we parked our jeeps, and entered a small establishment called *Le Café des Sept Coins.* Inside it was cheerful and warm, but the animated conversation ceased at our entry. There was a complete silence as we threaded our way past the crowded tables to the bar. Our blue uniforms were strange to the local populace. But the proprietor, an affable little man by the name of Marcel, singled me out for interrogation as I ordered a round of drinks in my halting French. I explained that we were fighter pilots of both the RAF and the RCAF.

Marcel held up his hand for silence and announced to his customers that he was greatly honoured with a visit from the Royal Air Force. Moreover, we were Spitfire pilots and that afternoon had been in action against the hated Germans. We had achieved a great victory, and so on.

All this was rendered with splendid Gallic zest. The best in the house was at our disposal.

'What food will you have?' asked Marcel.

'Steak,' replied the Canadians.

'And to follow?' enquired Marcel. 'I have plenty of provisions.'

'More steak!' said the Canadians. 'Medium rare.'

Madame and her two daughters emerged from the kitchen and the necessary introductions were made with a degree of formality. Soon tender steaks were placed before us and we fell to, since we were very hungry. Afterwards, as I sipped a liqueur and inhaled a good cigar, both provided by our generous host, I glanced round the table at my small band of Canadians, none of whom was more than 22 or 23 years of age. Their high spirits and vitality had responded to our pleasant surroundings and already they were engaged in deep conversation with the citizens of Louvain. For a few moments my own thoughts focused on the morning's fight with the 109s. I feared that Wally was dead. I drank a silent toast to his memory and the encounters with the Luftwaffe we had shared together.

As the evening wore on, the tempo increased and we were entertained by various songs from our Belgian friends. We responded with some of our more suitable ditties and towards midnight the café was heavy with smoke and warmth. Abruptly the swing doors burst open to admit several gendarmes headed by a *sergent de ville.* Their faces were solemn. What, the sergeant demanded, was all the commotion about? He could hear the din from the other side of the city square. Marcel explained the situation and we were introduced to the officers of the law. The tall sergeant threw back his heavy cape, reached for his hip pocket and produced a large notebook. For one uneasy moment we thought the book was to be used for official purposes, but the sergeant extracted a few franc notes, ordered a round of drinks, and proposed the health of the Royal Air Force!

Eventually, it was time to take our leave of this hospitable little tavern. We struggled into the two jeeps, feeling considerably lighter in heart than when we had left Le Culot. It was raining quite heavily as we sped through the deserted cobbled streets of Louvain. The second jeep roared past mine, swerved and heeled over at a dangerous angle as it negotiated a tricky bend in the road. Peering through the rain-lashed windscreen, I saw a body pitch out of the leading jeep directly in front of me. I swung the wheel over to the right and braked violently to avoid the unfortunate pilot in the road. My vehicle skidded out of control, struck the steep pavement at the edge of the road, pitched violently into the air and fell over on its side. Fortunately, we were all thrown clear and we hit the greasy cobbles in loose, relaxed bundles of flesh. Apart from a broken finger, a cracked head and a cut or two here and there, we were none the worse for our mishap. We heaved my jeep on to its four wheels, but before continuing our journey I issued strict convoy instructions to the other driver. We would proceed in line-astern at a steady pace at not more than thirty miles an hour, and there would be no overtaking. We arrived safely at Le Culot in the early hours of the morning, where we rousted the squadron's doctor from his warm bed to minister to our cuts and bruises. The injured were bandaged or sewn up to the accompaniment of cries of encouragement from their more fortunate comrades, but soon it was all over and I sent them packing to bed to catch a little sleep. The Doc had brewed up a pot of steaming coffee and we sipped a mug together after the others had departed. He opened the conversation.

'Bad thing about the CO. He will be hard to replace; the boys would follow him anywhere. What do you think happened?'

'Hard to say, Doc,' I replied. 'The sky's a big place once you're split up, but I think the Messerschmitt got him. It was always all or nothing with Wally.'

'Anyway, your party was a good thing and you certainly got it out of their systems. They'll be all right now.'

'Yes. I figured a good old-fashioned thrash was the only thing for them. Good-night, and thanks for patching up the lads'.

I walked across the wet grass to my caravan, undressed, removed a pained Sally from my bed and immediately fell into a deep sleep.

In 1949 the wreckage of a Spitfire was discovered on the outskirts of Wesel, just inside Germany – and the gallant Wally's remains were found within. The 28-year-old fearless Squadron Leader Henry Wallace McLeod DSO DFC & Bar – the 'Eagle of Malta' – was buried at Rheinberg. According to researchers, Wally had been shot down by the German ace Major Siegfried Freytag of JG77, and was the German's 101st victory.

Back on the ranch in New Jersey, Squadron Leader J. Danforth 'Danny' Browne DFC, who, when he had left us in Normandy, said he would not be returning to Europe because the girls in the US had better legs, sat in the cinema one evening and saw a newsreel about Allied progress in Holland and, like many other warriors, felt a strong urge to return to the exclusive comradeship of fighting men.

He had a return ticket on the *Queen Elizabeth* so he took a train to New York, boarded the great liner, with thousands of troops on board, and once in England instead of reporting to RCAF HQ in London made his way to Redhill, where he knew there was a daily Anson flight to Brussels Evere. On getting out of the old aeroplane at Brussels he was accosted by two men in civilian clothes who said they were from Scotland Yard, showed him their identification cards and said they would like a few words with him. They repaired to a room in a nearby hangar and one of the detectives spoke:

> 'You are Squadron Leader Browne?'
> 'Yes.'
>
> 'Did you just get off that aeroplane from Redhill?'
> 'Yes.'

> 'How did you get on that aeroplane without any authorisation papers?'
> 'I am a Squadron Leader and won the DFC in Normandy. I am well-known in 83 Group. When I left the wing last July, Wing Commander Johnnie Johnson said on my return he would give me a squadron and I am on my way to join him at Grave.'

There were some more questions in the same vein from the two detectives and eventually Danny said:

> 'I hope you are satisfied with my explanation, and if you are, I would like to phone Johnnie Johnson at Grave and arrange to be flown there.'

Dan phoned me at Grave with the good news and I sent Dagwood Phillips in our ancient Tiger Moth to collect the Squadron Leader. We expected him to return in time for dinner and I wanted to provide him a good meal. On some evenings I had seen the flighting mallard, and from my Spitfire had selected a pool where it was more than likely that the duck would alight. That evening for a few glorious minutes the mallard swung in thick and fast, and before it became too dark to shoot, Sally had retrieved half a dozen plump birds. On my way back I stopped the jeep, and in the light of the headlamps gathered a suitable quantity of mushrooms which flourished here in great abundance. When I arrived back at the caravan, Danny had already arrived. In addition to his return, it was a suitable evening for a party; on this very day the Wing had shot down its 200th enemy aircraft since its formation at the end of 1942.

We walked across the few yards which separated my caravan from the mess tent. Here we met the other squadron commanders, who were delighted to see Danny, and after we had filled our glasses we settled down to hear a highly spiced account of his activities in the States. The tent was crowded with the greater part of our 150 officers, but the buzz of conversation was interrupted by yet another unfamiliar sound in the evening sky which coincided with the bark of anti-aircraft fire. We flung ourselves to the ground as the night was shattered by a very adjacent and extremely loud explosion. Fortunately no one was injured, and investigation on the following morning proved the intruder to be a composite aircraft known as 'Mistletoe'. This unorthodox contraption consisted of a Junkers 88, well laden with high explosives, on the top of which was mounted a Messerschmitt 109. These two aircraft were so coupled to each other that the 109 pilot could release the unmanned bomber against selected targets. For various reasons, only small numbers of these composite aircraft were built, but it was another example of German ingenuity.

In mid-October I flew to England for a few days leave and on my return to rejoin the Canadians I was diverted to Brussels-Evere. The runway, I thought, looked narrow and short so I circled the airfield a couple of times before making my approach. Bill MacBrien met me and said the Wing had moved from Grave a few days previously because the surface of that grass airfield, beside the Maas, had become so wet that landings and take-offs were hazardous; also, the jet bombers of the Luftwaffe had continued to attack it with anti-personnel fragmentation bombs which made life unpleasant for one and all.

Bill told me that we could live in good houses in Brussels, provided they had been occupied by Germans or Belgian collaborators, and he had found a couple of apartments into which we moved with our batmen and dogs; my apartment had a small balcony from which I could see the airfield and so, for the moment, we gave up our buccaneering life under canvas and reverted to a vastly different world of hot baths and dinner parties. We soon found that there was a thriving black market, especially in cigarettes at five shillings each; fortunately the Canadians had ample supplies and the squadron commanders made sure that their Wing Commander Flying had his quota.

The Commander-in-Chief's wife, Lady Coningham, moved to Brussels and established an officers' club in an elegant mansion on the Avenue Louise. We had to wear our 'best blues' and Lady Coningham and her cohorts thoroughly scrutinised our Belgian girlfriends whenever we brought them along – 'Would you take that gel home to meet your mother and father?'

At *Chez Adrianne*, much frequented by Belgian fighter jocks, the standards were far less strict, the main disadvantage being that if Adrianne herself, a strapping buxom lass of thirty plus summers, took a fancy to you, you either had to move fast or face the music!

Lance Corporal Eric Sykes (later to win fame on stage and screen) had a girlfriend who ran a *maison de rendezvous*, a social establishment frequented by warriors and local young ladies in search of an evening's entertainment, including a few drinks, some dancing and, hopefully, a shared bed.

These happy sessions went on night after night and it was often very late when Eric and his love got themselves to bed. One night the party, including a few colonels and the odd brigadier, went on and on until the weary Lance Corporal shouted to Madam:

> 'Let's throw these buggers out and close the place, so that we can get some sleep!'

The black market was, however, not confined to cigarettes, as I found out one sunny afternoon at Evere. Suddenly, and without previous warning, a dozen Dakotas appeared overhead and proceeded to land. Our airmen guided them to various dispersals and I met the American Colonel when he came down the steps of the lead Dakota. He made no bones about the fact that they had taken jerrycans of petrol to the south of France and were returning with cases of cognac and could he have transport, please, to take his loot into Brussels. I hesitated and the Colonel said:

> 'Of course there will be a case for you.'
> 'Two,' I countered.

The entrepreneur did not hesitate: 'Two it is.' Soon they were on their way in a small convoy of RAF three tonners and the Dakotas took off, vanishing into the wide blue yonder. We opened a case and found it contained a dozen bottles of Remy Martin brandy. Dan began to figure how much the consignment was worth at £5 per bottle, and where were the Scotland Yard men on that sunny afternoon?!

After the failure at Arnhem we bedded down for the late autumn and winter of 1944. The Luftwaffe were occupied trying to halt the advancing Red Army from the east and attempting to reduce the American daylight bombing raids in the west, and our flying was largely confined to armed reconnaissance, when we searched for enemy vehicles, trains and anything that moved on the ground. I disliked this job because, apart from the murderous flak, it was a basic contradiction of the beauty and elegance of the Spitfire which was designed for air fighting.

The heavy Tempest, successor to the Typhoon, had arrived in 83 Group and the first Tempest Wing was commanded by my old friend Group Captain Jamie Jameson; they were based at Volkel, in Holland, close to the German front, so close in fact that two of his Tempests, one on the circuit and one preparing to land, were shot down by enemy flak. Much as I disliked beating up ground targets there was plenty of action, for, as Coningham said, the Army were in the habit of calling for the fighter-bombers whenever there was the slightest opposition on the ground.

To make matters worse, our trusty Spitfires IXBs were, for some reason I never found out, suddenly replaced by Spitfire XVIs with the Packard-Merlin engine made in the USA.

When we attacked ground targets we flew in squadron strength of twelve Spitfires because a Wing was far too cumbersome. For no apparent reason we began to lose pilots who sometimes had time to say: 'Engine on fire. Baling-out'.

Since they baled out over enemy territory it was difficult to find out the exact cause of the fires, and the early losses were thought to be from enemy flak – but when pilots began baling out when there was a complete absence of hostile ground fire, there was much room for thought and discussion. We began to suspect the Packard-Merlin, but all my enquiries failed to get the right answer. Subsequently we learned from Rolls-Royce that these failures were due to 'fatigue fracture' and that great company soon had an improved design in production.

I flew to Eindhoven to see Broadhurst and hopefully to get back our trusty Spitfire IXBs. He was not very helpful and said the engineers were working on the problem but for the present we would have to carry on. I said:

> 'When I was with 19 Squadron in September 1940, our eight-gun Spitfires were suddenly exchanged for Spitfires armed with 20mm cannon which did not work. The problem was put to Dowding who the next day flew to Duxford to see for himself, and that evening our eight-gun fighters were returned.'
>
> 'That was in England,' replied the AOC. 'Your old Spitfires have been returned to England and you can't have them back. Good morning.'

I had made my case and had been, rightly or wrongly, overruled, and in the military once you had lost you either resigned or, like me, got on with the job.

Bill MacBrien, the squadron commanders and I thought it would be a good thing if, like the Duke of Wellington before Waterloo, we held a grand ball to entertain our Belgian hosts and repay some of their lavish hospitality. So it was that in late December the 127 Wing Winter Ball took place and, like the Duke and his officers, we danced the night away, but it will be remembered that when the Duke was treading a measure with Lady Richmond an aide interrupted and told him that Napoleon was at Quatre Bras, but a few kilometres from Waterloo.

Chapter 10

'In the bleak midwinter'

The American Army in Europe was, as we saw in Normandy, good on the offensive but weak on the defensive. On 16 December 1944, when the renowned Field Marshal von Rundstedt launched three armies on a wide front through the hills and forests of the Ardennes, the Americans gave ground and asked for close air support to stop the dreaded Panzers. The weather, however, was so bad that our reconnaissance missions could not be flown and von Rundstedt was able to average a daily advance of more than twelve miles.

In Belgium there was much apprehension amongst the civil population as they did not relish another dose of German occupation with their foul Gestapo.

Much to the chagrin of Patton and other American generals, Eisenhower ordered Montgomery to take charge of all Allied ground forces, and his first question was what did the Americans have in reserve? There were no reserves and, as Monty said later: 'Everything was in the shop window!'

Fortunately, just before Christmas 1944, the clouds lifted and within two days the German columns were stopped – another example of the power and accuracy of our fighter-bombers, especially the Typhoons with their lethal rockets.

Once again we flew in squadron strength and patrolled Malmedy, St Vith and Bastogne. Our job was to hold off the Luftwaffe fighters while our fighter-bombers strafed columns of enemy vehicles on the few good roads in this part of the Ardennes. One day Danny Browne and I flew a two-man patrol over the battle area. Our squadrons were operating to a strict timetable and we had not intended to fly. But it was a grand day with sparkling sunshine and unlimited visibility. Soon we were over the snow-covered hilly terrain, flying fairly low but above the enemy's light flak.

Danny guarded the rear of our two Spitfires and I concentrated on searching ahead and below, for we were after the low-flying Focke-Wulfs, which were active again. Three miles above, vapour trails made intricate filigree patterns and below the hills were clothed in a concealing white blanket of frozen snow. Navigation was far more difficult than usual, for the highways and railroad merged into the surrounding countryside and only the unfrozen rivers and the country towns gave some clue to our position. From above, our grey-green Spitfires could easily be seen by an alert enemy pilot, as they were conspicuous against the backcloth of virgin snow. Every few seconds I yawed my Spitfire with coarse rudder so that I could help Danny search behind. Suddenly my Spitfire was rocked by an explosion. I heard the ugly crunches of heavy flak. Several bursts bracketed the Spitfire, and when I had zoomed away from the danger zone I dropped a wing and saw the guns below.

'Johnnie, you OK? That looked darned close to me.'

'I'm all right, Danny,' I said, 'Let's see what's going on below.'

We climbed our Spitfires high into the shielding sun, then stall-turned into a fast dive towards the shoulder of the wood where I had pin-pointed the flak positions; but they had drawn our attention to something far more important. On the far side of the wood was a long column of enemy vehicles, including tanks, self-propelled guns, staff cars and half-tracks. Doubtless it was a spearhead of a Panzer army. We climbed back a few thousand feet so that our radio transmissions would reach our ops room.

'Greycap to Kenway. Over Houffalize and have spotted enemy transports. Suggest you send two squadrons. I'll brief and head them to target. Over.'

'Kenway to Greycap. Will do. One of your squadrons has just taken off. We'll divert it and follow up with another. How long can you stay there?'

'Greycap to Kenway. We're good for another thirty minutes. Tell the chaps to hurry. Out.'

Presently the squadron commander broke the radio silence.

'Greycap from Green Leader. Understand you have some trade for us. What's the form?'

'Greycap to Green Leader. Rendezvous over Houffalize at 8,000 feet. I'll take you to the target.'

Our fourteen Spitfires were soon formed together, and I led the formation to where the enemy still crouched along a narrow road which meandered along the edge of the wood. The twelve Spitfires fell to their work and for a few minutes Danny and I watched the scene from above. Some flak opposed the first few attacks, but the guns were quickly silenced and the strafing continued almost at leisure. It was a sombre setting. Palls of thick black smoke curled upwards from the doomed column, making a strange contrast with the white hills whose ice-bound peaks glittered in the sunshine of the late afternoon. The hungry Spitfires plunged downwards with short, accurate bursts of cannon fire, then soared away to manoeuvre for another attack. Seizing an opportune moment, Danny and I strafed some half-tracks. Then we climbed away and set course for Evere as our petrol was running low. Before darkness fell the enemy columns had been written off – a half mile of blazing, ruined vehicles.

It was not a great occasion. Nothing like the destruction and carnage of the Falaise gap. But it was a fine example of the flexibility of our fighter-bomber squadrons and the speed with which we could concentrate our fire power in any particular sector. Not more than a few minutes had elapsed between the time I called for assistance and the moment when the first squadron made its appearance.

The weather was bad, grounding our fighter-bombers, and between 16 and 23 December 1944 von Rundstedt's advance averaged some 20 km per day. On Christmas Eve the weather improved, but even so the US Mustangs and Thunderbolts were unable to stop the advancing Panzers, partly because their close support techniques were not as good as ours and partly, more importantly, because they had no suitable fighter-bombers such as our rocket-firing Typhoons to deal with the Panzers. The Americans asked for our help and Coningham immediately agreed, provided they ceased to operate in the area, for we did not want clashes between Allied fighters because of faulty identification. This was at once agreed and Group Captain Desmond Scott (aged 26), took his 123 Wing into the American sector and helped to stop the enemy armoured columns.

Bastogne, a Belgian town, was held by the US Army and was a vital centre of the area's road network. It was occupied by the 101st Airborne Division commanded by Brigadier-General Anthony McAuliffe, and as the enemy drove westwards the Germans left behind forces to besiege and capture the town. By 22 December the defenders were low on ammunition, and air resupply was out of the question because of the foul weather which included heavy snow. The Germans demanded McAuliffe surrender but the courageous General, knowing that George Patton was on his way, simply replied, 'Nuts'.

As explained, by Christmas Eve the weather had improved to permit flying, but even so the US Mustangs and Thunderbolts were unable to stop the advancing Panzers, partly because their close support techniques were not as good as ours but, more importantly, they had no suitable fighter-bombers such as our rocket-firing Typhoons, to deal with the Panzers. The Americans asked for our help and Coningham immediately agreed provided they cease to operate in the area, for we did not want clashes between Allied fighters because of faulty identification. This was at once agreed and Group Captain Desmond Scott, took his 123 Wing into the American sector and within two days helped to stop the enemy armoured columns. This was another example of the power and accuracy of our fighter-bombers, especially the Typhoons with their lethal rockets.

Another most gallant Typhoon leader was Kit North-Lewis who, having fought courageously earlier in the war and also in Normandy and again during the airborne landings, was in Holland in September 1944. Kit and his pilots had supported the Guards Armoured Division as it began its dash to link up with the forces at Eindhoven. His Typhoons put down a rolling barrage on both sides of the road thus allowing the tanks to drive forward. His Wing also helped halt the German thrust through the Ardennes. On 26 December 1944 the weather having improved, his wing was ordered to deal with a dangerous German thrust towards a bridge over the Meuse. The wing attacked a large German force with both rockets and cannons. This close aerial support of British troops who were only a few hundred yards away stopped the Germans 'dead in their tracks' and within a few days the Battle of the Bulge was over.

Harry Broadhurst daily flew his Fieseler Storch from his mansion on the golf course to his Eindhoven Headquarters. Whenever he visited his squadrons in Holland and Belgium he flew the Storch with the minimum of fuel so that he could make short take-offs and landings of about twenty yards, and if the wind was suitable he would land across the runway instead of using its full length. One day he flew to Evere for a conference with Coningham, when Bill MacBrien met him before he drove into Brussels.

It was late afternoon when he took off for the return flight to Eindhoven. The little Storch took its usual short run and sprang into the air. Rocking in the stiff breeze, the pilot began to climb to a few hundred feet for his journey. When the Storch was just a few feet above some buildings, the engine stopped. Bill stood rooted to the ground as he watched the drama. Broadhurst tried to get down on the roof of a hanger, but unfortunately the hanger was practically gutted; all that remained of the once flat roof was a few charred beams. The little Storch bounced on these beams. Then it fell to the ground below. An ominous pall of dark smoke rose into the air. A few minutes later the Storch was little more than a pile of debris. But miraculously the group commander stood alongside it, without a scratch. He had run out of petrol, and snarled:

> 'Why didn't you get it refuelled?'

MacBrien, a regular officer in the RCAF, and very well aware of King's Regulations and Air Council Instructions, replied: 'That Sir is the pilot's responsibility!' Broadhurst then muttered something about getting another Storch from Italy!

Soon after Broadhurst's prang, Coningham's SASO phoned to say that on the following Sunday I was invited to lunch with the C-in-C and I was to bring a squadron commander. Thus the American, Dan Brown, was with me when we reported to Coningham's lavish mansion in the Avenue des Nations. A white-coated corporal showed us into an anteroom where half a dozen guests were already gathered. The C-in-C, vain and impeccably turned out, made the introductions to the Count of this, Baroness that… and so on. A sergeant, also white-coated, offered champagne in expensive-looking fluted glasses from a silver salver, while Coningham explained that the house had been occupied by a high-ranking German officer who had 'collected' the priceless paintings on the walls. The food was superb – oysters from Bergen-op-Zoom, roast partridge from the stubbles, and profiteroles, all served with fine wines. 'Mary' Coningham was an excellent host, keeping the conversation flowing round the table, and very attentive to his Belgian guests. After coffee, we were preparing to leave, but our host asked us to stay, and, after the other guests had left, put some searching and intelligent questions to us about air fighting, heights, turning circles and the remarkable Me262.

We drove back to Evere talking of the superb meal we had enjoyed while our brother officers had lunched off tinned stewed beef and hard biscuits. I thought of Montgomery, who, in his old corduroys and a jersey, had probably munched some bread and cheese in his bleak caravan and, like others, I decided Mary was overdoing it.

Early in the New Year, Group Captain 'Iron Bill' MacBrien returned to Canada and I was sorry to see him go. We had been together for the best part of two years and although he had only flown operational half-a-dozen times, he was an able and just commanding officer. I thought I stood a good chance of getting his job and was dismayed to learn that the unruly Stan Turner, of Douglas Bader's Tangmere Wing, was to be my next CO. I was not pleased about serving under Turner and after a few days I soon found that he had not improved – in fact the poacher had turned gamekeeper! He had only been at Petit Brogel a few days when he clapped two of my brightest Canadian pilots under close arrest for keeping the bar open after its proper closing time. I at once tackled Turner reminding him of his own misdeeds, including that at Catterick where he showed his displeasure at moving to that northern airfield by producing his revolver in the bar and firing through the ceiling – as a result both my pilots were merely admonished.

Since I could not get along with Turner I decided to take a few days leave in England to think about my next move, and I had only been at home a short time when 'Dingbat' Saunders, Commander-in-Chief, Fighter Command, phoned to say he thought I had done enough operational flying and would I like to join the recently formed Central Fighter Establishment as OC Tactics Branch in the rank of group captain. I replied that I would very much like that job, and he said he would arrange the posting. I sent a signal to Turner requesting a further forty-eight hours leave and eventually returned to Evere on a fine Saturday afternoon. Turner met me as I climbed out of the cockpit:

> 'I don't know what you've been up to in England, but if you hadn't returned today I had orders to place you under close arrest!'
>
> 'Who from?'
>
> 'Broady,' he replied.
>
> 'Well, if it's OK with you I think I should fly to Eindhoven and thrash this out with the AOC!'

Turner said it was OK with him so the next morning I stood before Broadhurst and asked what was the meaning of the close arrest instruction. He replied that there had been a flurry of signals between the Commander-in-Chief, Fighter Command and 'Mary' Coningham and our Commander-in-Chief was not amused about the attempt to prise me out of his command – hence the close arrest instruction to Turner.

I said that since I had a permanent commission it was important to get the highest possible rank before the war ended. Broadhurst agreed and then took the wind out of my sails when he said:

> 'On my recommendation the C-in-C has agreed that you are to have the next wing in this Group which I expect will be fairly soon. And now I should like you to stay for lunch. I believe O'Connor has managed to get a barrel of oysters from somewhere or other!'

I returned to the bleak airfield at Petit Brogel to learn that the next day Turner and I were to be at Eindhoven for a special briefing by Montgomery himself.

The Whitehall planner thought that the war against Germany would end in late 1944 and therefore the allotment of combat aeroplanes and the flow of trained aircrew had been reduced out of proportion to the effort required to carry on our daily operations. It would take some weeks to remedy these deficiencies and meanwhile Coningham instructed his group commanders to pay close attention to their accident rates.

So far in our trek across France and the Low Countries, whenever Spitfires were written off they were replaced the next day with a minimum of paper work; but now that we were bogged down for the winter there was time to examine these mishaps. A newly arrived Group Captain at Coningham's headquarters wrote a highly critical staff paper stating that 83 Group's accident rate was far higher than that in Fighter Command who operated similar fighters and fighter-bombers.

Coningham sent the paper to Broadhurst and asked for his comments. Broadhurst, the practical airman who, unlike his master, still flew operationally, was displeased and asked his SASO, Dermot Boyle, to draft a stiff reply pointing out that Fighter Command operated its fighters from permanent 'all-weather' airfields with concrete runways, and lit-up taxi tracks and dispersals – a far cry from his pock-marked, often soggy, airfields, with wire-mesh runways. Boyle, a good staff officer, wrote the paper, Broadhurst signed it and sent it to his Commander-in-Chief.

The Commander-in-Chief was not amused by his AOC's response and instructed that they should meet at Eindhoven to discuss the matter. Coningham opened the batting, saying the high accident rate could not be tolerated. Broadhurst said the comparison was unfair because it did not take account of the vastly different conditions between the UK airfields and those in Holland and Belgium: take this airfield, Eindhoven, he continued, operating three wings of fighter-bombers, a hundred plus aeroplanes, several times a day, plus communications aeroplanes, plus the army's 'spotter' planes, plus a stream of visitors and all flying from old, uneven brick runways that had been bombed many times and required constant patching. Further, his pilots often returned with flak damage which sometimes burst their tyres so that they swung off the runway and nosed-in; or they had to make wheels-up landings. His pilots were based near the battle zone and sometimes fast enemy jets, Me262s, sneaked in and dropped fragmentation bombers which had destroyed aeroplanes and killed airmen. Fighter Command operated in a different world and, concluded Broadhurst, the comparison was unjust.

The autocratic Coningham said that even allowing for the rough conditions there were far too many accidents and what was Broadhurst going to do about it? Broadhurst thought that Boyle might step in with a word; after all Boyle had written the paper, but the SASO remained silent. So, Broady, defending his pilots and never a man to give ground, thought the accident rate was acceptable. There followed heated words between the C-in-C and his AOC, and as the meeting ended Coningham snarled:

> 'Do something about it. Or I'll have you court-martialled!'

Harry Broadhurst and his senior staff officers lived well in a delightful country house alongside a golf course (handy for the Storch) a few miles from Eindhoven where on most Saturday evenings throughout the winter months he entertained his Group Captain and wing leaders. Thanks to Terry O'Connor, his Irish catering officer, there was an abundance of excellent food and wines when, of course, we could all relax and enjoy ourselves.

At one of these parties, Broady told us that we had only been in Normandy a few weeks when one of his senior officers came to see him, in a highly emotional state, and said could he fly an Anson to England because he had just heard that his wife's lover – a dashing young Group Captain serving in Italy – was in England and he, the husband, feared the game was on! Broady gave permission and found it very amusing when two hours later the Group Captain turned up for lunch: 'Their Ansons,' he chortled, 'must have passed each other in mid-Channel!'

Then there was the distinguished Typhoon leader who 'disappeared' when returning from a trip to England. In fact he had decided to spend the night at Manston, where he had some friends, but forgot to signal 83 Group and was reported as 'missing'. Broady was immediately informed but told his staff not to worry as the Typhoon maestro was probably in bed with some blonde. The next morning the pilot, realising his error, phoned his AOC, apologised and said he had spent a very pleasant evening with a young blonde!

At another of these convivial gatherings Broadhurst welcomed Bill MacBrien and me, and I said:

> 'Good to see you here. But I'm surprised you can tear yourselves away from the delights of Brussels!'
>
> 'You can't be serious?'

I replied that I was very serious and thought that we had lost something of the fine cutting edge we had in Normandy. Broadhurst looked thoughtful and said he would see what could be done.

We had no warning on the early morning of New Year's Day 1945 when the Luftwaffe struck at our crowded airfields to strafe the parked fighters. 438 and 439 Squadrons, both of the RCAF, were taxiing out when more enemy fighters appeared and joined in the carnage. Some of the Canadian pilots bravely tried to take off but were shot down and killed. Typhoons, artillery-spotting Austers and Dakotas were soon blazing on the ground. The few anti-aircraft guns were firing and there was much noise and confusion.

Flying Officer M.G. Croft of 124 Wing at Eindhoven recorded the attack:

> 'In exactly twenty-three and a half minutes our aircraft strength was depleted by 80%; stores of petrol, clothing and technical equipment almost totally destroyed and more than a hundred men killed or seriously wounded. Within a week the airfield was again back to normal working order, thanks to the speedy replacement of aircraft from England, but many years will yet pass before the healing passage of time finally erases from one's mind the memory of that dreadful moment.'

It was a beautiful day; cold and crisp with glistening frost, which scintillated in the bright rays of the morning sun. It appeared delightfully peaceful, as peaceful as it was possible with the preparations for battle well under way.

Six Typhoons from 143 Wing, who shared the drome with the Recce Wing and ourselves, were lining up at the end of the day. We were due to take off a few minutes after them. Meanwhile we were standing around in the dispersal hut whiling away the few minutes yet to go before we climbed into our machine. That waiting used to be hell; far worse than the diciest op. Imagination would gnaw at the foundations of one's confidence in the future; one began to think, and thinking opened the gates of fear. As we climbed into our machines though, all fears and doubts fled before the reawakened primeval urge to kill and to destroy.

But that morning, life did not proceed according to plan.

Without any warning, a bunch of Fw190s, flying at low-level, appeared over the airfield and proceeded to strafe the grounded aeroplanes.

A zipping stream of cannon shells crackled down the runway, mincing the six Typhoons into a heap of burning rubble … This first blast was the opening chord in a cataclysmic symphony of rending metal, exploding bombs, bursting shells and screaming engines. Faintly discernible, so faintly that one had to listen for it, as one listens for the dull pounding of the double bass in an orchestra, one could hear the Bofors gun over by

Intelligence section breaking out its feeble reply to the aggressors. We hadn't many guns, they had nearly all been moved down south to combat the 'buzz-bombs' a few days earlier.

Few of us on the Squadron saw much of the battle in progress; we were endeavouring to make ourselves as inconspicuous as possible. To see what was going on was just what we did not intend to do. Strangely, we felt that if we could not see the enemy, then the enemy could not see us. So whether we were safely ensconced in the Adjutant's slit trench, lying out in the open or on the floor of the dispersal hut, we buried our heads in our arms and prayed for invisibility. Actually the Huns were interested primarily in destroying the aircraft and stores, but nevertheless each one of us had the feeling that we had been singled out as a personal target.

I was on the floor of the dispersal hut with my head jammed against the side of a fireplace, which was of brick and very solid. One of the airmen had built it; how I blessed him for it that morning. If I raised my head my total range of vision consisted of about six bricks and I knew them intimately; an image of every crack and furrow was firmly impressed upon my mind. I remembered that I didn't feel scared, just empty, as if life, presumptuous of the future, had already departed my body. I could not prevent myself from wondering what it would be like to have a cannon shell rip through me, tearing flesh and bone with its jagged splinters of steel. Every time a plane dived down and the crackle of gunfire sounded in the immediate vicinity my flesh would contract about the empty void within me, waiting for what seemed the inevitable, but always the shells smacked their furrows either side of the hut or stopped a few yards short. I didn't realise it at the time but we were in quite a favourable position, being sandwiched between 137 and 181 Squadrons. They took a frightful pasting, whereas we escaped comparatively unscathed.

The pilots' crew room was the one building on our dispersal which wasn't hit. All the others were holed, but no-one was hurt, save one airman who suffered a flesh wound along his back.

Many had narrow escapes. Three fellows were sheltering behind a mound of earth about two feet high in which was erected the squadron flag. The flag, itself only three feet off the ground, had two shells through it!

The Adjutant's clerk, firmly wedged against the wall of the office with a table above him, escaped death by one inch when a cannon shell whanged though the wall, just that distance above his head. Another shell embedded itself in the inner wall of the slit trench much to the horror of the occupants. Among other units there were similar examples of miraculous escapes.

Two guards in bed in one of the hangars at 143 Wing remained completely unhurt when a 109 crashed into the building. An Fw190 crashed into a billet a short distance behind 181 dispersal and again the six occupants escaped unhurt.

Acts of bravery there were too. Who could forget the airman standing alone at the end of the runway, blazing away at the Huns with his Sten gun? The swine made three passes over him. Or the pilot from 137 who was caught landing? He opened up to go round again, shot down a Hun during his turn off the deck and immediately fell to the guns of one of the dozens of enemy aircraft in the circuit. Who could forget the airmen who removed rockets and ammunition from blazing aircraft without any regard for their own safety; or the people at the Recce Wing who removed the dead and tended the wounded during the height of the attack?

When the attacks eased off and only the friendly roar of Tempests and Spitfires filled the air, we emerged from our various hiding places and stood staring at the awful mess which but half an hour before was a well-equipped aerodrome. A thick pall of oily smoke covered everything, blotting out even the light of the sun. Visible at numerous points through the haze were the ruby coloured tongues of hungry flames, each group of which represented the site of an aircraft, no longer an object of powerful beauty, but a bubbling heap of molten metal. Wherever one looked there were burning and shattered aircraft spewing clouds of smoke into the air. There was a constant popping of ammunition as the flames ate their way into the magazines and now and then a throaty sigh would announce the passage of an ignited rocket.

We made a journey around the airfield to help with the transport of the wounded, our first stop being the Recce Wing who suffered the highest casualty rate. Being situated on the north side of the drome, from which direction most of the attacks were made, they endured the full weight of the cannon fire and as a result lost practically every aircraft they possessed.

143 Wing lost almost all their 'Tiffies', which owing to the limited amount of firm ground on their side of the field had to be dispersed in a line. It was too easy for the Hun. Their bomb dump also suffered hits, probably with bombs. It blew up about ten minutes after the raid was over, causing a gigantic smoke-ring which hung over the aerodrome like an oversized halo.

Although our airfield defences had been so reduced, the few guns remaining claimed about fifteen aircraft, which crashed in the vicinity. Two of the machines were quite near and we visited them. The first, which crashed behind our dispersal, was an Fw190. Bits of it were scattered far and wide over the ground, only the cockpit and its occupant remaining comparatively intact. Looking at the torn disfigured body of the pilot it seemed impossible that less than an hour before it had pulsed with life, had been afflicted with emotion or pain, harboured thoughts of home, or love, or perhaps of peace. Little plumes of smoke were curling up from the body, tainting the air with the smell of burning flesh. Of the other machine there was nothing remaining but a heap of ashes. The body of the pilot was squatting amid the wreckage, a shrunken effigy of a man minus hands and feet, burnt to the colour of dark coffee. From what we heard later, many German pilots came to a similar fate that morning. Thunderbolts, Tempests and Spitfires caught them as they made their way home, short of fuel and ammunition.

However devastating the raid may have been, it did not achieve its objective: the total crippling of the fighter strength of the Tactical Air Forces. Within two hours we had racked together sufficient aircraft for an 'op' and later carried out another.

Certainly the raid was well planned. Our control centre had no knowledge of the approaching aircraft: they flew at zero feet the whole way, being led to the Maas by a Junkers 88. The inexperience of many of the pilots engaged and the short notice given to them of the nature of the operation no doubt accounted for numbers of them missing their objective. Thus, Volkel, only a few miles north of us escaped with only a minor attack whereas we received more than our due share. Air gunnery was also wide and inaccurate; it was more the proximity of the target aircraft to one another that accounted for the heavy losses; perhaps also the loss of our defences had something to do with it.

If it were not for the loss of life, one could readily have acclaimed the raid as a valuable and necessary tonic to the over-confidence of all of us in the services. It may have been an expensive means of being brought back to reality, but it paid good dividends, as the world was soon to find out.

At his Eindhoven headquarters Broadhurst was discussing the raids with his SASO, Dermot Boyle, when the telephone rang. It was C-in-C 'Mary' Coningham on the line:

> 'What the hell are you doing Harry; I've got aeroplanes with black crosses on them flying over Brussels doing what they like.'
>
> Harry Broadhurst replied: 'You are lucky, sir. They are flying back and forth below my window!'

On this very day, 1 January 1945, a Canadian friend of mine, Paul Davoud, was handing over 143 (Typhoon) Wing to his fellow countryman Dean Nesbitt. They had completed some preliminaries – like signing for petty cash – and were strolling on the bustling Eindhoven airfield when two waves of Me109s and Fw190s dropped in at low-level and began to beat up the place. 438 and 439 Squadrons, both of the RCAF, were taxiing out for an operation when more waves of enemy fighters appeared and made determined and well-led strafing attacks. Some of the Canadian pilots bravely tried to take off but were shot down and killed.

Typhoons, Austers and transport aeroplanes were blazing on the ground. Anti-aircraft guns were firing and there was much noise and confusion. The two group captains, who had sought refuge in a slit trench, surveyed the shambles and Paul quietly said: 'Well Dean, I guess it's all yours now!'

Operation *Bodenplatte* was a bold stroke, but at Evere we saw for ourselves that the average German fighter pilot was not equal to the task. The shooting was atrocious, and the circuit at the Evere reminded us more of a bunch of beginners on their first solos than pilots of the frontline squadrons. The time factor was badly planned, for the basis of the strike should have been a sharp, concentrated attack. As it was, the long time spent over our airfields meant that we were able to scramble fighters from secure airfields and divert those already in the air. Both sides suffered about the same losses in aeroplanes, but the enemy lost far more pilots as he was operating over our territory. Strategically the operation was carried out at the wrong time; it should have been the prelude to the Ardennes offensive.

How very different from the handful of highly skilled German fighter and bomber pilots who in the late summer of 1940 made such a devastating low-level attack against Biggin Hill!

The important lesson of *Bodenplatte* was, and still is, that air superiority is never absolute. It is doubtful whether anyone has ever had such a degree of air superiority that we had at that time, and yet we were unable to prevent such an attack being launched and doing a considerable amount of damage to our aeroplanes on the ground.

Chapter 11

The Rhine Crossing

For the last time during the war we were summoned to Broady's headquarters to be briefed about Operation *Varsity*, the crossing of the Rhine. It was immediately apparent that here was a highly professional operation and integrated plan which clearly defined our tasks in support of our paratroopers and gliders – unlike the Arnhem fiasco.

I sat next to Charles Green, now a group captain, who wanted to know all about the enemy flak dispositions at Wesel, for it would fall to his Typhoon pilots to take out the German batteries. How, asked the AOC, did he propose to deal with this menace? The Rhodesian, victor of Mortain and Falaise, said it was really quite simple: we fly in three pairs, each pair separated by 1,000 yards. When the flak opens up at the leading pair, the second pair goes down in a shallow rocket attack. When other guns fire at the second pair they are dealt with by the last section of Typhoons!

The big mistake about Arnhem was that although it took place in our area of operations, Coningham had no control over the big airborne drop which, had it succeeded, might well have ended the war in 1944. Both planning and control were exercised from a combined headquarters in England. During the actual drop on 17 September 1944, and on all seven subsequent reinforcement and resupply operations, we of 2nd TAF were banned from Arnhem because the planners feared a clash between American and British fighters – despite that we had been fighting alongside each other for almost two years.

All the top brass from Eindhoven down were determined that our next big operation – the Rhine crossing – would be better planned and controlled than the Arnhem debacle, and our first briefing was from Montgomery himself who spoke in a cinema at Eindhoven to several hundred senior officers who would be at the sharp end. 'No Smoking' signs were well displayed and the Field Marshal made a somewhat dramatic entrance onto the stage; he was wearing a paratrooper's combat jacket in honour of his being appointed Colonel-in-Chief of the Parachute Regiment, and addressed us in his somewhat irritating high-pitched staccato voice.

The Northern Group of Armies, the Field Marshal explained, with the IX US Army on its right, all under his operational control, were to carry out Operation *Plunder* on 24 March 1945 to gain a firm bridgehead over the Rhine – as a base for later operations to isolate the industrial Ruhr. The First Allied Airborne Army would also take part in the battle.

We would cross the Rhine, the Field Marshal continued, on a front of two armies between Rheinberg and Rees. The IX Army on the right, Operation Flashpoint, and the British Second Army on the left, Operation *Plunder*. The town of Wesel and a Rhine crossing near Wesel would be secured by an airborne drop of US 18 Corps, Operation *Varsity*. The initial lodgement area on the east bank of the Rhine would be expanded with the IX US Army on the right, the Second British Army in the centre and the First Canadian Army on the left, all under my command so that further operations deeper into Germany could be developed.

The Field Marshal, the Master of the Battlefield, was heard in absolute silence. We would cross the Rhine, as planned, and the war would be won in a matter of weeks.

Broadhurst briefed his Airfield Commanders and Wing Leaders on their tasks during the crossing. The basis of the plan, prepared by Coningham's staff, was that only the Allied tactical air forces who knew the terrain, the location of our ground forces, and who could be closely controlled to meet the changing situation on the ground, would operate over the battle area and beyond.

The AOC explained that 83 Group had been made responsible for air supremacy over the Rhine and for fifty miles beyond. We were also responsible for anti-flak operations and for close support operations: on the front Second Army and the VIII US Airborne Corporals X if necessary; he could get additional help from 84 Group.

Fighter Command and the VIII US Air Force would escort the Airborne Air Forces from England to the battle area but these fighters would not be allowed to fly over the Rhine. Strategic bombers and fighters of the VIII US Air Force were only allowed to attack ground targets beyond the fifty-mile belt.

Bearing in mind the appalling situation at Arnhem, when fighter-bombers could not contact the beleaguered airborne troops, the *Varsity* planners had paid much attention to close air support which would be available from first light. The Americans would keep one squadron on patrol for one hour over the leading elements of each American assault division and would be available for air strikes. 83 Group would maintain one cab rank of four Typhoons over this advanced Control Centre on the west bank of the Rhine with two squadrons at readiness on the ground. There was one contact car with each of the two assaulting British divisions and two more with the airborne divisions. Immediate support requests from the four divisions were filtered at the advanced Control Centre and those accepted were passed to the patrolling cab rank and briefed by RAF controllers in the Contact Cars. There would be Contact Cars, also with RAF controllers, with Airborne Divisions.

On the morning of 23 March 1945, as the Allies mounted an airborne assault and amphibious crossing near Wesel on the Rhine.

From the cockpit of my Spitfire, *Varsity* looked pretty good, except the leading British transports and gliders arrived over their dropping zone seven minutes early and prevented the Typhoons from knocking out some enemy batteries. However, weaving between the slow Dakotas, the fighter-bombers pressed home their rocket attacks even after the first parachutes had spilled open. We were horrified to see several bursts of 88mm explode among our paratroopers as they swung helplessly from their sinking parachutes.

Kit North-Lewis was again commanding the Typhoons of 124 Wing against a strongpoint east of the town. The flak as usual was heavy and accurate and Kit's Typhoon was hit by anti-aircraft fire and the engine ceased. He crash-landed on a small island on the Rhine whereupon he was taken prisoner, but the Germans' situation got steadily worse during the night and his captors, realising the game was up, decided to surrender to him! A few days later he was awarded an immediate DSO. In the previous fourteen months he had flown 176 operational sorties during which time his own wing had 116 pilots killed or taken prisoner.

I led 127 Wing three times during the Rhine Crossing patrolling Rheine, Osnabrück and Münster. I saw the British and American airborne landings from my cockpit. Many tugs and gliders were shot down by flak, light flak causing the most casualties; however, there was no sign of enemy aircraft in the battle area throughout the day. I felt crossing the River Rhine was a great and long-awaited occasion. *Varsity* had been a great success. As I turned in with Sally on the floor beside me I was told the situation on the Rhine's far bank was well under control. Longfellow had written many years previously: 'Let us, then, be up and doing.' I felt that under Coningham's and Broadhurst leadership all of us in the Second Tactical Air Force had done exactly this and shown once again our mettle. As I fell to sleep

I remembered both the bravery and disgraceful planning at Arnhem and felt that the latter had been exonerated by today's Airborne operations. The final thrust had got off to an excellent start and I was determined, having been there at the tail end of the Battle of Britain, to see the end of this evil empire and Germany's unconditional surrender. The next day I was up early and 'at them', patrolling the 'Rhine battle area' and attacking enemy transport with my Canadians.

The following day Broadhurst called to tell me my days with the Canadians were over. I was to take over 125 Wing who were operating the latest Spitfire Mk XIV and Broady wanted me to move it to the first available airfield captured east of the Rhine. I said my farewells to all. It was two years since my association with the Canadians had started. There existed between us that special bond known only to those who have served and fought together. William Manchester summed it up when revisiting Sugar Hill in the Pacific after the Second World War: 'Men, I now knew, do not fight for flag or country, for the Marine Corps or glory or any other abstraction. They fight for one another.' Pilots also have a bond with nature, best expressed by the Irish poet William Butler Yeats in 1918 in his poem 'An Irish Airman Foresees His Death':

Nor law, nor duty bade me fight,
Nor public men, nor cheering crowds,
A lonely impulse of delight
Drove to this tumult in the clouds

The Spitfire squadrons of 125 Wing were the first to cross the Rhine and station themselves at Twente on the east bank of the Rhine at an airfield captured twenty-four hours earlier by the British Second Army. Although not as memorable as when I took the first aircraft to land in France shortly after the Normandy invasion, I was nevertheless pleased to be the Group Captain of the first operational airfield on the German side of the Rhine.

My Wing Commander (Flying) was George Keefer, a Canadian who had previously served with me at Kenley in 1943. George looked anxious, saying to me: 'I suppose you'll want your own Spit, just the same as when you were a Wing Leader.' I was now in overall command of the wing and no longer Wing Commander (Flying). It was George's job to lead the wing in the air and into battle, so I knew what he was getting at. I told him I had no intention of undermining his authority as the vital chain of command between the Wing Leader and his squadron commanders was paramount to me. Having said that I still needed to keep my hand in and be in the fight, so I told George that I reserved the right to occasionally lead a section or squadron and to lead the wing the first time it flew operationally over Berlin. It was a compromise that made us both happy.

On 5 April 1945, while first landing at Twente, I had a 'close shave', which was far too close for comfort at this late stage of the game. I had just switched off the Spitfire's engine when an Me109 suddenly appeared low overhead! The Hun saw me and turned for a strafing run. What a way to buy it, I thought, as I fell out of the cockpit and tried to make myself as small as possible under the Spitfire's wing alongside an airman. We heard two gun reports in quick succession, then a large explosion as the enemy aircraft ploughed in. A jeep arrived and I was driven across the airfield so that I could warmly congratulate the RAF Regiment Bofors gun crew which had just saved our lives.

I moved from Twente airfield on the east bank of the Rhine in Holland to Celle in Germany on 16 April 1945 and flew my first operational sortie the next day in a Spitfire XIV having flown the faithful Spitfire IX since late March 1943. We all knew the war would shortly be over but until the final whistle blew we would attack the Hun at every opportunity. Two days later while leading the wing, George Keefer and his number two destroyed eleven Me109s on the runway at Parchim preparing to take off. The next day George destroyed an Me109 and the wing got another. On both occasions I flew in the wing as a lowly pilot and the vital chain of command agreed with George was never breeched.

On the same day that George and his wing man destroyed eleven Me109s, the popular Squadron Leader Terry Spencer, CO of 350 Squadron, was shot down by flak while attacking a tanker in Weimar Bay. His Spitfire burst into flames and crashed and I feared this gallant leader would not survive. As Terry was lost, I led his squadron for the last two operations that I flew in the Second World War in Europe.

On 25 April, I flew over Berlin at two thousand feet with the Aussie Flight Lieutenant Tony Gaze, with whom I had last flown in Bader's Wing at Tangmere in 1941. The German capital was covered by thick cloud, forcing us down even lower. Masses of refugees filled the roads to the west, all fleeing the Soviet advance from the east. Suddenly Tony's voice crackled in my headphones: 'Fifty-plus at two o'clock, Greycap. Same level. More behind.' I asked if they were 'Huns' and Tony replied 'probably Russians'. They were, and flying Yaks, about a hundred of them, in a loose flying formation. Every few minutes a handful of them broke away, attacked something in the city and then re-joined their comrades. We were not allowed to fly over Berlin again as there could have been an awful mix up with the Russians, but as I turned away I noticed the city was nicely aflame.

The next day was my last operation and I led Terry's squadron again on a one-hundred-minute uneventful fighter sweep over Weimar where Terry had been lost. I thought about him and was saddened, but fortune favoured the brave because a few days later Terry walked into the Mess burned, knocked about but undaunted. I quickly telephoned Broady who agreed an immediate DFC for Terry and I pinned a roughly cut out cardboard replica to his tunic and the party began as our war ended.

Germany surrendered unconditionally on 8 May 1945, twelve days after my last operational flight. I had been lucky to survive for I had flown Spitfires operationally for some four and a quarter years since joining 19 Squadron at Duxford in August 1940. I felt no satisfaction in the enemy pilots and ground forces that I had destroyed, but only immense pride in a job well done by all with whom I had the good fortune to serve, whatever their rank.

Chapter 12

Looking back

By the Second World War's end I had flown some 1,492 hours piloting Spitfires since finishing pilot training at Hawarden on 23 August 1940.

We all knew war was inevitable by the tail end of the thirties, and the prevailing attitude amongst RAF pilots in late 1939 is well summed up by the words of an old Irish prayer:

> 'God give us strength for the storms of our journey.'

It was during the dying days of the war that I fully realised how evil Hitler's diabolical regime had been. We were stationed at Celle and the German concentration camp at Belsen was but a few miles away. I saw the ghastly ovens and the long, filthy, corridors of the mostly Jewish prisoners' wooden huts. I was unable to distinguish the dead from the dying and saw hundreds of corpses, reminding me of skeletons clothed in soiled rags, as the bulldozers pushed them into mass graves. The scene was as if it was taken straight out of Dante's *Inferno* and frankly defies my description. The nearest German town was but a few miles from Belsen and Celle and the locals claimed that they knew nothing of what had gone on at Belsen. This infuriated us all so I immediately arranged for the local elders along with some adult civilians to be taken to Belsen to witness first-hand the Nazi genocide. Belsen left an indelible image on my mind as it could have so easily occurred on British soil had the Battle of Britain not been won. I thought briefly and warmly of Bader and his joking, but nevertheless often repeated serious jibe: 'we cannot allow the Hun to come over here bombing our cricket pitches' and it made me feel slightly better for a job well done by the Allies, albeit sad at the countless civilians of both sides who had perished in the conflict which was largely not of their making.

My relationship with Douglas Bader can be best summed up as initially 'Master and Servant' and later as 'He whom propaganda has made mighty, no man may readily cast aside.' Stated simply, I was an apprentice to Bader and learnt my early air fighting tactics from him for which I was immensely grateful. He was already a hero, a Wing Commander and ex Cranwell, and I a lowly Pilot Officer commissioned from the ranks. I was not of his social class and frankly in awe of him. He drilled into me his three rules. Firstly, 'If you have the height, you control the battle.' Secondly, 'If you come out of the sun, the Hun cannot see you,' and lastly, 'If you hold your fire until you are very close, you seldom miss.' Some have said he was too arrogant and ambitious but I have always held that loyalty is sacrosanct amongst fighter pilots and we agreed to disagree on the tactics of the 'Big Wing'. After the war I was very saddened when I learnt of Douglas's involvement with Air Vice-Marshal Trafford Leigh-Mallory in the downfall of both Air Vice-Marshal Keith Park and Air Chief Marshal Sir Hugh Dowding, who were both ultimately responsible for winning the Battle of Britain. It is best that I sum up this sorry incident in a letter from Keith Park dated 23 October 1956 to a close friend, Flight Lieutenant J. Hunt:

'Thank you very much for your letter of October 10th, and for the Press Cutting about the book written by Group Captain Johnson.

'You said that my 11 Group chaps have wondered why I have not written my own account of the Battle of Britain. For your personal information, my reply is that I do not wish to hurt the friends and relatives of some very high-ranking officers still very much alive.

'During the Battle of Britain there were two Air Marshals at Air Ministry who very much wanted Lord Dowding's job at HQ Fighter Command. At the same time, Dowding was very unpopular with the CAS, Newall, who was very friendly with the aspiring Air Marshals at Air Ministry. Dowding was so highly thought of by the Cabinet that his position appeared to be unassailable, until the conspirators at Air Ministry discovered an Air Vice-Marshal in No 12 Group who badly wanted my job commanding 11 Group. Consequently, in October, when the Battle had been won, it was brought to the attention of the Air Secretary that Air Vice-Marshal Leigh-Mallory claimed that the tactical handling of 11 Group Fighters had been faulty, and that the mass formation tactics of his Group would have been more successful. The trouble was that neither Dowding nor I took seriously this criticism of my fighter tactics, because we were so confident that we had been right in the method of winning the Battle.

'Imagine the surprise and anger of Dowding when, in October, 1940, he was summoned to attend an Air Council Meeting with me, to justify my fighter tactics in the face of critics from 12 Group. This meeting was arranged without the knowledge or approval of Dowding, and I was asked to explain to the Meeting the reasons for my fighter tactics. As will be seen from the Official History of the RAF, this criticism after the event was used by the retiring CAS and his Air Marshals as an excuse for getting rid of Dowding. Of course, being the First Lieutenant and his tactical commander throughout the Battle of Britain, I was banished to a Training Command. The result was that Air Marshal Sholto Douglas, from Air Ministry, replaced Dowding in November, 1940, and, shortly after, I was replaced by his close friend, Leigh-Mallory from 12 Group, whose malicious criticism had been used by the ambitious Air Marshals at Air Ministry.

'Should I pass on before I have an opportunity of writing a book, then I give you full permission to publish this letter so that ex-11 Group Members will know why a small section of the Air Ministry listened to the criticism of 11 Fighter Group, after the Battle had been well and truly won.'

Douglas Bader had been in Leigh-Mallory's Group and accompanied him to that fateful meeting in October 1940 at the Air Ministry. It was Bader who championed the Big Wing, thereby giving Leigh-Mallory the necessary support from an ex-Cranwell and active fighter pilot and squadron leader. Douglas Bader and I never agreed on the Big Wing – indeed when writing the foreword to my autobiography *Wing Leader* he wrote, '…apart from your dissertation on Battle of Britain strategy, with which I cordially disagree!' He did not 'pull the trigger' on Dowding nor Park, that was Leigh-Mallory's doing, but in March 1941 he got his Wing under Leigh-Mallory's command. Leigh-Mallory took Bader to that historic meeting managing the politics well. If only Dowding and Park had read the political nuances better at that historic meeting and taken 'Sailor' Malan along to counter Douglas's 'expert' and somewhat dubious Battle of Britain air fighting opinions the RAF would have had Dowding and Park in more worthwhile positions for the storms ahead.

One final, last, look back: was Normandy the right place for the great Allied Invasion?

Despite our overwhelming air power, it took three months to drive the Germans out of the province. During the severe July gales, the Mulberry Harbour was badly damaged, our supplies were reduced and there was such a petrol shortage that some wings were temporarily grounded. Once we left Normandy and leap-frogged to Paris, Brussels and Eindhoven, all our food, ammunition and petrol had to be delivered from the Mulberry Harbour to our various locations by the famous 'Red Ball' convoys – big trucks driven hard, day and night by tough Negroes. We depended on the 'Red Ball' convoys until the port of Antwerp was cleared and opened many months after D-Day.

From an airman's point of view the open, flat terrain of the Pas de Calais would have been better than the Normandy *bocage* because in the former there were far fewer hiding places for the much-feared Tiger and Panther tanks, with their formidable 88mm guns, which until they came out could not be found from the air. The Mulberry harbour could have been positioned along the coast until a port was available, and there were ample airfields in South East England to accommodate our fighter wings. The formidable strength of the German army, especially the Panzer divisions near the Pas-de-Calais, would have probably stopped Montgomery, but then Patton might have broken out and liberated Paris earlier? History is full of 'what ifs', of course, but the fact, I suppose, is that victory always comes at a certain cost, and against such a foul empire as Hitler's, only Total Victory at any cost was acceptable – fortunately, I survived. All too many did not.

Air Vice-Marshal Johnnie Johnson's WW2 Service Record

JAMES EDGAR 'Johnnie' JOHNSON

WW2 SERVICE and COMBAT RECORDS, HONOURS and AWARDS

Personal Number 83267	**Service Record**			
Date	**Unit**	**Group**	**Duties**	**Rank**
10/8/1940	7 Operational Training Unit		Operational Training	
2/9/1940	19 Squadron		Flying	
5/9/1940	616 Squadron		Flying	
13/9/1941	616 Squadron		Flying	Fg/Off
9/7/1942	610 Squadron		Flying	
13/7/1942	610 Squadron		Flying to Command	Sqn/Ldr
16/3/1943	Kenley		Flying	Wg/Cdr
8/7/1943	17 Fighter Wing	83	Flying	Wg/Cdr
13/9/1943	HQ 11 Group		Plans	Wg/Cdr
6/3/1944	22 (Fighter) Wing	83	Flying Wing Leader	Wg/Cdr
20/4/1944	17 (Fighter) Wing HQ	83	Flying	Wg/Cdr
12/7/1944	127 Wing HQ	83	Operations General Duties	Wg/Cdr
4/4/1945	125 Wing	83	To Command	Gp/Capt
14/7/1945	124 Wing	83	Flying	Gp/Capt

Johnnie Johnson's Aerial Combat Claims

1941

15 Jan	½ Do17 Damaged	Spitfire IA	K4477	Near North Coates	616 Sqn
26 Jun	Me109E Destroyed	Spitfire IIA	P7837	Gravelines	616 Sqn
04 Jul	Me109E Damaged	Spitfire IIA	P7828	5m inland Gravelines	616 Sqn
06 Jul	Me109E Destroyed	Spitfire IIA	P7838	S Dunkirk	616 Sqn
14 Jul	Me109F Destroyed	Spitfire VB	P8707	Fauquembergues	616 Sqn
21 Jul	Me109 Probable	Spitfire IIA	P7837	Merville	616 Sqn
23 Jul	Me109 Damaged	Spitfire IIA	P7837	10m inland Boulogne	616 Sqn
09 Aug	Me109F Destroyed	Spitfire VB	W3334	Béthune	616 Sqn
09 Aug	½ Me109F Destroyed	Spitfire VB	W3334	Béthune	616 Sqn
21 Aug	Me109E Probable	Spitfire VB	W3457	10 m E Le Touquet	616 Sqn
21 Sep	2 Me109Fs Destroyed	Spitfire VB	W3428	Near Le Touquet	616 Sqn

1942

15 Apr	Fw190 Damaged	Spitfire VB	BM121	10 m E Le Touquet	616 Sqn
19 Aug	Fw190 Destroyed	Spitfire VB	EP215	Dieppe	610 Sqn
19 Aug	⅓ Me109F Destroyed	Spitfire VB	EP215	Dieppe	610 Sqn
19 Aug	½ Fw190 Damaged	Spitfire VB	EP215	Dieppe	610 Sqn
20 Aug	Fw190 Probable	Spitfire VB	EP215	Off French coast	610 Sqn

1943

13 Feb	Fw190 Probable	Spitfire VB	EP121	SW Boulogne	610 Sqn
03 Apr	Fw190 Destroyed	Spitfire IX	EN398	E Montreuil	Kenley Wg
05 Apr	3 Fw190s Damaged	Spitfire IX	EN398	Ostend-Ghent	Kenley Wg
11 May	Fw190 Destroyed	Spitfire IX	EN398	Gravelines	Kenley Wg
13 May	Fw190 Destroyed	Spitfire IX	EN398	Berck-Le Touquet	Kenley Wg
13 May	⅓ Fw190 Destroyed	Spitfire IX	EN398	Mid-Channel	Kenley Wg
14 May	Fw190 Destroyed	Spitfire IX	EN398	Nieuport	Kenley Wg
01 Jun	½ Me109 Destroyed	Spitfire IX	EN398	Somme Estuary	Kenley Wg
15 Jun	2 Fw190s Destroyed	Spitfire IX	EN398	Yvetot	Kenley Wg
17 Jun	Fw190 Destroyed	Spitfire IX	EN398	Ypres-St Omer	Kenley Wg
24 Jun	Fw190 Damaged	Spitfire IX	EN398	St Omer	Kenley Wg
24 Jun	Fw190 Destroyed	Spitfire IX	EN398	S of Fécamp	Kenley Wg
27 Jun	Fw190 Destroyed	Spitfire IX	EN398	W of St Omer	Kenley Wg
15 Jul	Me109G Destroyed	Spitfire IX	EN398	Blangy-Senarpont	Kenley Wg
25 Jul	Me109G Destroyed	Spitfire IX	EN398	E of Schipol	Kenley Wg
29 Jul	Me109G Damaged	Spitfire IX	EN398	SW Amsterdam	Kenley Wg
30 Jul	Me109 Destroyed	Spitfire IX	EN398	W of Schipol	Kenley Wg
12 Aug	½ Me109 Destroyed	Spitfire IX	EN398	Axel	127 Wg

12 Aug	½ Me109 Destroyed	Spitfire IX	EN398	Axel	127 Wg
17 Aug	¼ Me110 Destroyed	Spitfire IX	EN398	N of Ghent	127 Wg
23 Aug	Fw190 Destroyed	Spitfire IX	EN398	Gosnay	127 Wg
26 Aug	Fw190 Destroyed	Spitfire IX	MA573	SW Rouen	127 Wg
04 Sep	Fw190 Destroyed	Spitfire IX	MA573	NW Roubaix	127 Wg
05 Sep	Me109 Damaged	Spitfire IX	EN398	Daynze	127 Wg

1944

28 Mar	½ Ju 88 on ground	Spitfire IXB	MK392	Dreux Airfield	144 Wg
25 Apr	2 Fw190s Destroyed	Spitfire IXB	MK392	Laon	144 Wg
05 May	Fw190 Destroyed	Spitfire IXB	MK392	Douai	144 Wg
16 Jun	Fw190 Destroyed	Spitfire IXB	MK392	NE Villers-Bocage	144 Wg
22 Jun	Me109 Destroyed	Spitfire IXB	MK392	7m W of Argentan	144 Wg
28 Jun	2 Me109s Destroyed	Spitfire IXB	MK392	S of Caen	144 Wg
30 Jun	Me109 Destroyed	Spitfire IXB	NH380	E of Grace	144 Wg
05 Jul	2 Fw190s Destroyed	Spitfire IXB	MK392	Alençon	144 Wg
20 Jul	Fw190 Damaged	Spitfire IXB	MK392	S of Argentan	127 Wg
23 Aug	2 Fw190s Destroyed	Spitfire IXB	MK392	Senlis	127 Wg
27 Sep	Me109 Destroyed	Spitfire IXB	MK392	Rees on Rhine	127 Wg

Officially, Johnnie's number of aerial victories was thirty-eight-and-a-half. Johnnie, however, personally approved the list above, compiled from details in his log book. The statistics ultimately arrived at from this data are: thirty-four enemy aircraft personally destroyed, with a further seven shared, three probably destroyed with a further two shared 'probables', ten damaged and another three shared; one shared destroyed on the ground. Thirty of Johnnie's aerial combats concerned Fw190s, twenty-five Me109s, and one an Me110. Only once did he engage a German bomber, this being his first combat, on 15 January 1941, a kill shared with Cocky Dundas. In total, therefore, Johnnie opened fire on fifty-seven enemy aircraft. His total number of flying hours by 8 May 1945 was 1,741, 1,628.40 as first pilot and 785.40 of which were operational. This represents some 700 operational sorties.

The foregoing list indicates that Johnnie's most successful combat tour was in 1943, leading the Kenley Wing which was subsequently redesignated 127 Wing. During that period, Johnnie claimed fourteen enemy aircraft destroyed while flying Spitfire EN398. This statistic makes that machine the most successful Spitfire of all. Unfortunately, however, this historic airframe cannot be found preserved in a museum – it was unceremoniously scrapped in 1949.

Johnnie Johnson's Decorations & Awards

Companion of the Order of Bath
Commander of the British Empire
Distinguished Service Order with Bars for second and third awards
Distinguished Flying Cross with Bar for second award
1939-45 Star
Air Crew Europe Star with Battle of Britain, France and Germany clasp
Defence Medal 1939-45
War Medal 1939-45
Queen's Korea Medal
United Nations Korea Medal
General Service Medal
1953 Coronation Medal
Air Efficiency Award
Belgian Order of Leopold 1
Bclgian Croix dc Gucrrc, with Palm
French Legion of Honour
American Legion of Merit
American Distinguished Flying Cross
American Air Medal

Abbreviations

A/C	aircraft
ALG	advanced landing ground
CAS	Chief of the Air Staff
E/A	enemy aircraft
PSP	perforated steel planking
R/T	radio telephone
SASO	Senior Air Staff Officer
TAF	Tactical Air Force
Tiffy	RAF slang for Typhoon

Acknowledgements

Firstly, I will forever be indebted to my friend Chris Johnson, Johnnie's youngest son, for gifting me the copyright to his august father's 1942 diary, this unpublished manuscript, and photographs. Without Chris's generosity and our shared desire to see awareness raised of Johnnie's inspirational story, and maintain its currency, this and other books would never have happened.

My great friend and publisher Martin Mace is a real pleasure to work with, as are the whole team at Pen & Sword.

Bibliography

Published & Secondary Sources

Bader, G/C Sir DRS, *Fight for the Sky*, Sidgwick & Jackson, London, 1973

Bracken, R, *Spitfire: The Canadians*, Boston Mills Press, Boston, 1995

Brickhill, P, *Reach for the Sky*, William Collins, London, 1954

D'Este, C, *Decision in Normandy: The Real Story of Montgomery and the Allied Campaign*, Penguin, London, 1983

Douglas-Home, C, *Rommel*, Weidenfeld & Nicholas, London, 1973

Dundas, G/C Sir HSL, *Flying Start*, Stanley Paul, London, 1988

Foreman, J, *1941: Part One*, Air Research Publications, New Malden, 1993

Foreman, J, *1941: Part Two*, Air Research Publications, New Malden, 1994

Foreman, J, *1944: Over the Beaches*, Air Research Publications, New Malden, 1994

Galland, A, *The First and the Last: Germany's Fighter Force in the Second World War*, Methuen, London, 1954

Godefroy, Wg Cdr Dr HC, *Lucky Thirteen*, Croom Helm, London, 1983

Johnson, AVM JE, *Wing Leader*, Chatto & Windus, London, 1956

Johnson, AVM JE, *Full Circle*, Chatto & Windus, London, 1964

Johnson, AVM JE, & Lucas, Wg Cdr PB, *Courage in the Skies*, Stanley Paul, London, 1992

Johnson, AVM JE & Lucas, W/C PB, *Winged Victory*, Stanley Paul & Co., London, 1995

Price, Dr A, *The Spitfire Story*, Arms & Armour Press, London, 1995

Sarkar, D, *Spitfire Ace of Aces: The Wartime Story of Johnnie Johnson*, Amberley Publishing, Stroud, 2011

Sarkar, D, *Arnhem 1944: The Human Tragedy of the Bridge Too Far*, Pen & Sword, Barnsley, 2019

Unpublished

Johnson Papers.
Interviews of AVM JE Johnson & Sqn Ldr Danforth Browne, Dilip Sarkar Archive.
Pilot's Flying Log Book, AVM JE Johnson

The National Archives

Operations Records Books

350 Squadron	AIR 27/1746
403 Squadron	AIR 27/1783
416 Squadron	AIR 27/1816
421 Squadron	AIR 27/1828
441 Squadron	AIR 27/1881
442 Squadron	AIR 27/1882
443 Squadron	AIR 27/1883
125 Wing	AIR 26/185
127 Wing	AIR 26/187
144 Wing	AIR 26/209

Combat Reports

AVM JE Johnson	AIR50/402
403 Squadron	AIR 50/138
416 Squadron	AIR 50/145
421 Squadron	AIR 50/147
441 Squadron	AIR 50/152
442 Squadron	AIR 50/153
443 Squadron	AIR 50/154
125 Wing	AIR 50/431
127 Wing	AIR 50/433
144 Wing	AIR 50/442

Films

Johnnie Johnson: This is Your Life, Thames Television, 8 May 1985

Websites

dilipsarkarauthor.com	Dilip Sarkar's personal website
jjhousing.co.uk	The Johnnie Johnson Housing Trust
douglasbaderfoundation.com	The Douglas Bader Foundation
nationalarchives.gov.uk	The National Archives

Other Books by Dilip Sarkar

(in order of publication)

Spitfire Squadron: No 19 Squadron at War, 1939-41
The Invisible Thread: A Spitfire's Tale
Through Peril to the Stars: RAF Fighter Pilots Who Failed to Return, 1939-45
Angriff *Westland: Three Battle of Britain Air Raids Through the Looking Glass*
A Few of the Many: Air War 1939-45, A Kaleidoscope of Memories
Bader's Tangmere Spitfires: The Untold Story, 1941
Bader's Duxford Fighters: The Big Wing Controversy
Missing in Action: Resting in Peace?
Guards VC: Blitzkrieg 1940
Battle of Britain: The Photographic Kaleidoscope, Volumes I-IV
Fighter Pilot: The Photographic Kaleidoscope
Group Captain Sir Douglas Bader: An Inspiration in Photographs
Johnnie Johnson: Spitfire Top Gun, Parts I & II
Battle of Britain: Last Look Back
Spitfire! Courage & Sacrifice
Spitfire Voices: Heroes Remember
The Battle of Powick Bridge: Ambush a Fore-thought
Duxford 1940: A Battle of Britain Base at War
The Few: The Battle of Britain in the Words of the Pilots
Spitfire Manual 1940
The Last of the Few: Eighteen Battle of Britain Pilots Tell Their Extraordinary Stories
Hearts of Oak: The Human Tragedy of HMS *Royal Oak*
The Sinking of HMS Royal Oak *In the Words of the Survivors (reprint of Hearts of Oak)*
Spitfire Voices: Life as a Spitfire Pilot in the Words of the Veterans
How the Spitfire Won the Battle of Britain
Spitfire Ace of Aces: The True Wartime Story of Johnnie Johnson

OTHER BOOKS BY DILIP SARKAR

Douglas Bader
Fighter Ace: The Extraordinary Life of Douglas Bader, Battle of Britain Hero (reprint of above)
Spitfire: The Photographic Biography
Hurricane Manual 1940
River Pike
The Final Few: The Last Surviving Pilots of the Battle of Britain Tell Their Stories
Arnhem 1944: The Human Tragedy of the Bridge Too Far
Spitfire! The Full Story of a Unique Battle of Britain Fighter Squadron
Battle of Britain 1940: The Finest Hour's Human Cost
Letters from The Few: Unique Memories of the Battle of Britain
Johnnie Johnson's 1942 Diary: The Wartime Diary of the Spitfire Ace of Aces

Index